D0380232

AT HOME ON THE EARTH

AT HOME
ON THE
EARTH

BECOMING NATIVE TO OUR PLACE

A Multicultural Anthology

EDITED BY

DAVID LANDIS BARNHILL

UNIVERSITY OF CALIFORNIA PRESS

BERKELEY   LOS ANGELES   LONDON

University of California Press
Berkeley and Los Angeles, California

University of California Press, Ltd.
London, England

Library of Congress Cataloging-in-Publication Data

At home on the earth : becoming native to our place :
  a multicultural anthology / edited by David Landis
  Barnhill.
      p.   cm.
    Includes bibliographical references.
    ISBN 0-520-21483-8 (alk. paper). —
    ISBN 0-520-21684-9 (pbk.: alk. paper)
    1. Landscape—United States—Literary
collections.   2. Human ecology—United States—
Literary collections.   3. Indian philosophy—
United States—Literary collections.   4. Place
(Philosophy)—United States—Literary collections.
5. Philosophy of nature—United States—Literary
collections.   6. Geographical perception—United
States—Literary collections.   I. Barnhill, David
Landis.
  PS509.L3A7   1999
  917.3'001—dc21   98-33876
                                              CIP
Manufactured in the United States of America
9 8 7 6 5 4 3 2 1

The paper used in this publication meets the
minimum requirements of American National
Standard for Information Sciences—Permanence
of Paper for Printed Library Materials, ANSI
Z39.48-1984.

FOR GARY SNYDER
AND WENDELL BERRY

CONTENTS

PART TWO: PLACES TO LIVE

HOMESTEADING

RANCHING

FARMING

LIVING BETWEEN CITY AND COUNTRY

PREFACE

Our relationship to the earth is *radical:* it lies at the root of our consciousness and our culture and of any sense of a rich life and right livelihood. What is the proper relationship with the land? How can we
achieve it?

The essays in this volume explore our intrinsic relationship with
the earth as well as our alienation from it and the violence we have
done to it. But the principal focus is on the possibilities of being at home
on the earth: finding place, reinhabitation, and becoming native. The essays articulate how we fit in nature and how we can work with it. If we
are to create a culture that lives in harmony with the earth, if we are to
overcome our alienation from nature, we all need to find our path toward
becoming true inhabitants of place.

Nature writing is one of the central ways we have of discovering and
walking that path. It is profoundly conservative: conserving the earth,
which conserves us all. It is also, as Thoreau knew so well, deeply subver-
sive, for it points to views and ways of life that diverge fundamentally from
what dominates our times.

Creating an anthology is a peculiar task, for it is an attempt to be creative
with other people's works. My deepest thanks go to the contributors to
this volume for their continuing efforts in helping us move toward a new
sanity and an old wisdom in our relationship with nature. I owe a great
deal to my editor Doug Arava regarding both the original conception and
the final design of the book. His interest in the project has demonstrated
a personal as well as professional commitment to the topic. I also have

benefited from discussions with John Elder and Ben Orlove. Any anthologist is indebted to precursors, and we are living in a remarkably rich age for collections of nature writing. I am grateful to other editors for their labors of love, and John A. Murray deserves special thanks. We all benefit from the work of a dedicated few, including organizations, and the Orion Society and Planet Drum Foundation have been especially significant contributors to a new vision of the earth. Guilford College has been a place where a professor can explore new and interdisciplinary topics; I doubt if I could have completed this project at many other institutions.

There is an old Chinese saying that a poet or painter should walk ten thousand miles and read ten thousand books. Today we might add "and sit ten thousand hours in front of the computer." Gratitude to my family for indulging me in all of these endeavors, and for walking some of those miles with me. And finally, although he is not included in this volume, Kenneth Rexroth has been an enormous influence on me and our culture as a whole. Anyone interested in nature, the sacred, and social justice is deeply indebted to him.

David Landis Barnhill

INTRODUCTION

It is 6:30 a.m. and the sun has begun to filter through the cornstalks and seep into the woods. I have finished morning yoga by the garden and have moved to my little meditation grove. I settle into position, let body and mind center themselves, as the sounds of the woods sink into me. Less than a mile to my left is a bulldozer rumbling loudly. From far to my right, the drone of the freeway drifts in. I sit arced by oaks and hickories; birds and squirrels rustle all around; and beneath me is rock and soil and millions of years of time. Occasionally a jet streams overhead.

My home stands on a lot that is slightly less than one acre. At the back is a tiny piece of woods, part of a ribbon of trees that links neighbors for half a mile. Each year a pine falls in a summer storm as the hardwoods are coming to predominate through the natural process of succession. At the edge of the woods is a hutch for my wife Phyllis's Angora rabbits. Near the compost pile, a path curls off, courses through trees and ground vines, and passes by a slanting rock. This is my meditation spot, no cliff edge above timberline but a seat of stillness nonetheless. At the base of the rock is a flat stone about one foot wide, shaped like a triangle with the top bent leftward. To its right is a knotty-barked tree that angles sharply away and then rises skyward in delicate curves. It is an *Ailanthus altissima,* "Tree of Heaven," an exotic that spreads aggressively through suckers and that I just as aggressively root out in order for the maples and dogwoods to thrive.

But this particular *Ailanthus* I have come to like. With the two rocks, it creates a dynamic balance that recalls the Zen gardens I have visited in Japan. And perhaps we have something in common. I too am an outsider

1

here, though I hesitate to use the word exotic for me, let alone "heaven." My kind is an invader, competing with the indigenous inhabitants. And there are far too many of us, spreading cancerously throughout this area. Yet the solution is not removal but naturalization, to live in a way that allows other beings to thrive and the natural systems to flow. This process is a long and difficult one, and we do not yet understand it very well. But the goal is finally to live with—and as—this place.

After meditation, and still somewhat within it, I begin my brief morning work in the garden. It is late summer, and much of the labor involves returning the plants to the soil that gave them life. The leaves from last fall that I used as mulch through spring and summer disappear into the soil. Soon they too will be wholly of this ground, to hold next spring's water and the roots of new peas. I shovel in spent corncobs, bean scraps, and clippings from the lawn, turning this year into the future. It is a ritual I have done in the clay of Palo Alto, in the post-glacial soil near Seattle's Lake Union, and in the duff of a cleared forest twenty miles north of Everett. Each place it is the same; each place it is unique. Here in the central piedmont—the "foot" of the Blue Ridge Mountains, the Uwharria bioregion—the earth is a sandy clay that through most of the summer bakes hard but in a sudden storm weeps sand, the dirt more orange than the proverbial red. But after ten years of working with the garden's growth, this soil has turned a rich brown.

Soon the recurrent summer thunderstorm will soak the soil. Some of the water will be taken in by the plants, the leaves giving it back to the air, which will return it to the earth. Some of the water will seep and trickle and fall to creek and stream, to river, and to the sea. The water's path shapes the land and the mind, forming the geography of the intricate and infinite community of this place. Watershed consciousness has become an increasingly important aspect of a vision of nature that is new to most Americans: feeling yourself to be a part not of a city or state but of a drainage system, a community defined by the water's converging flow within a single river system. Nearby to the east, for instance, Greensboro lies in the Haw River basin, while a few miles to the west Winston-Salem lies in the Yadkin River drainage. My own town of Kernersville, however, is located in an unusual way, for it lies in no watershed, or more accurately, in three of them. The rain that falls through my land moves through Smith Creek west into the Yadkin River, curling back southeast to meander (with the new name Pee Dee) through the coastal plain of South Carolina. A few more miles east of my land, the Deep River begins as a trickle, flowing southeast into the Haw River, on into Cape Fear River and the Atlantic. The Haw River itself begins as an intermittent stream a few miles north across a number of indistinguishable hills. And a few hundred yards west of the Haw's source, rain slips north through Belews Creek, into the Dan River and Virginia, then east into the Roanoke River and on to the sea.

Most everyone lives in a single watershed, which can give a very physical sense of unity: enwrapped by a home valley, a community pulled together in water's downward flow. But the multiple watersheds of Kernersville can make one feel tippy, about to fall in any direction, just as a momentary shower might fall into any or all of the three major drainages. Yet this multiplicity can give rise to a feeling of centeredness rather than imbalance. In Asian countries the land has been seen in terms of a Buddhist mandala—a map of the spiritual cosmos. With this perspective, Kernersville becomes an empty center, streams spinning out north, south, east, and west, beginning from nothing and drawn finally toward the endless sea.

Our multiple watershed setting is not, of course, a primary concern in this town. Classical theology saw nature as a book, reading its symbols in order to understand the mind of the heavenly author. Our culture reads nature like a map, defined by roads leading to roads leading to places of money, the land merely blank flat space. For a heavenly vision of nature we have substituted one that is not earthly but commercial, and the enormous power of this perspective resides in its blindness to the earth and to our embeddedness in nature.

There is another kind of vision. The eyes feel the curve and slope of the earth as it flows, following the water to the sea. The mind follows as well, wondering what creek lies below, what stream below that, what river. It is a geographic vision. What is here does not end here; all is unbroken. Place molds the sensual mind.

When the roadmap mentality controls politics, as it almost always does, we get roads and more roads, as well as the malls and gas stations that spring up alongside. Kernersville, alas, is such a town. When my family first came here Kernersville still had the flavor of a southern small town: slow stores, tobacco and hay fields, and an old downtown. In the last ten years shopping centers have appeared seemingly out of thin air, new ones built even as the last one stands half empty. Fast-food chains follow in their wake. Recently, the town forced its planning director out of office. According to one report, the town elders did not consider him sufficiently "user friendly"— he didn't automatically give in to the demands of the developers.

My land lies just outside the city limits so my voice is not politically legitimate in town, at least until after the developers have secured their desires and the land is annexed. Just beyond my bedroom window begins an old tobacco field that dips and curves, edged by streambed woods. In the first few years after I arrived here, Mr. Clodfelter would work the fields with a team of Percherons as well as by tractor. Phyllis and I would walk through the weeds and trees to fields and ponds further on. The old farmer is gone now, the land is being scraped clean, and no one asks where the animals that lived there will go. Soon the houses will start rising, and Kernersville, as they say, will have grown.

It is Saturday morning, and Phyl and I decide to walk with Smith Creek, making our own path along the water. Tall oaks and maples rise, and a sycamore has toppled onto the meadow, its shallow root mass upright like a wall. Gazing at the stream I imagine millennia of coursing water; looking straight ahead I see the circled concrete monuments rising from the new sewer line. Pipe and stream, suburban efflux and the rain's landflow.

I hear the trickle of the creek, the far hum of cars. A great blue heron rises behind us and slowly wings upstream.

We come across an old pond, dug out long ago. We walk along its grassy edge and find two more, turn left to come upon three others. They were fish spawning ponds, and the path between them runs under an arch of oaks. How long will they remain this way? In two hundred years will they be circles of swampy meadow, seen so often in the northern woods we visit in the summer? As we look back at the clustered water, a large flock of Canadian geese curves toward us. The two lead birds extend their wings, held motionless in the air. Slowly they settle on the water nearby. Other geese disappear onto the next pond past some trees. Then another flock startles us overhead, flying toward the city. Beyond the call of the geese is the sound of their wingbeats through an empty sky.

We turn and slowly head toward home. This is our place: fields, woods, and garden. But like all places, it has a subtle spatial multiplicity. When I meditate on my rock, my body holds in mind a cliff edge at White Pass in the northern Cascades where I gazed on ridge upon ridge at sunset. Our garden holds not only strawberries and worms but also the tactile memories of other gardens, the particular way the soil would crumble in your hand. I gaze at the rolling pasture along Old Winston Road through a mist-like vision of the California coast range, a redwing blackbird calling in the crackling grass. Further back, but still present, are the words of the Japanese poet Bashō writing about his beloved Yoshino hills that recalled the mountains of Chinese poets before him.

Back home, Phyl and I stroll the path through our little woods. A downy woodpecker is searching for food and a squirrel raucously asserts his territory. Slowly, last year's leaves are turning into forest duff; slowly a young maple is reaching skyward. Out in the falling and rising light, the garden goes through its cycles as well. My days, too, pass like water.

The essays in this book are now also part of my living here, part of the grain of this place. They explore with uncommon sensitivity what it means to be at home on the earth. There is no one way to do so; there are various kinds of settings in which this can and must be accomplished. Some authors speak of painful loss, others of the work that preserves what we have. Some articulate a future vision, others write of vital memories. But they all share a sense that human identity and human goodness are intimately tied to the land one lives in. What we make of ourselves and of our society is linked to what we make of the earth, and how we let the earth make us.

Much nature writing has emphasized the beauty, integrity, and necessity of wilderness. But the notions of wild and wilderness often have been accompanied by dichotomies: wilderness versus civilization, wild versus domesticated, pristine wilderness versus active human presence. While Western culture has traditionally given positive value to the second set of terms, there is a growing tendency to hold that wilderness has primal worth. In many ways this is a healthy change. But still this belief is often based on the old assumptions: that nature and humans are distinct, and that nature is healthy only when it is free of human interference.

To think instead about being in place is to assume that there is at least the possibility of living *with* the land and its processes. The essays in this volume center on this underlying and overwhelming concern: how can we live in place, truly inhabit the earth, and become native to our land? If we are to arrest our destructiveness and overcome our sense of estrangement, we need to ask this question with wisdom and honesty and humility.

All questions have a context; in this book it is North America. The particularities of history, geography, and culture shape our relationship to the land, and these authors present their own American experience of place, inevitably different from that of, say, England or Japan. But there is no one American sense of place, no one way to be native here. The essays in this book offer a rich variegation of views, authors, styles, and contexts. As in an ecosystem, diversity yields richness.

A sense of place was first developed on this continent by Paleo-Indians. We have precious little knowledge of their ways, though as John Hanson Mitchell suggests, it may be possible to link imaginatively to those ancient cultures. But we are certainly able to learn about—and, one hopes, from—the later cultures of Native Americans. The book begins with essays by two of our most outstanding American Indian writers, and both accentuate the links between culture and nature. N. Scott Momaday discusses the historical development among Native Americans of a moral relationship with the land, in which humans fit within the patterns of nature and see the earth as sacred. Such a view is grounded in a sense of the earth's beauty and feelings of wonder and delight. The result is a culture in which humans invest themselves in the landscape and incorporate the land into their experience. Leslie Marmon Silko also speaks of how Native Americans traditionally see themselves interwoven with nature. Pueblo Indians are not viewers of a landscape but participants in a system of relationships, something we can see in their pictorial art and myths. Their oral tradition highlights the unique details of specific places and their cultural meanings, yielding an interactive intimacy with the land they live in.

European culture arrived in the Americas to find peoples who had a deep sense of being at home on the earth. The European response was to claim and tame, to exploit and destroy—both the land and the people. This violent, tragic stance continues to this day, although in ways less overt than the genocide of the Indians and the slaughter of the bison. Development and progress (ironic terms that have replaced the notion of manifest destiny) contribute to the ongoing destruction of the environment and our continuing alienation from the land. All Americans, past and present, suffer from this—whether it is an African-American moving to a northern city or a white man homesteading in Alaska. In the second section, bell hooks and John Haines serve as witnesses to the loss of place. They write of the earth's vitality and wonder, its animating spirit. hooks speaks of how African-Americans lost their rootedness in the land in the great migration to the North, and how estrangement from the body accompanies estrangement from the earth. Haines senses the ghosts that abide following the vast destruction of wild Alaska. Yet both find hope in signs of sanity and of healing.

Two of our most compelling voices of this sanity and healing are Wendell Berry and Scott Russell Sanders. In the third section they offer overviews of the need and possibility of becoming at home on the earth. Berry recalls the violence and placelessness of the European supplanters of the Native Americans, contrasting a road cut into the earth by European settlers with an Indian footpath. Walking in the woods at his Kentucky farm, he becomes conscious of creation at work and what creation requires of us. The holiness of nature teaches us that we must become stewards, but not in an arrogant sense of managing creation. Being a steward of nature involves becoming its follower and apprentice. Sanders, like Berry, underscores the importance of staying put in one's place, resisting the dogma of rootlessness that lies behind the "unsettling of America." Sanders argues that the human inclination to wander can be reconciled with the need to settle down. Even nomads are deeply connected to the land they travel through. The question as Sanders frames it is "whether we belong to the land, through our loyalty and awareness." Like hooks, he sees the necessity of healing, which comes "from aligning yourself with the grain of your place and answering to its needs."

The ideal, then, is not an amorphous oneness with nature but a perceptive and particularized harmony with one's own local area. Bioregionalism has been a widespread movement in this direction. As Gary Snyder explains, bioregionalism stresses that our love of nature must be grounded in a specific place. By remaining long enough, we can become at home in the land, whether country or city. Bioregionalism is not parochialism but a balance between cosmopolitan pluralism and local consciousness. Such a view can lead to a rich sense of the history—and story—of one's place. Thomas Berry offers a story of the Hudson River bioregion where he once lived. Geology and human history, ancient Native American cultures and European settlers, are elements of the single, ongoing narrative of the land, which includes both tragic destruction and the possibility of a renewed sense of being at home on the earth.

How can we develop this sense of being in place, members of a biore-gion and its interspecies community? One way, as Snyder and others have suggested, is to draw on the wisdom of the native cultures of America. But European-Americans are caught in a difficult paradox. Models of native living are right here and we need to learn from them, yet there are pro-found limits to that learning, and inauthentic imitation and cultural ap-propriation are all too common. The fourth section explores the possibil-ities and difficulties inherent in attempts to learn from a Native American sense of place. Melissa Nelson sees a creative challenge in integrating her European and Ojibwe Indian heritages. She has been influenced by Asian mysticism and deep ecology, and she affirms the potential value of Euro-pean rationality. In Native American traditions she finds a way to overcome the nature/culture split by taking a "kin-centric" view, with the natural world as an extended family. Ultimately, however, traditional wisdom is not the exclusive province of Native American culture, for we all have earth-based spiritual traditions in our past. The knowledge we need, Nelson claims, "is really a deeper knowledge of the self within a wider ecocultural context." In this way, all of us can come to honor the place where we live.

Terry Tempest Williams considers the Navajo relation to the land and, like Momaday and Silko, emphasizes the importance of stories in that re-lationship. Those stories inform her teaching and writing, but she recog-nizes that she cannot become Navajo. Yet a respectful familiarity with Navajo culture helps to create her own stories and her own sense of place. Richard Nelson, while hunting deer on an island in the Pacific Northwest, recalls his time spent living with native peoples in Alaska. He evokes his profound struggle over his peculiar cultural location, caught between his identities as a modern European-American and as a person drawn to the views and practices of tribal cultures. While rejecting the idea that he could become an Indian and maintaining a degree of agnosticism toward specific native beliefs about animal spirits, he succeeds in incorporating some of their central values into his life.

These two authors speak for many European-Americans who feel that we can neither presume to become Indian nor dismiss the possibility of learning from native cultures. As is so often the case, the complexities of language can cause problems. The word "native" has several meanings. It can designate a group or a culture that is indigenous, as in Native Amer-ican. It also can refer to anyone born in a place, and in this sense all but first generation immigrants are native. But we can use the term "native" in another way, a way that is central to our search for a more responsible relation to the earth. It can point to an individual's way of living and state of mind, referring to someone who realizes a deep embeddedness in nature, who has a subtle understanding of the land and an abiding identity with place usually found in aboriginal people. Terry Tempest Williams and Richard Nelson, as well as Gary Snyder in the concluding section, suggest that non-indigenous people can develop the ability to consider native cultures as living elders and to learn from their wisdom. But can non-indigenous people really presume to become native? One way to help us consider that question is to avoid the seductive simplicity of absolute terms. Perhaps it is better to say that it is not a matter of being either native or invader—or being in place or not—but of relative degrees. What kind of nativeness is possible and to what extent can we become native to the land?

There is an important reason to consider nativeness to be at least a possibility for non-indigenous people: the earth needs it. It needs people who live in a native way, who consider themselves people of the land. European-Americans have been so destructive to this continent and its indigenous peoples in large part because we have rejected the notion that we are native to the earth. We have insisted on our transcendence and so devastation has followed in our path. To seek a new sense of nativeness—a slow and stumbling process to be sure—is one of the ways we can begin to live well with the earth and all its peoples.

One can live at home on the earth in many different types of places. Part Two presents essays that highlight this diversity. John Haines homesteaded in Alaska in order to return to an older and simpler existence where he entered the original mystery of things, the great past out of which we came. He finds the land and the spirit of place are not passive but *make* people. Sharon Butala and Gretel Ehrlich offer different kinds of reflections on ranching. Butala recounts her return to rural Saskatchewan, which she had left for school and career. She describes her husband as a true rural man whose character and consciousness have been molded by a life spent completely immersed in nature. But even though she is not fully rural in this sense, she recognizes how nature has shaped her as she too has become a rancher. Ehrlich vividly depicts how living on a ranch can be trying and painful, with death an accepted aspect of life. Yet she shows how living in such an open land also involves an interdependent community, necessary for survival. With deepened sensitivity, her experience of the land and the movements of her mind become profoundly interwoven.

Farming is another traditional location for cultivating a sense of being at home on the earth. David Mas Masumoto recalls walking with a scientist in the spring fields, seeking a child-like innocence and curiosity of vision that will allow him to see the ever new world of his peach orchard. He is attempting to develop an alternative style of farming that works more with than against nature. It is a family farm begun by his grandfather, and his eight-year-old daughter tries to grow her own little garden. As she accepts the fact that her plants are dying, she helps her father learn to fail amid the returning green of nature's abundance. A breeze jingles a fūrin bell and he recalls the Japanese saying that the bamboo's strength comes from its ability to bend with the blowing wind. Sue Hubbell, who owns a honeybee farm in the Ozarks of Missouri, reflects on participating in nature's processes. Managing a woodlot involves her in determining what should grow there and what should be removed, which leads her to attend closely to the cycles of life and death. She sees such interaction—which she calls "meddling"—as being a part of life's circle, and her actions have reverberations throughout the whole web of nature.

We are used to associating living close to the land with rural areas, yet most of us live in or near towns and cities. We need to learn to develop a sense of place there as well. The next essays suggest how one can become at home on the earth in more urbanized areas. Rick Bass offers an account of his upbringing in the hill country of Texas on the west edge of Houston. In his youth, he explored the de facto wilderness between encroaching subdivisions while the men in the family went further into the wild to hunt. Though his father worked in the city, he and his family maintained an intimate connection with the hill country. They developed a sense of the real language of the earth; now in the act of memory, Bass's own language intersects with the language of the land he grew up in. As in the cases of the Kiowa and Pueblo Indians, stories helped bring culture and nature together, clarifying the allegiance his family owes the land. Bass feels his soul cutting down through the bedrock, and the hill country indelibly marks him: he too is becoming the earth. Robert Finch reflects on the various changes that take place in nature, including in his hometown on Cape Cod. Human ways of inhabiting also change, and Cape Cod, like the outskirts of Kernersville, is being transformed from rural to suburban. In this context, which Finch calls "subrural," what is it to be part of the land? While a bird is born to the condition in which it lives, Finch says, we have yet to truly arrive at our places. What we need to discover is "entrance." Cutting paths into the maze of nature does not give true entry. Instead he suggests that a clue to our arrival may be found in the call of a bird. John Hanson Mitchell finds entrance in developing a more subtle sense of time that can link a small town such as Scratch Flat with the distant past. In the American Indian sense of ceremonial time, distinctions between past, present, and future dissolve and the long history of the local area reveals itself. Mitchell recounts how his apprenticeship with Native Americans allows him to develop a deep sense of place through imaginatively experiencing the last fifteen thousand years.

Increasingly, the sense of place has come to include the city. Perhaps especially in such a setting, the sense of the land can become complex. Peter Sauer speaks of the substantial manipulation of nature in the city—in particular how a brook has been moved underground—as well as how nature continues to impinge. In his view the city can be seen as a point of connection, between nature and urban life, what is alive and what is found in museums, a park and a street, west and east. Even New York City takes on the character of place. Far from this megalopolis is Seattle, where Alan Thein Durning has returned with his family after establishing a successful career as an environmental researcher in Washington, D.C. He sees his home city as one part of the Pacific Northwest, and his family attempts to establish a sense of community with local neighbors and the whole bioregion.

Urban living offers cultural interaction, and often other places merge into the consciousness of the local area. Richard Rodriguez recalls his upbringing in Sacramento. Mexico was a continuing presence for his family, as Ireland was for his classmates and for his priest, and India was for his uncle. The history of California, both Mexican and American, also pervades his sense of his place. Sacramento in the 1950s turned away from the land and toward development. But the roots of elm trees created cracks in the sidewalk as nature continued to be part of the city. And the memories of a city boy's experience with family, cultures, and nature still animate his life.

From reminiscences we turn to a dream of the future. Fantasy, especially in the form of ecotopia, has become an important subgenre in nature writing. As Durning sees the beginnings of a bioregional city in Seattle, Starhawk offers a vision of a fully developed one. Urban life has become both more complex and more harmonious, with a mixture of races and cultures, of nature and human artifact, of spontaneity and ritual, of the local and the global. Community, with other humans and with nature, predominates.

With the diversity of these essays, there is no way to bring them all together or provide a true conclusion. But this book ends with three essays that speak in very different ways to many of the themes and issues in the volume. Gary Snyder critiques various views of nature, not only the exploiters but also those who attempt to preserve a pristine wilderness. He argues for a view in which nature and culture are linked, agreeing with those who claim that what we call "nature" is culturally determined. But the reality of suffering in nature remains paramount. He presents a history of the reinhabitory move of bioregionalism and reviews Native American attitudes toward place. We need to consider our continent as Turtle Island, he says, and ultimately we all can claim the term "native."

Alice Walker articulates a vision of a responsive universe, a central idea in the notion of place. The way we interact with the earth directly affects how it interacts with us. At her place in the country, she has learned that we can become intimate with the animals and plants where we live and establish a communion. But there is a political dimension here, for nature also responds generously to all, including the efforts of the military-industrial complex to generate deadly substances. The land's responsiveness requires us to be responsible. We can teach peace by bringing the American Indian sense of the divinity of nature to the politics of war.

Native American Linda Hogan lovingly describes dwellings she finds in the Southwest, including the architecture of bees. She recounts the birdhouses of an Italian immigrant and the deterioration of a house after people abandon it. Throughout the essay she celebrates the interaction of nature and human habitation within the "deeper, wider nest of earth that houses us all." At the end she discovers a bird's nest that has woven in it a thread from her skirt and a hair from her daughter's head, part of "the maze of the universe, holding us."

These essays point out many of the central themes and issues in current discussions of becoming at home on the earth. The interconnection between nature and culture is perhaps most central: we shape nature as nature shapes us. Community and family often play a more prominent role than accounts of the heroic individual in the wilderness. Stories are threads that tie us to the land and to each other. The experience of place also can involve a complex sense of time, from personal memories that shape present experience to a mystical perception of ancient times. Space, too, is complex, for one's local place in some sense includes others. Underlying such an experience of the land is a strong sense of the vitality and the holiness of ongoing creation, which can be enriched by exposure to various religions, including Asian and Native American.

But living in place and becoming native to the land is not a simple endeavor. The authors speak of obstacles, both personal and social. A number of the essays point to how our current economic system and its ideologies of growth and individualism run counter to a sane and sustainable relationship to the land and to each other. Bioregionalism, as Snyder notes, involves a political critique of the modern view of the nation-state, and Walker points out the links between the need for peace with nature and peace with other people. Though these essays focus on personal experience and vision, they are political in a fundamental way. It is not surprising that many of the authors are active in struggles against the prevailing powers. A crucial issue for the future is how personal reflections on being at home on the earth, such as those expressed so well by these authors, can be combined effectively with political action.

So we are engaged in an ongoing struggle, a search for a new relation to the earth. It is also an old relationship: to be in and of place, to truly inhabit the land rather than just live on it. Why is it important? The answer is all around us in the destruction of habitats, species, and individual beings, often done out of ignorance, greed, and fear. The answer is also inside us, in a psychological rupture from the physical matrix of our life—nature and our bodies. And the answer is in the way we treat each other: our debasement and abuse of nature is linked with our debasement and abuse of people. To heal the social and the psychological, we need to heal our relationship with the earth. And vice versa. As Buddhism teaches, all of life is a mutual co-arising: everything conditions and is conditioned by everything else.

This volume presents some of the most important recent explorations of these concerns. The essays here do not provide a systematic analysis; they offer no simple solutions. But they give us openings. And they invite us to take our own path.

Part One

LIVING IN PLACE

AMERICANS NATIVE
TO THIS LAND

N. Scott Momaday

A FIRST AMERICAN
VIEWS HIS LAND

> *First Man*
> *behold:*
> *the earth*
> *glitters*
> *with leaves;*
> *the sky*
> *glistens*
> *with rain.*
> *Pollen*
> *is borne*
> *on winds*
> *that low*
> *and lean*
> *upon*
> *mountains.*
> *Cedars*
> *blacken*
> *the slopes—*
> *and pines.*

N. Scott Momaday is a Kiowa Indian who lives in Arizona. Raised on a reservation, he was educated at Stanford University, where he taught before becoming
a professor at the University of Arizona. His novels include *House Made of Dawn,*
and he has published volumes of poetry as well as personal and tribal memories, such as *The Way to Rainy Mountain.* In the following selection, Momaday
examines the Native American attitude toward nature. It is at once moral and

aesthetic, grounded in a sense of beauty and wonder while yielding ethical imperatives. The relationship is reciprocal, as humans become invested in the landscape and appropriate the land into their experience. Through the functioning of imagination, nature and culture become intertwined.

One hundred centuries ago. There is a wide, irregular landscape in what is now northern New Mexico. The sun is a dull white disk, low in the south; it is a perfect mystery, a deity whose coming and going are inexorable. The gray sky is curdled, and it bears very close upon the earth. A cold wind runs along the ground, dips and spins, flaking drift from a pond in the bottom of a ravine. Beyond the wind the silence is acute. A man crouches in the ravine, in the darkness there, scarcely visible. He moves not a muscle; only the wind lifts a lock of his hair and lays it back along his neck. He wears skins and carries a spear. These things in particular mark his human intelligence and distinguish him as the lord of the universe. And for him the universe is especially *this* landscape; for him the landscape is an element like the air. The vast, virgin wilderness is by and large his whole context. For him there is no possibility of existence elsewhere.

Directly there is a blowing, a rumble of breath deeper than the wind, above him, where some of the hard clay of the bank is broken off and the clods roll down into the water. At the same time there appears on the skyline the massive head of a long-horned bison, then the hump, then the whole beast, huge and black on the sky, standing to a height of seven feet at the hump, with horns that extend six feet across the shaggy crown. For a moment it is poised there; then it lumbers obliquely down the bank to the pond. Still the man does not move, though the beast is now only a few steps upwind. There is no sign of what is about to happen; the beast meanders; the man is frozen in repose.

Then the scene explodes. In one and the same instant the man springs to his feet and bolts forward, his arm cocked and the spear held high, and the huge animal lunges in panic, bellowing, its whole weight thrown violently into the bank, its hooves churning and chipping earth into the air, its eyes gone wide and wild and white. There is a moment in which its awful, frenzied motion is wasted, and it is mired and helpless in its fear, and the man hurls the spear with his whole strength, and the point is driven into the deep, vital flesh, and the bison in its agony staggers and crashes down and dies.

This ancient drama of the hunt is enacted again and again in the landscape. The man is preeminently a predator, the most dangerous of all. He hunts in order to survive; his very existence is simply, squarely established upon that basis. But he hunts also because he can, because he has the means; he has the ultimate weapon of his age, and his prey is plentiful. His relationship to the land has not yet become a moral equation.

But in time he will come to understand that there is an intimate, vital link between the earth and himself, a link that implies an intricate network of rights and responsibilities. In some unimagined future he will understand that he has the ability to devastate and perhaps destroy his environment. That moment will be one of extreme crisis in his evolution.

The weapon is deadly and efficient. The hunter has taken great care in its manufacture, especially in the shaping of the flint point, which is an extraordinary thing. A larger flake has been removed from each face, a groove that extends from the base nearly to the tip. Several hundred pounds of pressure, expertly applied, were required to make these grooves. The hunter then is an artisan, and he must know how to use rudimentary tools. His skill, manifest in the manufacture of this artifact, is unsurpassed for its time and purpose. By means of this weapon is the Paleo-Indian hunter eminently able to exploit his environment.

Thousands of years later, about the time that Columbus begins his first voyage to the New World, another man, in the region of the Great Lakes, stands in the forest shade on the edge of a sunlit brake. In a while a deer enters into the pool of light. Silently the man fits an arrow to a bow, draws aim, and shoots. The arrow zips across the distance and strikes home. The deer leaps and falls dead.

But this latter-day man, unlike his ancient predecessor, is only incidentally a hunter; he is also a fisherman, a husbandman, even a physician. He fells trees and builds canoes; he grows corn, squash, and beans, and he gathers fruits and nuts; he uses hundreds of species of wild plants for food, medicine, teas, and dyes. Instead of one animal, or two or three, he hunts many, none to extinction as the Paleo-Indian may have done. He has fitted himself far more precisely into the patterns of the wilderness than did his ancient predecessor. He lives on the land; he takes his living from it; but he does not destroy it. This distinction supports the fundamental ethic that we call conservation today. In principle, if not yet in name, this man is a conservationist.

These two hunting sketches are far less important in themselves than is that long distance between them, that whole possibility within the dimension of time. I believe that in that interim there grew up in the mind of man an idea of the land as sacred.

> At dawn
> eagles
> lie and
> hover
> above
> the plain
> where light
> gathers
> in pools.
> Grasses
> shimmer
> and shine.
> Shadows
> withdraw
> and lie
> away
> like smoke.

"The earth is our mother. The sky is our father." This concept of nature, which is at the center of the Native American worldview, is familiar to us all. But it may well be that we do not understand entirely what that concept is in its ethical and philosophical implications.

I tell my students that the American Indian has a unique investment in the American landscape. It is an investment that represents perhaps thirty thousand years of habitation. That tenure has to be worth something in itself—a great deal, in fact. The Indian has been here a long time; he is at home here. That simple and obvious truth is one of the most important realities of the Indian world, and it is integrated in the Indian mind and spirit.

How does such a concept evolve? Where does it begin? Perhaps it begins with the recognition of beauty, the realization that the physical world *is* beautiful. We don't know much about the ancient hunter's sensibilities. It isn't likely that he had leisure in his life for the elaboration of an aesthetic ideal. And yet the weapon he made was beautiful as well as functional. It has been suggested that much of the minute chipping along the edges of his weapon served no purpose but that of aesthetic satisfaction.

A good deal more is known concerning that man of the central forests. He made beautiful boxes and dishes out of elm and birch bark, for example. His canoes were marvelous, delicate works of art. And this aesthetic perception was a principle of the whole Indian world of his time, as indeed it is of our time. The contemporary Native American is a man whose strong aesthetic perceptions are clearly evident in his arts and crafts, in his religious ceremonies, and in the stories and songs of his rich oral tradition. This, in view of the pressures that have been brought to bear upon the Indian world and the drastic changes that have been effected in its landscape, is a blessing and an irony.

Consider for example the Navajos of the Four Corners area. In recent years an extensive coal-mining operation has mutilated some of their most sacred land. A large power plant in that same region spews a contamination into the sky that is visible for many miles. And yet, as much as any people of whom I have heard, the Navajos perceive and celebrate the beauty of the physical world.

There is a Navajo ceremonial song that celebrates the sounds that are made in the natural world, the particular voices that beautify the earth:

> Voice above,
> Voice of thunder,
> Speak from the
> dark of clouds;
> Voice below,
> Grasshopper voice,
> Speak from the
> green of plants;
> So may the earth
> be beautiful.

There is in the motion and meaning of this song a comprehension of the world that is peculiarly native, I believe, that is integral in the Native American mentality. Consider: The singer stands at the center of the natural world, at the source of its sound, of its motion, of its life.

Nothing of that world is inaccessible to him or lost upon him. His song is filled with reverence, with wonder and delight, and with confidence as well. He knows something about himself and about the things around him —and he knows that he knows. I am interested in what he sees and hears; I am interested in the range and force of his perception. Our immediate impression may be that his perception is narrow and deep—vertical. After all, "voice above . . . voice below," he sings. But is it vertical only? At each level of his expression there is an extension of his awareness across the whole landscape. The voice above is the voice of thunder, and thunder rolls. Moreover, it issues from the impalpable dark clouds and runs upon their horizontal range. It is a sound that integrates the whole of the atmosphere. And even so, the voice below, that of the grasshopper, issues from the broad plain and multiplicity of plants. And of course the singer is mindful of much more than thunder and insects; we are given in his song the wide angle of his vision and his hearing—and we are given the testimony of his dignity, his trust, and his deep belief.

This comprehension of the earth and air is surely a matter of morality, for it brings into account not only man's instinctive reaction to his environment but the full realization of his humanity as well, the achievement of his intellectual and spiritual development as an individual and as a race.

In my own experience I have seen numerous examples of this regard for nature. My grandfather Mammedaty was a farmer in his mature years; his grandfather was a buffalo hunter. It was not easy for Mammedaty to be a farmer; he was a Kiowa, and the Kiowas never had an agrarian tradition. Yet he had to make his living, and the old, beloved life of roaming the plains and hunting the buffalo was gone forever. Even so, as much as any man before him, he fitted his mind and will and spirit to the land; there was nothing else. He could not have conceived of living apart from the land.

In *The Way to Rainy Mountain* I set down a small narrative that belongs in the oral tradition of my family. It indicates something essential about the Native American attitude toward the land:

"East of my grandmother's house, south of the pecan grove, there is buried a woman in a beautiful dress. Mammedaty used to know where she is buried, but now no one knows. If you stand on the front porch of the house and look eastward towards Carnegie, you know that the woman is buried somewhere within the range of your vision. But her grave is unmarked. She was buried in a cabinet, and she wore a beautiful dress. How beautiful it was! It was one of those fine buckskin dresses, and it was decorated with elk's teeth and beadwork. That dress is still there, under the ground."

It seems to me that this statement is primarily a declaration of love for the land, in which the several elements—the woman, the dress, and this plain—are at last become one reality, one expression of the beautiful in nature. Moreover, it seems to me a peculiarly Native American expression in this sense: that the concentration of things that are explicitly remembered—the general landscape, the simple, almost abstract nature of the burial, above all the beautiful dress, which is wholly singular in kind (as well as in its function within the narrative)—is especially Indian in character. The things that are *not* explicitly remembered—the woman's name, the exact location of her grave—are the things that matter least in the special view of the storyteller. What matters here is the translation of the woman into the landscape, a translation particularly signified by means of the beautiful and distinctive dress, an *Indian* dress.

When I was a boy, I lived for several years at Jemez Pueblo, New Mexico. The Pueblo Indians are perhaps more obviously invested in the land than are other people. Their whole life is predicated upon a thorough perception of the physical world and its myriad aspects. When I first went there to live, the cacique, or chief, of the Pueblos was a venerable old man with long, gray hair and bright, deep-set eyes. He was entirely dignified and imposing—and rather formidable in the eyes of a boy. He excited my imagination a good deal. I was told that this old man kept the calendar of the tribe, that each morning he stood on a certain spot of ground near the center of the town and watched to see where the sun appeared on the skyline. By means of this solar calendar did he know and announce to his people when it was time to plant, to harvest, to perform this or that ceremony. This image of him in my mind's eye—the old man gazing each morning after the ranging sun—came to represent for me the epitome of that real harmony between man and the land that signifies the Indian world.

One day when I was riding my horse along the Jemez River, I looked up to see a long caravan of wagons and people on horseback and on foot. Men, women, and children were crossing the river ahead of me, moving out to the west, where most of the cultivated fields were, the farmland of the town. It was a wonderful sight to see, this long procession, and I was immediately deeply curious. I wanted to investigate, but it was not in me to do so at once, for that racial reserve, that sense of propriety that is deep-seated in Native American culture, stayed me, held me up. Then I saw someone coming toward me on horseback, galloping. It was a friend of mine, a boy of my own age. "Come on," he said. "Come with us." "Where are you going?" I asked casually. But he would not tell me. He simply laughed and urged me to come along, and of course I was very glad to do so. It was a bright spring morning, and I had a good horse under me, and the prospect of adventure was delicious. We moved far out across the eroded plain to the farthest fields at the foot of a great red mesa, and there we planted two large fields of corn. And afterward, on the edge of the fields, we sat on blankets and ate a feast in the shade of a cottonwood grove. Later I learned it was the cacique's fields we planted. And this is an ancient tradition at Jemez. The people of the town plant and tend and harvest the cacique's fields, and in the winter the hunters give to him a portion of the meat that they bring home from the mountains. It is as if the cacique is himself the translation of man, every man, into the landscape.

I have not forgotten that day, nor shall I forget it. I remember the warm earth of the fields, the smooth texture of seeds in my hands, and the brown water moving slowly and irresistibly among the rows. Above all I remember the spirit in which the procession was made, the work was done, and the feasting was enjoyed. It was a spirit of communion, of the life of each man in relation to the life of the planet and of the infinite distance and silence in which it moves. We made, in concert, an appropriate expression of that spirit.

One afternoon an old Kiowa woman talked to me, telling me of the place in Oklahoma in which she had lived for a hundred years. It was the place in which my grandparents, too, lived; and it is the place where I was born. And she told me of a time even further back, when the Kiowas came down from the north and centered their culture in the red earth of the southern plains. She told wonderful stories, and as I listened, I began to feel more and more sure that her voice proceeded from the land itself. I asked her many things concerning the Kiowas, for I wanted to understand all that I could of my heritage. I told the old woman that I had come there to learn from her and from people like her, those in whom the old ways were preserved. And she said simply: "It is good that you have come here." I believe that her word "good" meant many things; for one thing it meant *right,* or *appropriate.* And indeed it was appropriate that she should speak of the land. She was eminently qualified to do so. She had a great reverence for the land, and an ancient perception of it, a perception that is acquired only in the course of many generations.

It is this notion of the appropriate, along with that of the beautiful, that forms the Native American perspective on the land. In a sense these considerations are indivisible; Native American oral tradition is rich with songs and tales that celebrate natural beauty, the beauty of the natural world. What is more appropriate to our world than that which is beautiful?

> At noon
> turtles
> enter
> slowly
> into
> the warm
> dark loam.
> Bees hold
> the swarm.
> Meadows
> recede
> through planes
> of heat
> and pure
> distance.

Very old in the Native American worldview is the conviction that the earth is vital, that there is a spiritual dimension to it, a dimension in which man rightly exists. It follows logically that there are ethical imperatives in this matter. I think: Inasmuch as I am in the land, it is appropriate that I should affirm myself in the spirit of the land. I shall celebrate my life in the world and the world in my life. In the natural order man invests himself in the landscape and at the same time incorporates the landscape into his own most fundamental experience. This trust is sacred.

The process of investment and appropriation is, I believe, preeminently a function of the imagination. It is accomplished by means of an act of the imagination that is especially ethical in kind. We are what we imagine ourselves to be. The Native American is someone who thinks of himself, imagines himself in a particular way. By virtue of his experience his idea of himself comprehends his relationship to the land.

And the quality of this imagining is determined as well by racial and cultural experience. The Native American's attitudes toward this landscape have been formulated over a long period of time, a span that reaches back to the end of the Ice Age. The land, *this* land, is secure in his racial memory.

In our society as a whole we conceive of the land in terms of ownership and use. It is a lifeless medium of exchange; it has for most of us, I suspect, no more spirituality than has an automobile, say, or a refrigerator. And our laws confirm us in this view, for we can buy and sell the land, we can exclude each other from it, and in the context of ownership we can use it as we will. Ownership implies use, and use implies consumption.

But this way of thinking of the land is alien to the Indian. His cultural intelligence is opposed to these concepts; indeed, for him they are all but inconceivable quantities. This fundamental distinction is easier to understand with respect to ownership than to use, perhaps. For obviously the Indian does use, and has always used, the land and the available resources in it. The point is that *use* does not indicate in any real way his idea of the land. "Use" is neither his word nor his idea. As an Indian I think: "You say that I *use* the land, and I reply, yes, it is true; but it is not the first truth. The first truth is that I *love* the land; I see that it is beautiful; I delight in it; I am alive in it."

In the long course of his journey from Asia and in the realization of himself in the New World, the Indian has assumed a deep ethical regard for the earth and sky, a reverence for the natural world that is antipodal to that strange tenet of modern civilization that seemingly has it that man must destroy his environment. It is this ancient ethic of the Native American that must shape our efforts to preserve the earth and the life upon and within it.

At dusk
the gray
foxes
stiffen
in cold;
blackbirds

are fixed
in white
branches.
Rivers
follow
the moon,
the long
white track
of the
full moon.

Leslie Marmon Silko

LANDSCAPE, HISTORY, AND THE PUEBLO IMAGINATION

Leslie Marmon Silko grew up in the Laguna Pueblo Reservation and continues to live in the Southwest. She is a poet and the author of the celebrated novel *Ceremony*. In the following essay, Silko focuses on the importance of cultural imagination in the Pueblo relationship to nature. Myth, story, and naming have been ways to maintain an intimate and interactive connection with the earth. The oral tradition has highlighted the unique details of specific locales and their meanings for the tribe, helping to link nature and culture and ground them in a clear sense of place. In such a tradition, the land becomes an aid to a culture's spiritual development.

From a High Arid Plateau in New Mexico

You see that after a thing is dead, it dries up. It might take weeks or years, but eventually if you touch the thing, it crumbles under your fingers. It goes back to dust. The soul of the thing has long since departed. With the plants and wild game the soul may have already been borne back into bones and blood or thick green stalk and leaves. Nothing is wasted. What cannot be eaten by people or in some way used must then be left where other living creatures may benefit. What domestic animals or wild scavengers can't eat will be fed to the plants. The plants feed on the dust of these few remains.

The ancient Pueblo people buried the dead in vacant rooms or partially collapsed rooms adjacent to the main living quarters. Sand and clay used to construct the roof make layers many inches deep once the roof has collapsed. The layers of sand and clay make for easy grave-digging. The vacant room fills with cast-off objects and debris. When a vacant room has filled deep enough, a shallow but adequate grave can be scooped in a far corner. Archaeologists have remarked over formal burials complete with elaborate funerary objects excavated in trash middens of abandoned rooms. But the rocks and adobe mortar of collapsed walls were valued by the ancient people. Because each rock had been carefully selected for size and shape, then chiseled to an even face. Even the pink clay adobe melting with each rainstorm had to be prayed over, then dug and carried some distance. Corn cobs and husks, the rinds and stalks and animal bones were not regarded by the ancient people as filth or garbage. The remains were merely resting at a midpoint in their journey back to dust. Human remains are not so different. They should rest with the bones and rinds where they all may benefit living creatures—small rodents and insects—until their return is completed. The remains of things—animals and plants, the clay and the stones—were treated with respect. Because for the ancient people all these things had spirit and being.

The antelope merely consents to return home with the hunter. All phases of the hunt are conducted with love. The love the hunter and the people have for the Antelope People. And the love of the antelope who agree to give up their meat and blood so that human beings will not starve. Waste of meat or even the thoughtless handling of bones cooked bare will offend the antelope spirits. Next year the hunters will vainly search the dry plains for antelope. Thus it is necessary to return carefully the bones and hair, and the stalks and leaves to the earth who first created them. The spirits remain close by. They do not leave us.

The dead become dust, and in this becoming they are once more joined with the Mother. The ancient Pueblo people called the earth the Mother Creator of all things in this world. Her sister, the Corn Mother, occasionally merges with her because all succulent green life rises out of the depths of the earth.

Rocks and clay are part of the Mother. They emerge in various forms, but at some time before, they were smaller particles or great boulders. At a later time they may again become what they once were. Dust.

A rock shares this fate with us and with animals and plants as well. A rock has being or spirit, although we may not understand it. The spirit may differ from the spirit we know in animals or plants or in ourselves. In the end we all originate from the depths of the earth. Perhaps this is how all beings share in the spirit of the Creator. We do not know.

From the Emergence Place

Pueblo potters, the creators of petroglyphs and oral narratives, never conceived of removing themselves from the earth and sky. So long as the human consciousness remains *within* the hills, canyons, cliffs, and the plants, clouds, and sky, the term *landscape,* as it has entered the English language, is misleading. "A portion of territory the eye can comprehend in a single view" does not correctly describe the relationship between the human being and his or her surroundings. This assumes the viewer is somehow *outside* or *separate from* the territory he or she surveys. Viewers are as much a part of the landscape as the boulders they stand on. There is no high mesa edge or mountain peak where one can stand and not immediately be part of all that surrounds. Human identity is linked with all the elements of Creation through the clan: you might belong to the Sun Clan or the Lizard Clan or the Corn Clan or the Clay Clan.* Standing deep within the natural world, the ancient Pueblo understood the thing as it was—the squash blossom, grasshopper, or rabbit itself could never be created by the human hand. Ancient Pueblos took the modest view that the thing itself (the landscape) could not be improved upon. The ancients did not presume to tamper with what had already been created. Thus *realism,* as we now recognize it in painting and sculpture, did not catch the imaginations of Pueblo people until recently.

The squash blossom itself is *one thing:* itself. So the ancient Pueblo potter abstracted what she saw to be the key elements of the squash blossom— the four symmetrical petals, with four symmetrical stamens in the center. These key elements, while suggesting the squash flower, also link it with the four cardinal directions. By representing only its intrinsic form, the squash flower is released from a limited meaning or restricted identity. Even in the most sophisticated abstract form, a squash flower or a cloud or a lightning bolt became intricately connected with a complex system of relationships which the ancient Pueblo people maintained with each other, and with the populous natural world they lived within. A bolt of light-

---

* Clan—*A social unit composed of families sharing common ancestors who trace their lineage back to the Emergence where their ancestors allied themselves with certain plants or animals or elements.*

ning is itself, but at the same time it may mean much more. It may be a messenger of good fortune when summer rains are needed. It may deliver death, perhaps the result of manipulations by the Gunnadeyahs, destructive necromancers. Lightning may strike down an evil-doer. Or lightning may strike a person of good will. If the person survives, lightning endows him or her with heightened power.

Pictographs and petroglyphs of constellations or elk or antelope draw their magic in part from the process wherein the focus of all prayer and concentration is upon the thing itself, which, in its turn, guides the hunter's hand. Connection with the spirit dimensions requires a figure or form which is all-inclusive. A "lifelike" rendering of an elk is too restrictive. Only the elk *is* itself. A *realistic* rendering of an elk would be only one particular elk anyway. The purpose of the hunt rituals and magic is to make contact with *all* the spirits of the Elk.

The land, the sky, and all that is within them—the landscape—includes human beings. Interrelationships in the Pueblo landscape are complex and fragile. The unpredictability of the weather, the aridity and harshness of much of the terrain in the high plateau country explain in large part the relentless attention the ancient Pueblo people gave the sky and the earth around them. Survival depended upon harmony and cooperation not only among human beings, but among all things—the animate and the less animate, since rocks and mountains were known to move, to travel occasionally.

The ancient Pueblos believed the Earth and the Sky were sisters (or sister and brother in the post-Christian version). As long as good family relations are maintained, then the Sky will continue to bless her sister, the Earth, with rain, and the Earth's children will continue to survive. But the old stories recall incidents in which troublesome spirits or beings threaten the earth. In one story, a malicious ka'tsina, called the Gambler, seizes the Shiwana, or Rainclouds, the Sun's beloved children.* The Shiwana are snared in magical power late one afternoon on a high mountain top. The Gambler takes the Rainclouds to his mountain stronghold where he locks them in the north room of his house. What was his idea? The

---

* Ka'tsina—*Ka'tsinas are spirit beings who roam the earth and who inhabit kachina masks worn in Pueblo ceremonial dances.*

Shiwana were beyond value. They brought life to all things on earth. The Gambler wanted a big stake to wager in his games of chance. But such greed, even on the part of only one being, had the effect of threatening the survival of all life on earth. Sun Youth, aided by old Grandmother Spider, outsmarts the Gambler and the rigged game, and the Rainclouds are set free. The drought ends, and once more life thrives on earth.

Through the Stories We Hear Who We Are

All summer the people watch the west horizon, scanning the sky from south to north for rain clouds. Corn must have moisture at the time the tassels form. Otherwise pollination will be incomplete, and the ears will be stunted and shriveled. An inadequate harvest may bring disaster. Stories told at Hopi, Zuni, and at Acoma and Laguna describe drought and starvation as recently as 1900. Precipitation in west-central New Mexico averages fourteen inches annually. The western pueblos are located at altitudes over 5,600 feet above sea level, where winter temperatures at night fall below freezing. Yet evidence of their presence in the high desert plateau country goes back ten thousand years. The ancient Pueblo people not only survived in this environment, but many years they thrived. In A.D. 1100 the people at Chaco Canyon had built cities with apartment buildings of stone five stories high. Their sophistication as sky-watchers was surpassed only by Mayan and Incan astronomers. Yet this vast complex of knowledge and belief, amassed for thousands of years, was never recorded in writing.

Instead, the ancient Pueblo people depended upon collective memory through successive generations to maintain and transmit an entire culture, a worldview complete with proven strategies for survival. The oral narrative, or "story," became the medium in which the complex of Pueblo knowledge and belief was maintained. Whatever the event or the subject, the ancient people perceived the world and themselves within that world as part of an ancient continuous story composed of innumerable bundles of other stories.

The ancient Pueblo vision of the world was inclusive. The impulse was to leave nothing out. Pueblo oral tradition necessarily embraced all levels of human experience. Otherwise, the collective knowledge and beliefs comprising ancient Pueblo culture would have been incomplete. Thus stories about the Creation and Emergence of human beings and animals into this World continue to be retold each year for four days and four nights during the winter solstice. The "humma-hah" stories related events from the time long ago when human beings were still able to communicate with animals and other living things. But, beyond these two preceding categories, the Pueblo oral tradition knew no boundaries. Accounts of the appearance of the first Europeans in Pueblo country or of the tragic encounters between Pueblo people and Apache raiders were no more and no less important than stories about the biggest mule deer ever taken or adulterous couples surprised in cornfields and chicken coops. Whatever happened, the ancient people instinctively sorted events and details into a loose narrative structure. Everything became a story.

Traditionally everyone, from the youngest child to the oldest person, was expected to listen and to be able to recall or tell a portion, if only a small detail, from a narrative account or story. Thus the remembering and retelling were a communal process. Even if a key figure, an elder who knew much more than others, were to die unexpectedly, the system would remain intact. Through the efforts of a great many people, the community was able to piece together valuable accounts and crucial information that might otherwise have died with an individual.

Communal storytelling was a self-correcting process in which listeners were encouraged to speak up if they noted an important fact or detail omitted. The people were happy to listen to two or three different versions of the same event or the same humma-hah story. Even conflicting versions of an incident were welcomed for the entertainment they provided. Defenders of each version might joke and tease one another, but seldom were there any direct confrontations. Implicit in the Pueblo oral tradition was the awareness that loyalties, grudges, and kinship must always influence the narrator's choices as she emphasizes to listeners this is the way *she* has always heard the story told. The ancient Pueblo people sought a communal truth, not an absolute. For them this truth lived somewhere within the web of differing versions, disputes over minor points, outright contradictions tangling with old feuds and village rivalries.

A dinner-table conversation, recalling a deer hunt forty years ago when the largest mule deer ever was taken, inevitably stimulates similar memories in listeners. But hunting stories were not merely after-dinner entertainment. These accounts contained information of critical importance about behavior and migration patterns of mule deer. Hunting stories carefully described key landmarks and locations of fresh water. Thus a deer-hunt story might also serve as a "map." Lost travelers, and lost piñon-nut gatherers, have been saved by sighting a rock formation they recognize only because they once heard a hunting story describing this rock formation.

The importance of cliff formations and water holes does not end with hunting stories. As offspring of the Mother Earth, the ancient Pueblo people could not conceive of themselves within a specific landscape. Location, or "place," nearly always plays a central role in the Pueblo oral narratives. Indeed, stories are most frequently recalled as people are passing by a specific geographical feature or the exact place where a story takes place. The precise date of the incident often is less important than the place or location of the happening. "Long, long ago," "a long time ago," "not too long ago," and "recently" are usually how stories are classified in terms of time. But the places where the stories occur are precisely located, and prominent geographical details recalled, even if the landscape is well-known to listeners. Often because the turning point in the narrative involved a peculiarity or special quality of a rock or tree or plant found only at that place. Thus, in the case of many of the Pueblo narratives, it is impossible to determine which came first: the incident or the geographical feature which begs to be brought alive in a story that features some unusual aspect of this location.

There is a giant sandstone boulder about a mile north of Old Laguna, on the road to Paguate. It is ten feet tall and twenty feet in circumference. When I was a child, and we would pass this boulder driving to Paguate village, someone usually made reference to the story about Kochininako, Yellow Woman, and the Estrucuyo, a monstrous giant who nearly ate her. The Twin Hero Brothers saved Kochininako, who had been out hunting rabbits to take home to feed her mother and sisters. The Hero Brothers had heard her cries just in time. The Estrucuyo had cornered her in a cave too small to fit its monstrous head. Kochininako had already thrown to the Estrucuyo all her rabbits, as well as her moccasins and most of her clothing. Still the creature had not been satisfied. After killing the Estrucuyo with their bows and arrows, the Twin Hero Brothers slit open the Estrucuyo and cut out its heart. They threw the heart as far as they could. The monster's heart landed there, beside the old trail to Paguate village, where the sandstone boulder rests now.

It may be argued that the existence of the boulder precipitated the creation of a story to explain it. But sandstone boulders and sandstone formations of strange shapes abound in the Laguna Pueblo area. Yet most of them do not have stories. Often the crucial element in a narrative is the terrain—some specific detail of the setting.

A high dark mesa rises dramatically from a grassy plain fifteen miles southeast of Laguna, in an area known as Swanee. On the grassy plain one hundred and forty years ago, my great-grandmother's uncle and his brother-in-law were grazing their herd of sheep. Because visibility on the plain extends for over twenty miles, it wasn't until the two sheepherders came near the high dark mesa that the Apaches were able to stalk them. Using the mesa to obscure their approach, the raiders swept around from both ends of the mesa. My great-grandmother's relatives were killed, and the herd lost. The high dark mesa played a critical role: the mesa had compromised the safety which the openness of the plains had seemed to assure. Pueblo and Apache alike relied upon the terrain, the very earth herself, to give them protection and aid. Human activities or needs were maneuvered to fit the existing surroundings and conditions. I imagine the last afternoon of my distant ancestors as warm and sunny for late September. They might have been traveling slowly, bringing the sheep closer to Laguna in preparation for the approach of colder weather. The grass was tall and only beginning to change from green to a yellow which matched the late-afternoon sun shining off it. There might have been comfort in the warmth and the sight of the sheep fattening on good pasture which lulled my ancestors into their fatal inattention. They might have had a rifle whereas the Apaches had only bows and arrows. But there would have been four or five Apache raiders, and the surprise attack would have canceled any advantage the rifles gave them.

Survival in any landscape comes down to making the best use of all available resources. On that particular September afternoon, the raiders made better use of the Swanee terrain than my poor ancestors did. Thus the high dark mesa and the story of the two lost Laguna herders became inextricably linked. The memory of them and their story resides in part with the high black mesa. For as long as the mesa stands, people within the family and clan will be reminded of the story of that afternoon long ago. Thus the continuity and accuracy of the oral narratives are reinforced by the landscape—and the Pueblo interpretation of that landscape is *maintained*.

The Migration Story: An Interior Journey

The Laguna Pueblo migration stories refer to specific places—mesas, springs, or cottonwood trees—not only locations which can be visited still, but also locations which lie directly on the state highway route linking Paguate village with Laguna village. In traveling this road as a child with older Laguna people I first heard a few of the stories from that much larger body of stories linked with the Emergence and Migration.* It may be coincidental that Laguna people continue to follow the same route which, according to the Migration story, the ancestors followed south from the Emergence Place. It may be that the route is merely the shortest and best route for car, horse, or foot traffic between Laguna and Paguate villages. But if the stories about boulders, springs, and hills are actually remnants from a ritual that retraces the creation and emergence of the Laguna Pueblo people as a culture, as the people they became, then continued use of that route creates a unique relationship between the ritual-mythic world and the actual, everyday world. A journey from Paguate to Laguna down the long incline of Paguate Hill retraces the original journey from the Emergence Place, which is located slightly north of the Paguate village. Thus the landscape between Paguate and Laguna takes on a deeper significance: the landscape resonates the spiritual or mythic dimension of the Pueblo world even today.

Although each Pueblo culture designates a specific Emergence Place—usually a small natural spring edged with mossy sandstone and full of cattails and wild watercress—it is clear that they do not agree on any single location or natural spring as the one and only true Emergence Place. Each Pueblo group recounts its own stories about Creation, Emergence, and Migration, although they all believe that all human beings, with all the animals and plants, emerged at the same place and at the same time.†

---

* The Emergence—*All the human beings, animals, and life which had been created emerged from the four worlds below when the earth became habitable.*

The Migration—*The Pueblo people emerged into the Fifth World, but they had already been warned they would have to travel and search before they found the place they were meant to live.*

† Creation—*Tse'itsi'nako, Thought Woman, the Spider, thought about it, and everything she thought came into being. First she thought of three sisters for herself, and they helped*

Natural springs are crucial sources of water for all life in the high desert plateau country. So the small spring near Paguate village is literally the source and continuance of life for the people in the area. The spring also functions on a spiritual level, recalling the original Emergence Place and linking the people and the spring water to all other people and to that moment when the Pueblo people became aware of themselves as they are even now. The Emergence was an emergence into a precise cultural identity. Thus the Pueblo stories about the Emergence and Migration are not to be taken as literally as the anthropologists might wish. Prominent geographical features and landmarks which are mentioned in the narratives exist for ritual purposes, not because the Laguna people actually journeyed south for hundreds of years from Chaco Canyon or Mesa Verde, as the archaeologists say, or eight miles from the site of the natural springs at Paguate to the sandstone hilltop at Laguna.

The eight miles, marked with boulders, mesas, springs, and river crossings, are actually a ritual circuit or path which marks the interior journey the Laguna people made: a journey of awareness and imagination in which they emerged from being within the earth and from everything included in earth to the culture and people they became, differentiating themselves for the first time from all that had surrounded them, always aware that interior distances cannot be reckoned in physical miles or in calendar years.

The narratives linked with prominent features of the landscape between Paguate and Laguna delineate the complexities of the relationship which human beings must maintain with the surrounding natural world if they hope to survive in this place. Thus the journey was an interior process of the imagination, a growing awareness that being human is somehow different from all other life—animal, plant, and inanimate. Yet we are all from the same source: the awareness never deteriorated into Cartesian duality, cutting off the human from the natural world.

The people found the opening into the Fifth World too small to allow them or any of the animals to escape. They had sent a fly out through the small hole to tell them if it was the world which the Mother Creator had

---

her think of the rest of the Universe, including the Fifth World and the four worlds below. The Fifth World *is the world we are living in today. There are four previous worlds below this world.*

promised. It was, but there was the problem of getting out. The antelope tried to butt the opening to enlarge it, but the antelope enlarged it only a little. It was necessary for the badger with her long claws to assist the antelope, and at last the opening was enlarged enough so that all the people and animals were able to emerge up into the Fifth World. The human beings could not have emerged without the aid of antelope and badger. The human beings depended upon the aid and charity of the animals. Only through interdependence could the human beings survive. Families belonged to clans, and it was by clan that the human being joined with the animal and plant world. Life on the high arid plateau became viable when the human beings were able to imagine themselves as sisters and brothers to the badger, antelope, clay, yucca, and sun. Not until they could find a viable relationship to the terrain, the landscape they found themselves in, could they *emerge*. Only at the moment the requisite balance between human and *other* was realized could the Pueblo people become a culture, a distinct group whose population and survival remained stable despite the vicissitudes of climate and terrain.

Landscape thus has similarities with dreams. Both have the power to seize terrifying feelings and deep instincts and translate them into images—visual, aural, tactile—into the concrete where human beings may more readily confront and channel the terrifying instincts or powerful emotions into rituals and narratives which reassure the individual while reaffirming cherished values of the group. The identity of the individual as a part of the group and the greater Whole is strengthened, and the terror of facing the world alone is extinguished.

Even now, the people at Laguna Pueblo spend the greater portion of social occasions recounting recent incidents or events which have occurred in the Laguna area. Nearly always, the discussion will precipitate the retelling of older stories about similar incidents or other stories connected with a specific place. The stories often contain disturbing or provocative material, but are nonetheless told in the presence of children and women. The effect of these inter-family or inter-clan exchanges is the reassurance for each person that she or he will never be separated or apart from the clan, no matter what might happen. Neither the worst blunders or disasters nor the greatest financial prosperity and joy will ever be permitted to isolate anyone from the rest of the group. In the ancient times, cohesiveness was all that stood between extinction and survival, and, while the individual certainly was recognized, it was always as an individual simultaneously bonded to family and clan by a complex bundle of custom and ritual. You are never the first to suffer a grave loss or profound humiliation. You are never the first, and you understand that you will probably not be the last to commit or be victimized by a repugnant act. Your family and clan are able to go on at length about others now passed on, others older or more experienced than you who suffered similar losses.

The wide deep arroyo near the Kings Bar (located across the reservation borderline) has over the years claimed many vehicles. A few years ago, when a Viet Nam veteran's new red Volkswagen rolled backwards into the arroyo while he was inside buying a six-pack of beer, the story of his loss joined the lively and large collection of stories already connected with that big arroyo. I do not know whether the Viet Nam veteran was consoled when he was told the stories about the other cars claimed by the ravenous arroyo. All his savings of combat pay had gone for the red Volkswagen. But this man could not have felt any worse than the man who, some years before, had left his children and mother-in-law in his station wagon with the engine running. When he came out of the liquor store his station wagon was gone. He found it and its passengers upside down in the big arroyo. Broken bones, cuts and bruises, and a total wreck of the car. The big arroyo has a wide mouth. Its existence needs no explanation. People in the area regard the arroyo much as they might regard a living being, which has a certain character and personality. I seldom drive past that wide deep arroyo without feeling a familiarity with and even a strange affection for this arroyo. Because as treacherous as it may be, the arroyo maintains a strong connection between human beings and the earth. The arroyo demands from us the caution and attention that constitute respect. It is this sort of respect the old believers have in mind when they tell us we must respect and love the earth.

Hopi Pueblo elders have said that the austere and, to some eyes, barren plains and hills surrounding their mesa-top villages actually help to nurture the spirituality of the Hopi *way*. The Hopi elders say the Hopi people might have settled in locations far more lush where daily life would not have been so grueling. But there on the high silent sandstone mesas that overlook the sandy arid expanses stretching to all horizons, the Hopi elders say the Hopi people must "live by their prayers" if they are to survive. The Hopi way cherishes the intangible: the riches realized from interaction and interrelationships with all beings above all else. Great abundances of material things, even food, the Hopi elders believe, tend to lure human attention away from what is most valuable and important. The views of the Hopi elders are not much different from those elders in all the Pueblos.

The bare vastness of the Hopi landscape emphasizes the visual impact of every plant, every rock, every arroyo. Nothing is overlooked or taken for granted. Each ant, each lizard, each lark is imbued with great value simply because the creature is there, simply because the creature is alive in a place where any life at all is precious. Stand on the mesa edge at Walpai and look west over the bare distances toward the pale blue outlines of the San Francisco peaks where the ka'tsina spirits reside. So little lies between you and the sky. So little lies between you and the earth. One look and you know that simply to survive is a great triumph, that every possible resource is needed, every possible ally—even the most humble insect or reptile. You realize you will be speaking with all of them if you intend to last out the year. Thus it is that the Hopi elders are grateful to the landscape for aiding them in their quest as spiritual people.

THE LOSS OF PLACE

Wendell Berry

From

A NATIVE HILL

Wendell Berry is a poet, novelist, essayist, and farmer. Brought up in rural Kentucky, he became an established poet in New York City and then decided to return to his homeland to begin a life of sustainable farming, exquisite poetry, and incisive cultural criticism. His book *The Unsettling of America: Culture and Agriculture* is a powerful indictment of contemporary culture. He has expanded that critique and articulated his vision of right livelihood in various collections of essays such as *The Gift of Good Land;* among his many volumes of poetry is *Selected Poems of Wendell Berry.* His writings explore the intersection of nature and humanity, and their deep religious sensibility has been influenced by Confucianism as well as an earth-centered Christianity. Berry's development of the ideal of stewardship is marked by humility, responsibility, and joy. The following selection is an excerpt from an early long essay titled "A Native Hill." That essay begins with an autobiographical sketch of his family's tenure on the land and his early life, his work at various universities, and his return to Kentucky. Berry then considers the violent history of European settlement and the resistance to nature exemplified by the building of a road, which he contrasts to Native American footpaths. For another excerpt from this essay, which suggests an alternative to this tragic heritage, see the following section, "The Possibility of Place."

I know of no better key to what is adverse in our heritage in this place than the account of "The Battle of the Fire-Brands," quoted in Collins' *History of Kentucky* "from the autobiography of Rev. Jacob Young, a Methodist minister." The "Newcastle" referred to is the present-day New Castle, the county seat of Henry County. I give the quote in full:

> The costume of the Kentuckians was a hunting shirt, buckskin pantaloons, a leathern belt around their middle, a scabbard, and a big knife

fastened to their belt; some of them wore hats and some caps. Their feet were covered with moccasins, made of dressed deer skins. They did not think themselves dressed without their powder-horn and shot-pouch, or the gun and the tomahawk. They were ready, then, for all alarms. They knew but little. They could clear ground, raise corn, and kill turkeys, deer, bears, and buffalo; and, when it became necessary, they understood the art of fighting the Indians as well as any men in the United States.

Shortly after we had taken up our residence, I was called upon to assist in opening a road from the place where Newcastle now stands, to the mouth of Kentucky river. That country, then, was an unbroken forest; there was nothing but an Indian trail passing the wilderness. I met the company early in the morning, with my axe, three days' provisions, and my knapsack. Here I found a captain, with about 100 men, all prepared to labor; about as jovial a company as I ever saw, all good-natured and civil. This was about the last of November, 1797. The day was cold and clear. The country through which the company passed was delightful; it was not a flat country, but, what the Kentuckians called, rolling ground—was quite well stored with lofty timber, and the undergrowth was very pretty. The beautiful canebrakes gave it a peculiar charm. What rendered it most interesting was the great abundance of wild turkeys, deer, bears, and other wild animals. The company worked hard all day, in quiet, and every man obeyed the captain's orders punctually.

About sundown, the captain, after a short address, told us the night was going to be very cold, and we must make very large fires. We felled the hickory trees in great abundance; made great log-heaps, mixing the dry wood with the green hickory; and, laying down a kind of sleepers under the pile, elevated the heap and caused it to burn rapidly. Every man had a water vessel in his knapsack; we searched for and found a stream of water. By this time, the fires were showing to great advantage; so we warmed our cold victuals, ate our suppers, and spent the evening in hearing the hunter's stories relative to the bloody scenes of the Indian war. We then heard some pretty fine singing, considering the circumstances.

Thus far, well; but a change began to take place. They became very rude, and raised the war-whoop. Their shrill shrieks made me tremble. They chose two captains, divided the men into two companies, and commenced fighting with the fire-brands—the log heaps having burned down. The only law for their government was, that no man should throw a brand without fire on it—so that they might know how to dodge. They fought, for two or three hours, in perfect good nature; till brands became scarce, and they began to violate the law. Some were severely wounded, blood began to flow freely, and they were in a fair way of commencing a fight in earnest. At this moment, the loud voice of the captain rang out above the din, ordering every man to retire to rest. They dropped their weapons of warfare, rekindled the fires, and laid down to sleep. We finished our road according to directions, and returned home in health and peace.

The significance of this bit of history is in its utter violence. The work of clearing the road was itself violent. And from the orderly violence of that labor, these men turned for amusement to disorderly violence. They were men whose element was violence; the only alternatives they were aware of were those within the comprehension of main strength. And let us acknowledge that these were the truly influential men in the history of Kentucky, as well as in the history of most of the rest of America. In comparison to the fatherhood of such as these, the so-called "founding fathers" who established our political ideals are but distant cousins. It is not John Adams or Thomas Jefferson whom we see night after night in the magic mirror of the television set; we see these builders of the road from New Castle to the mouth of the Kentucky River. Their reckless violence has glamorized all our trivialities and evils. Their aggressions have simplified our complexities and problems. They have cut all our Gordian knots. They have appeared in all our disguises and costumes. They have worn all our uniforms. Their war whoop has sanctified our inhumanity and ratified our blunders of policy.

To testify to the persistence of their influence, it is only necessary for me to confess that I read the Reverend Young's account of them with delight; I yield a considerable admiration to the exuberance and extravagance of their fight with the firebrands; I take a certain pride in belonging to the same history and the same place that they belong to—though I know that they represent the worst that is in us, and in me, and that their presence in our history has been ruinous, and that their survival among us promises ruin.

"They knew but little," the observant Reverend says of them, and this is the most suggestive thing he says. It is surely understandable and pardonable, under the circumstances, that these men were ignorant by the standards of formal schooling. But one immediately reflects that the American Indian, who was ignorant by the same standards, nevertheless knew how to live in the country without making violence the invariable mode of his relation to it; in fact, from the ecologist's or the conservationist's point of view, he did it *no* violence. This is because he had, in place of what we would call education, a fully integrated culture, the content of which was a highly complex sense of his dependence on the earth. The same, I believe, was generally true of the peasants of certain old agricultural societies, particularly in the Orient. They belonged by an intricate awareness to the earth they lived on and by, which meant that they respected it, which meant that they practiced strict economies in the use of it.

The abilities of those Kentucky road builders of 1797 were far more primitive and rudimentary than those of the Stone Age people they had driven out. They could clear the ground, grow corn, kill game, and make war. In the minds and hands of men who "know but little"—or little else—all of these abilities are certain to be destructive, even of those values and benefits their use may be intended to serve.

On such a night as the Reverend Young describes, an Indian would have made do with a small shelter and a small fire. But these road builders, veterans of the Indian War, "felled the hickory trees in great abundance; made great log-heaps . . . and caused [them] to burn rapidly." Far from making a small shelter that could be adequately heated by a small fire, their way was to make no shelter at all, and heat instead a sizable area of the landscape. The idea was that when faced with abundance one should consume abundantly—an idea that has survived to become the basis of our present economy. It is neither natural nor civilized, and even from a "practical" point of view it is to the last degree brutalizing and stupid.

I think that the comparison of these road builders with the Indians, on the one hand, and with Old World peasants on the other, is a most suggestive one. The Indians and the peasants were people who belonged deeply and intricately to their places. Their ways of life had evolved slowly in accordance with their knowledge of their land, of its needs, of their own relation of dependence and responsibility to it. The road builders, on the contrary, were *placeless* people. That is why they "knew but little." Having left Europe far behind, they had not yet in any meaningful sense arrived in America, not yet having *devoted* themselves to any part of it in a way that would produce the intricate knowledge of it necessary to live in it without destroying it. Because they belonged to no place, it was almost inevitable that they should behave violently toward the places they came to. We *still* have not, in any meaningful way, arrived in America. And in spite of our great reservoir of facts and methods, in comparison to the deep earthly wisdom of established peoples we still know but little.

But my understanding of this curiously parabolic fragment of history will not be complete until I have considered more directly that the occasion of this particular violence was the building of a road. It is obvious that one who values the idea of community cannot speak against roads without risking all sorts of absurdity. It must be noticed, nevertheless, that the predecessor to this first road was "nothing but an Indian trail passing the wilderness"—a path. The Indians, then, who had the wisdom and the grace to live in this country for perhaps ten thousand years without destroying or damaging any of it, needed for their travels no more than a footpath; but their successors, who in a century and a half plundered the area of at least half its topsoil and virtually all of its forest, felt immediately that they had to have a road. My interest is not in the question of whether or not they *needed* the road, but in the fact that the road was then, and is now, the most characteristic form of their relation to the country.

The difference between a path and a road is not only the obvious one. A path is little more than a habit that comes with knowledge of a place. It is a sort of ritual of familiarity. As a form, it is a form of contact with a known landscape. It is not destructive. It is the perfect adaptation, through experience and familiarity, of movement to place; it obeys the natural contours; such obstacles as it meets it goes around. A road, on the other hand, even the most primitive road, embodies a resistance against the landscape. Its reason is not simply the necessity for movement, but haste. Its wish is to *avoid* contact with the landscape; it seeks so far as possible to go over the country, rather than through it; its aspiration, as we see clearly in the example of our modern freeways, is to be a bridge; its tendency is to translate place into space in order to traverse it with the least effort. It is destructive, seeking to remove or destroy all obstacles in its way. The primitive road advanced by the destruction of the forest; modern roads advance by the destruction of topography.

That first road from the site of New Castle to the mouth of the Kentucky River—lost now either by obsolescence or metamorphosis—is now being crossed and to some extent replaced by its modern descendant known as I-71, and I have no wish to disturb the question of whether or not *this* road was needed. I only want to observe that it bears no relation whatever to the country it passes through. It is a pure abstraction, built to serve the two abstractions that are the poles of our national life: commerce and expensive pleasure. It was built, not according to the lay of the land, but according to a blueprint. Such homes and farmlands and woodlands as happened to be in its way are now buried under it. A part of a hill near here that would have caused it to turn aside was simply cut down and disposed of as thoughtlessly as the pioneer road builders would have disposed of a tree. Its form is the form of speed, dissatisfaction, and anxiety. It represents the ultimate in engineering sophistication, but the crudest possible valuation of life in this world. It is as adequate a symbol of our relation to our country now as that first road was of our relation to it in 1797.

bell hooks

TOUCHING THE EARTH

I wish to live because life has within it that which is good, that which is beautiful, and that which is love. Therefore, since I have known all these things, I have found them to be reason enough and—I wish to live. Moreover, because this is so, I wish others to live for generations and generations and generations and generations.

LORRAINE HANSBERRY,
To Be Young, Gifted, and Black

bell hooks was born and raised in rural Kentucky and is now a professor of English at City College of New York. A major figure in African-American feminism, she is a practicing Buddhist particularly influenced by Thich Nhat Hanh. The following essay is from her book *Sisters of the Yam: Black Women and Self-Recovery*, which brings together eros and contemplation. In "Touching the Earth," hooks reflects on the history of the African-American relationship with nature. Despite the horrors of slavery and segregation, there was a deep connection between blacks and the soil in the rural South. The sense of wonder and reverence for life cultivated there was largely lost in the migration to the North. The result was estrangement from the self, the body, and the earth. But a spiritual recovery is possible in a recognition of the tie between black self-healing and the healing of our relationship with the earth. Such a view allows us to see both our bodies and the land as sacred.

When we love the earth, we are able to love ourselves more fully. I believe this. The ancestors taught me it was so. As a child I loved playing in dirt, in that rich Kentucky soil, that was a source of life. Before I understood anything about the pain and exploitation of the southern system of sharecropping, I understood that grown-up black folks loved the land. I could stand with my grandfather Daddy Jerry and look out at fields of growing vegetables, tomatoes, corn, collards, and know that this was his handiwork. I could see the look of pride on his face as I expressed wonder and awe at the magic of growing things. I knew that my grandmother Baba's backyard garden would yield beans, sweet potatoes, cabbage, and yellow squash, that she too would walk with pride among the rows and rows of growing vegetables showing us what the earth will give when tended lovingly.

From the moment of their first meeting, Native American and African people shared with one another a respect for the life-giving forces of nature, of the earth. African settlers in Florida taught the Creek Nation runaways, the "Seminoles," methods for rice cultivation. Native peoples taught recently arrived black folks all about the many uses of corn. (The hotwater cornbread we grew up eating came to our black southern diet from the world of the Indian.) Sharing the reverence for the earth, black and red people helped one another remember that, despite the white man's ways, the land belonged to everyone. Listen to these words attributed to Chief Seattle in 1854:

> How can you buy or sell the sky, the warmth of the land? The idea is strange to us. If we do not own the freshness of the air and the sparkle of the water, how can you buy them? Every part of this earth is sacred to my people. Every shining pine needle, every sandy shore, every mist in the dark woods, every clearing and humming insect is holy in the memory and experience of my people . . . We are part of the earth and it is part of us. The perfumed flowers are our sisters; the deer, the horse, the great eagle, these are our brothers. The rocky crests, the juices in the meadows, the body heat of the pony, and man—all belong to the same family.

The sense of union and harmony with nature expressed here is echoed in testimony by black people who found that even though life in the new world was "harsh, harsh," in relationship to the earth one could be at peace. In the oral autobiography of granny midwife Onnie Lee Logan, who lived all her life in Alabama, she talks about the richness of farm life—growing vegetables, raising chickens, and smoking meat. She reports:

> We lived a happy, comfortable life to be right outa slavery times. I didn't know nothin else but the farm so it was happy and we was happy . . . We couldn't do anything else but be happy. We accept the days as they come and as they were. Day by day until you couldn't say there was any great hard time. We overlooked it. We didn't think nothin about it. We just went along. We had what it takes to make a good livin and go about it.

Living in modern society, without a sense of history, it has been easy for folks to forget that black people were first and foremost a people of the land, farmers. It is easy for folks to forget that at the first part of the 20th century, the vast majority of black folks in the United States lived in the agrarian south.

Living close to nature, black folks were able to cultivate a spirit of wonder and reverence for life. Growing food to sustain life and flowers to please the soul, they were able to make a connection with the earth that was ongoing and life-affirming. They were witnesses to beauty. In Wendell Berry's important discussion of the relationship between agriculture and human spiritual well-being, *The Unsettling of America,* he reminds us that working the land provides a location where folks can experience a sense of personal power and well-being:

> We are working well when we use ourselves as the fellow creature of the plants, animals, material, and other people we are working with. Such work is unifying, healing. It brings us home from pride and despair, and places us responsibly within the human estate. It defines us as we are: not too good to work without our bodies, but too good to work poorly or joylessly or selfishly or alone.

There has been little or no work done on the psychological impact of the "great migration" of black people from the agrarian south to the industrialized north. Toni Morrison's novel *The Bluest Eye* attempts to fictively document the way moving from the agrarian south to the industrialized north wounded the psyches of black folk. Estranged from a natural world, where there was time for silence and contemplation, one of the "displaced" black folks in Morrison's novel, Miss Pauline, loses her capacity to experience the sensual world around her when she leaves southern soil to live in a northern city. The south is associated in her mind with a world of sensual beauty most deeply expressed in the world of nature. Indeed, when she falls in love for the first time she can name that experience only by evoking images from nature, from an agrarian world and near wilderness of natural splendor:

> When I first seed Cholly, I want you to know it was like all the bits of color from that time down home when all us chil'ren went berry picking after a funeral and I put some in the pocket of my Sunday dress, and they mashed up and stained my hips. My whole dress was messed with purple, and it never did wash out. Not the dress nor me. I could feel that purple deep inside me. And that lemonade Mama used to make when Pap came in out of the fields. It be cool and yellowish, with seeds floating near the bottom. And that streak of green them june bugs made on the tress that night we left from down home. All of them colors was in me. Just sitting there.

Certainly, it must have been a profound blow to the collective psyche of black people to find themselves struggling to make a living in the industrial north away from the land. Industrial capitalism was not simply changing the nature of black work life, it altered the communal practices that were so central to survival in the agrarian south. And it fundamentally altered black people's relationship to the body. It is the loss of any capacity to appreciate her body, despite its flaws, Miss Pauline suffers when she moves north.

The motivation for black folks to leave the south and move north was both material and psychological. Black folks wanted to be free of the overt racial harassment that was a constant in southern life and they wanted access to material goods—to a level of material well-being that was not available in the agrarian south where white folks limited access to the spheres of economic power. Of course, they found that life in the north had its own perverse hardships, that racism was just as virulent there, that it was much harder for black people to become landowners. Without the space to grow food, to commune with nature, or to mediate the starkness of poverty with the splendor of nature, black people experienced profound depression. Working in conditions where the body was regarded solely as a tool (as in slavery), a profound estrangement occurred between mind and body. The way the body was represented became more important than the body itself. It did not matter if the body was well, only that it appeared well.

Estrangement from nature and engagement in mind/body splits made it all the more possible for black people to internalize white-supremacist assumptions about black identity. Learning contempt for blackness, southerners transplanted in the north suffered both culture shock and soul loss. Contrasting the harshness of city life with an agrarian world, the poet Waring Cuney wrote this popular poem in the 1920s, testifying to lost connection:

> She does not know her beauty
> She thinks her brown body
> has no glory.
> If she could dance naked,
> Under palm trees
> And see her image in the river
> She would know.
> But there are no palm trees on the street,
> And dishwater gives back no images.

For many years, and even now, generations of black folks who migrated north to escape life in the south, returned down home in search of a spiritual nourishment, a healing, that was fundamentally connected to reaffirming one's connection to nature, to a contemplative life where one could take time, sit on the porch, walk, fish, and catch lightning bugs. If we think of urban life as a location where black folks learned to accept a mind/body split that made it possible to abuse the body, we can better understand the growth of nihilism and despair in the black psyche. And we can know that when we talk about healing that psyche we must also speak about restoring our connection to the natural world.

Wherever black folks live we can restore our relationship to the natural world by taking the time to commune with nature, to appreciate the other creatures who share this planet with humans. Even in my small New York City apartment I can pause to listen to birds sing, find a tree and watch it. We can grow plants—herbs, flowers, vegetables. Those novels by African-American writers (women and men) that talk about black migration from the agrarian south to the industrialized north describe in detail the way folks created space to grow flowers and vegetables. Although I come from country people with serious green thumbs, I have always felt that I could not garden. In the past few years, I have found that I can do it—that many gardens will grow, that I feel connected to my ancestors when I can put a meal on the table of food I grew. I especially love to plant collard greens. They are hardy, and easy to grow.

In modern society, there is also a tendency to see no correlation between the struggle for collective black self-recovery and ecological movements that seek to restore balance to the planet by changing our relationship to nature and to natural resources. Unmindful of our history of living harmoniously on the land, many contemporary black folks see no value in supporting ecological movements, or see ecology and the struggle to end racism as competing concerns. Recalling the legacy of our ancestors who knew that the way we regard land and nature will determine the level of our self-regard, black people must reclaim a spiritual legacy where we connect our well-being to the well-being of the earth. This is a necessary dimension of healing. As Berry reminds us:

> Only by restoring the broken connections can we be healed. Connection is health. And what our society does its best to disguise from us is how ordinary, how commonly attainable, health is. We lose our health—and create profitable diseases and dependencies—by failing to see the direct connections between living and eating, eating and working, working and loving. In gardening, for instance, one works with the body to feed the body. The work, if it is knowledgeable, makes for excellent food. And it makes one hungry. The work thus makes eating both nourishing and joyful, not consumptive, and keeps the eater from getting fat and weak. This health, wholeness, is a source of delight.

Collective black self-recovery takes place when we begin to renew our relationship to the earth, when we remember the way of our ancestors. When the earth is sacred to us, our bodies can also be sacred to us.

John Haines

SHADOWS AND VISTAS

There are shadows over the land. They come out of the ground,
from the dust and the tumbled bones of the earth . . .

from The Stars, the Snow, the Fire

John Haines lived for several decades on a homestead in northern Alaska. He
has taught at many universities and now lives in Montana. *The Owl in the Mask of
the Dreamer* offers his collected poems, and he has published various collections
of essays, including *Living Off the Country: Essays on Poetry and Place*. In the following selection, Haines portrays changes that have taken place since he first
arrived in the Alaskan backcountry. Like his other essays on nature, this one
exhibits a sharp eye for beauty and a deep but shadowed sense of nature's enduring value amid the destructiveness of our time. His vision is grounded in the concrete, "the hard, irreducible world of natural things"—evidence of living the rigors
of homesteading in Alaska. His vision is also profoundly spiritual, attending to "the
original mystery of things." Such sensitivity makes the destruction of nature intensely
painful, but it is also necessary for developing an abiding sense of living in place.

I begin with "Shadows" as a way of speaking. Laurens van der Post, in *The
Lost World of the Kalahari,* acknowledges that he believes in ghosts, in the
spirit of the life that the land once held but which cannot be found any
longer. Van der Post was looking for the Bushman, who for him signified
a lost Africa, one that he had been told about as a boy; but all he could
find of it was the changed land itself and a few sites where decades before
the Bushman had camped and hunted. According to an old African of his
household, from whom he had learned much, the Bushman disappeared
because *he would not be tamed.*

I recall an afternoon in October many years ago, when I stood on the edge of that high overlook near Maclaren Summit in the Alaska Range and gazed down onto the wide sweep of the Maclaren River Basin. The cold, late afternoon sun came through broken clouds, and the tundra below me was patched with sunlight. The river, a thin, silvery-blue thread, twisted through the subdued autumn coloration of the land, stretching far up into the dark and gloomy hills on which the first light snow had fallen.

I was entirely alone at that moment; no traffic disturbed the gravel road a few yards behind me. The land before me seemed incredibly vast and empty. But it was not empty. Far below me, a few scattered caribou were feeding in the meadows of the river basin, their brown, white-maned forms dispersed among the bogs and ponds, moving slowly upriver toward the mountains. They were the first individuals of a herd that would appear later.

I felt as if I were looking down on a landscape elementary to our being, and that nothing had occurred to change it since the last of the continental ice melted from the earth, and the first grasses and shrubs began to grow; and very slowly the animals moved north into the newly restored land, finding their way, feeding on the fresh, undisturbed forage for the first time.

That image has remained with me as one sure glimpse into our past. Even the road that crossed the river on a tiny bridge in the distance did not break the continuity of the feeling I had then. It was all part of an essential vista, a sheer sense of the land in its original presence. On that afternoon, when the guns of the hunters along the road were silent and no cars passed, I easily slipped back a thousand years into a twilight approaching winter; a dusk in which I and a few others, following the game herds upriver, would find meat, fire and shelter.

That was well over thirty years ago, when the tundra life along the Denali road was still fairly abundant. I have looked over that same view a number of times since, but I have not seen the caribou feeding as they were then. And yet I know that their ghosts are there, that the land contains them and refuses in some mysterious way to give them up, though to the surface view the land appears to be empty.

It is not simply nostalgia, I think, that compels me to believe that this vista, its possibility, needs to be kept. We need it as a kind of model of life, whose images we are bound in some way to resurrect and imitate, even when the original has been destroyed. It is not so much a matter of saving a species, a particular herd and its habitat, but of saving something essential of life and ourselves. And not only our immediate selves, you and I, but those others who were here before us and will come after us, and whose land and nature we have so easily confiscated and misused to our longstanding peril.

It is foolish to believe that we erase life by killing it off, by driving into extinction the remaining game, by paving over the grazing grounds, cutting the forests, and pretending to ourselves that it did not matter after all. Too bad, we say, but let's get on with the business of things. Vanquished in one place, life springs back in another, as at the present time, in spite of all sophistication in transport and communication, coyotes are barking in the Los Angeles suburbs, and as all the killed and vanished life, animal and people, continues in one way or another to haunt us and question our wasting passage through the world.

As a friend of mine remarked to me some years ago, when in the course of conversation we both remarked on the great physical presence of Kluane Lake in the Yukon: "That place," she exclaimed, "really has spirit!" It does indeed.

And what does that mean? That places, lands, regions, watersheds, etc., all have a life, a felt quality of their own, which we can call *spirit,* and we cannot kill that spirit without destroying something in ourselves. A degraded land inevitably produces a degraded people. It is in fact ourselves we are destroying, a possibility of life that once gone will be a long time returning. I say "a long time" and not that it will never come back, because I do not hold with the view that we have the power to destroy life on earth forever. That notion is a part of our problem, a part of our arrogance and self-bemusement. We have got it backwards. Life has the power to destroy *us,* and to do so with our connivance, using our own misaligned means and purposes. A few degrees of climate change, a few more inches of topsoil lost, and our descendants may read the record for themselves.

Is it destined to be a law with us, an iron and withering rule, that anything that cannot be tamed, domesticated and put to use, shall die? A river, a patch of woodland, a wolf, a small tribe of hunting people? And all the while we preserve a few wretched specimens in a zoo, a controlled park or reservation, or as a collection of images on film, part of an ever-growing catalogue of fossil life.

You can kill off the original inhabitants, most of the world's wildlife, and still live on the land. But I doubt that we can live fully on that land accompanied only by crowds of consumers like ourselves and a few hybrid domesticated animals turned into producing machines. A sure poverty will follow us, an inner desolation to match the devastation without. And having rid the earth of wilderness, of wild things generally, we will look to outer space, to other planets, to find their replacements there.

Today, most of us are familiar with a continuing effort to save some part of a wild heritage, to rethink our lives in relation to the land we drive and park on and from which we draw what certainty we have. And we know the forces assembled in opposition to this effort: there is no need to name or rank them, they all flock under the flag of an ever more questionable progress and enterprise, whose hidden name is poverty.

On the occasion of a visit to New England in the 1930s, T. S. Eliot wrote the following:

> My local feelings were stirred very sadly by my first view of New England, on arriving from Montreal, and journeying all day through the beautiful desolate country of Vermont. These hills had once, I suppose, been covered with primeval forest; the forest was razed to make sheep pasture for the English settlers; now the sheep are gone, and most of the descendants of the settlers; and a new forest appeared blazing with the melancholy glory of October maple and beech and birch scattered among the evergreens; and after this process of scarlet and gold and purple wilderness you descend to the sordor of the half-dead milltowns of southern New Hampshire and Massachusetts. It is not necessarily those lands which are most fertile or most favored in climate that seem to me the happiest, but those in which a long struggle of adaptation between man and his environment has brought out the best qualities of both; in which the landscape has been moulded by numerous generations of one race, and in which the landscape has in turn moulded the race to its own character. And those New England mountains seemed to me to give evidence of a human success so meager and transitory as to be more desperate than the desert.

Certainly, Eliot's description and the feeling it evokes could with a little effort be transferred to many an Alaskan urban landscape, be it Mountain View, North Pole, Soldotna, or one of those lost highway settlements in which it seems as if all the unwanted debris and waste of American life had somehow blown there to settle into an impervious drift composed of tarpaper, crushed plastic, ripped shingles and foundered hopes. I suppose there are few more unreal and depressing prospects than some of the housing sites, the outlying developed properties in Anchorage and Fairbanks. And what is unreal will sooner or later disappear, the transitory inspiration of a people come to plunder and leave. Van der Post, in another of his books, remarks on the physical fact of Africa as being by far the most exciting thing about that continent. And for him a definite sadness lay in the fact that it had not yet produced the people and the towns worthy of it. By comparison with its physical self, everything else was drab and commonplace.

We who have learned to call this north country home are only at the beginning of a struggle of adaptation between ourselves and the land, and if the evidence so far seems pretty meager, there's a long road yet to travel. The prospect of an Alaska in which a million or so people are on the prowl with guns, snowmachines, airboats and four-wheelers, is not only terrifying, it is finally unacceptable. An environmental ethic, believed in, practiced and enforced, is not just an alternative, it is the only one, though another name for it may be self-restraint. And it is sometimes possible to sense, behind all the noise and confrontation, a genuine urge toward a real satisfaction, a sane kind of plenitude, a fullness of spirit and being.

And we are all in it together, poet and plumber, even those so far unconscious people out there on the peripheries; and especially those in the halls of academe—our humanists, who surely ought to care but who seem often not to. Mired in their coursework, busily teaching (but what are they teaching?), satisfied to draw their salaries, to save for retirement, to drink the water, breathe the air and burn the fuel, without a whisper of protest or encouragement.

You may ask what these remarks of mine have to do with immediate politics and practical tasks—the issues, the problems that many of you understand as well as or better than I do. And I have no ready answer, no claim that poetic imagery, the personal mythologies of which a writer is sometimes the master, can solve anything. And yet without that dimension of imagination, the instilled power to think and to visualize that poetry, for example, nourishes in us, the solutions, the resolved difficulties seem bound to lack a necessary human element.

So it is a matter of language also, of words common and uncommon, that with something of their original freshness and power have the ability to restore a much-needed sense of reality and reveal to us a few essential things with clarity and concreteness.

Not long ago I saw a marsh hawk, a harrier, hunting the Tanana River islands below Richardson, the first spring arrival of its kind. And that bird was, in a vivid way, rather like a ghost with its grey and white plumage slanting in the spring sunlight as it hovered and sailed over the winter-brown willows and frost-seared grasses. A real spirit, if you like, come back to claim its territory, as it or its ancestors have returned to those flats and adjacent meadows for far longer than our race has existed or can easily imagine. A small but definite image to end on, and returning me halfway to that glimpse into the Maclaren River Basin I described earlier, haunted as I am by its persistent contours, and by what seems sometimes destined to become a vanished hope on earth.

> And to think, from this diminished perspective in time, from this long vista of empty light and deepening shade, that so small and refined a creature could fill an uncertain niche in the world; and that its absence would leave, not just a momentary gap in nature, but a lack in one's own existence, one less possibility of being.
>
> As if we were to look out on a cherished landscape, hoping to see on the distant, wrinkled plain, among the cloud-shadows passing over its face, groups of animals feeding and resting; and in the air above them a compact flock of waterfowl swiftly winging its way to a farther pond; and higher still, a watchful hawk on the wind. To look, straining one's eyesight, noting each detail of lake, meadow and bog; and to find nothing, nothing alive and moving. Only the wind and the distance, the silence of a vast, creatureless earth.*

---

* John Haines, "Shadows," from *The Stars, the Snow, the Fire* (St. Paul, Minn.: Graywolf Press, 1989), pp. 178–179.

THE POSSIBILITY
OF PLACE

Wendell Berry

From

A NATIVE HILL

This second selection from Wendell Berry's "A Native Hill" presents an alternative to the violent imposition of human culture on nature seen in the excerpt in the section "The Loss of Place." As Berry walks through the woods, he becomes increasingly aware of creation at work. He articulates his sense of stewardship as being a life of humble apprenticeship to creation rather than a claim of being the crown of creation and master of nature. By practicing this discipline and art, it is possible to become a true member of nature's household—an image rooted in the term *eco* ("house") and suggesting how the human and the natural are interwoven. While primarily rooted in Christianity, this vision has deep affinities with Confucianism and the Chinese aesthetic tradition, which have influenced Berry's thought. Berry's complex view of stewardship centers on "thinking little": cultivating the skills of living in continuous harmony with one's local place.

I start down from one of the heights of the upland, the town of Port Royal at my back. It is a winter day, overcast and still, and the town is closed in itself, humming and muttering a little, like a winter beehive.

The dog runs ahead, prancing and looking back, knowing the way we are about to go. This is a walk well established with us—a route in our minds as well as on the ground. There is a sort of mystery in the establishment of these ways. Any time one crosses a given stretch of country with some frequency, no matter how wanderingly one begins, the tendency is always toward habit. By the third or fourth trip, without realizing it, one is following a fixed path, going the way one went before. After that, one may still wander, but only by deliberation, and when there is reason to hurry, or when the mind wanders rather than the feet, one returns to the old route. Familiarity has begun. One has made a relationship with the landscape, and the form and the symbol and the enactment of the relationship is the path. These paths of mine are seldom worn on the ground. They are habits of mind, directions and turns. They are as personal as old shoes. My feet are comfortable in them.

From the height I can see far out over the country, the long open ridges of the farmland, the wooded notches of the streams, the valley of the river opening beyond, and then more ridges and hollows of the same kind.

Underlying this country, nine hundred feet below the highest ridgetops, more than four hundred feet below the surface of the river, is sea level. We seldom think of it here; we are a long way from the coast, and the sea is alien to us. And yet the attraction of sea level dwells in this country as an ideal dwells in a man's mind. All our rains go in search of it and, departing, they have carved the land in a shape that is fluent and falling. The streams branch like vines, and between the branches the land rises steeply and then rounds and gentles into the long narrowing fingers of ridgeland. Near the heads of the streams even the steepest land was not too long ago farmed and kept cleared. But now it has been given up and the woods is returning. The wild is flowing back like a tide. The arable ridgetops reach out above the gathered trees like headlands into the sea, bearing their human burdens of fences and houses and barns, crops and roads.

Looking out over the country, one gets a sense of the whole of it: the ridges and hollows, the clustered buildings of the farms, the open fields, the woods, the stock ponds set like coins into the slopes. But this is a surface sense, an exterior sense, such as you get from looking down on the roof of a house. The height is a threshold from which to step down into the wooded folds of the land, the interior, under the trees and along the branching streams.

I pass through a pasture gate on a deep-worn path that grows shallow a little way beyond, and then disappears altogether into the grass. The gate has gathered thousands of passings to and fro that have divided like the slats of a fan on either side of it. It is like a fist holding together the strands of a net.

Beyond the gate the land leans always more steeply toward the branch. I follow it down, and then bear left along the crease at the bottom of the slope. I have entered the downflow of the land. The way I am going is the way the water goes. There is something comfortable and fit-feeling in this, something free in this yielding to gravity and taking the shortest way down. The mind moves through the watershed as the water moves.

As the hollow deepens into the hill, before it has yet entered the woods, the grassy crease becomes a raw gully, and along the steepening slopes on either side I can see the old scars of erosion, places where the earth is gone clear to the rock. My people's errors have become the features of my country.

It occurs to me that it is no longer possible to imagine how this country looked in the beginning, before the white people drove their plows into it. It is not possible to know what was the shape of the land here in this hollow when it was first cleared. Too much of it is gone, loosened by the plows and washed away by the rain. I am walking the route of the departure of the virgin soil of the hill. I am not looking at the same land the firstcomers saw. The original surface of the hill is as extinct as the passenger pigeon. The pristine America that the first white man saw is a lost continent, sunk like Atlantis in the sea. The thought of what was here once and is gone forever will not leave me as long as I live. It is as though I walk knee-deep in its absence.

The slopes along the hollow steepen still more, and I go in under the trees. I pass beneath the surface. I am enclosed, and my sense, my interior sense, of the country becomes intricate. There is no longer the possibility of seeing very far. The distances are closed off by the trees and the steepening walls of the hollow. One cannot grow familiar here by sitting and looking as one can up in the open on the ridge. Here the eyes become dependent on the feet. To see the woods from the inside one must look and move and look again. It is inexhaustible in its standpoints. A lifetime will not be enough to experience it all. Not far from the beginning of the woods, and set deep in the earth in the bottom of the hollow, is a rock-walled pool not a lot bigger than a bathtub. The wall is still nearly as straight and tight as when it was built. It makes a neatly turned narrow horseshoe, the open end downstream. This is a historical ruin, dug here either to catch and hold the water of the little branch, or to collect the water of a spring whose vein broke to the surface here—it is probably no longer possible to know which. The pool is filled with earth now, and grass grows in it. And the branch bends around it, cut down to the bare rock, a torrent after heavy rain, other times bone dry. All that is certain is that when the pool was dug and walled there was deep topsoil on the hill to gather and hold the water. And this high up, at least, the bottom of the hollow, instead of the present raw notch of the stream bed, wore the same mantle of soil as the slopes, and the stream was a steady seep or trickle, running most or all of the year. This tiny pool no doubt once furnished water for a considerable number of stock through the hot summers. And now it is only a lost souvenir, archaic and useless, except for the bitter intelligence there is in it. It is one of the monuments to what is lost.

Wherever one goes along the streams of this part of the country, one is apt to come upon this old stonework. There are walled springs and pools. There are the walls built in the steeper hollows where the fences cross or used to cross; the streams have drifted dirt in behind them, so that now where they are still intact they make waterfalls that have scooped out small pools at their feet. And there used to be miles of stone fences, now mostly scattered and sifted back into the ground.

Considering these, one senses a historical patience, now also extinct in the country. These walls were built by men working long days for little wages, or by slaves. It was work that could not be hurried at, a meticulous finding and fitting together, as though reconstructing a previous wall that had been broken up and scattered like puzzle pieces along the stream beds. The wall would advance only a few yards a day. The pace of it could not be borne by most modern men, even if the wages could be afforded. Those men had to move in closer accord with their own rhythms, and nature's, than we do. They had no machines. Their capacities were only those of flesh and blood. They talked as they worked. They joked and laughed. They sang. The work was exacting and heavy and hard and slow. No opportunity for pleasure was missed or slighted. The days and the years were long. The work was long. At the end of this job the next would begin. Therefore, be patient. Such pleasure as there is, is here, now. Take pleasure as it comes. Take work as it comes. The end may never come, or when it does it may be the wrong end.

Now the men who built the walls and the men who had them built have long gone underground to be, along with the buried ledges and the roots and the burrowing animals, a part of the nature of the place in the minds of the ones who come after them. I think of them lying still in their graves, as level as the sills and thresholds of their lives, as though resisting to the last the slant of the ground. And their old walls, too, re-enter nature, collecting lichens and mosses with a patience their builders never conceived of.

Like the pasture gates, the streams are great collectors of comings and goings. The streams go down, and paths always go down beside the streams. For a while I walk along an old wagon road that is buried in leaves—a fragment, beginningless and endless as the middle of a sentence on some scrap of papyrus. There is a cedar whose branches reach over this road, and under the branches I find the leavings of two kills of some bird of prey. The most recent is a pile of blue jay feathers. The other has been rained on and is not identifiable. How little we know. How little of this was intended or expected by any man. The road that has become the grave of men's passages has led to the life of the woods.

> And I say to myself: Here is your road
> without beginning or end, appearing
> out of the earth and ending in it, bearing
> no load but the hawk's kill, and the leaves
> building earth on it, something more
> to be borne. Tracks fill with earth
> and return to absence. The road was worn
> by men bearing earth along it. They have come
> to endlessness. In their passing
> they could not stay in, trees have risen
> and stand still. It is leading to the dark,
> to mornings where you are not. Here
> is your road, beginningless and endless as God.

Now I have come down within the sound of the water. The winter has been rainy, and the hill is full of dark seeps and trickles, gathering finally, along these creases, into flowing streams. The sound of them is one of the elements, and defines a zone. When their voices return to the hill after their absence during summer and autumn, it is a better place to be. A thirst in the mind is quenched.

I have already passed the place where water began to flow in the little stream bed I am following. It broke into the light from beneath a rock ledge, a thin glittering stream. It lies beside me as I walk, overtaking me and going by, yet not moving, a thread of light and sound. And now from below comes the steady tumble and rush of the water of Camp Branch—whose nameless camp was it named for?—and gradually as I descend the sound of the smaller stream is lost in the sound of the larger.

The two hollows join, the line of the meeting of the two spaces obscured even in winter by the trees. But the two streams meet precisely as two roads. That is, the stream *beds* do; the one ends in the other. As for the meeting of the waters, there is no looking at that. The one flow does not end in the other, but continues in it, one with it, two clarities merged without a shadow.

All waters are one. This is a reach of the sea, flung like a net over the hill, and now drawn back to the sea. And as the sea is never raised in the earthly nets of fishermen, so the hill is never caught and pulled down by the watery net of the sea. But always a little of it is. Each of the gathering strands of the net carries back some of the hill melted in it. Sometimes, as now, it carries so little that the water seems to flow clear; sometimes it carries a lot and is brown and heavy with it. Whenever greedy or thoughtless men have lived on it, the hill has literally flowed out of their tracks into the bottom of the sea.

There appears to be a law that when creatures have reached the level of consciousness, as men have, they must become conscious of the creation; they must learn how they fit into it and what its needs are and what it requires of them, or else pay a terrible penalty: the spirit of the creation will go out of them, and they will become destructive; the very earth will depart from them and go where they cannot follow.

My mind is never empty or idle at the joinings of streams. Here is the work of the world going on. The creation is felt, alive and intent on its materials, in such places. In the angle of the meeting of the two streams stands the steep wooded point of the ridge, like the prow of an upturned boat—finished, as it was a thousand years ago, as it will be in a thousand years. Its becoming is only incidental to its being. It will be because it is. It has no aim or end except to be. By being, it is growing and wearing into what it will be. The fork of the stream lies at the foot of the slope like hammer and chisel laid down at the foot of a finished sculpture. But the stream is no dead tool; it is alive, it is still at its work. Put your hand to it to learn the health of this part of the world. It is the wrist of the hill.

Perhaps it is to prepare to hear some day the music of the spheres that I am always turning my ears to the music of streams. There is indeed a music in streams, but it is not for the hurried. It has to be loitered by and imagined. Or imagined *toward,* for it is hardly for men at all. Nature has a patient ear. To her the slowest funeral march sounds like a jig. She is satisfied to have the notes drawn out to the lengths of days or weeks or months. Small variations are acceptable to her, modulations as leisurely as the opening of a flower.

The stream is full of stops and gates. Here it has piled up rocks in its path, and pours over them into a tiny pool it has scooped at the foot of its fall. Here it has been dammed by a mat of leaves caught behind a fallen limb. Here it must force a narrow passage, here a wider one. Tomorrow the flow may increase or slacken, and the tone will shift. In an hour or a week that rock may give way, and the composition will advance by another note. Some idea of it may be got by walking slowly along and noting the changes as one passes from one little fall or rapid to another. But this is a highly simplified and diluted version of the real thing, which is too complex and widespread ever to be actually heard by us. The ear must imagine an impossible patience in order to grasp even the unimaginableness of such music.

But the creation is musical, and this is a part of its music, as bird song is, or the words of poets. The music of the streams is the music of the shaping of the earth, by which the rocks are pushed and shifted downward toward the level of the sea.

And now I find lying in the path an empty beer can. This is the track of the ubiquitous man Friday of all our woods. In my walks I never fail to discover some sign that he has preceded me. I find his empty shotgun shells, his empty cans and bottles, his sandwich wrappings. In wooded places along roadsides one is apt to find, as well, his overtraveled bedsprings, his outcast refrigerator, and heaps of the imperishable refuse of his modern kitchen. A year ago, almost in this same place where I have found his beer can, I found a possum that he had shot dead and left lying, in celebration of his manhood. He is the true American pioneer, perfectly at rest in his assumption that he is the first and the last whose inheritance and fate this place will ever be. Going forth, as he may think, to sow, he only broadcasts his effects.

As I go on down the path alongside Camp Branch, I walk by the edge of croplands abandoned only within my own lifetime. On my left are the south slopes where the woods is old, long undisturbed. On my right, the more fertile north slopes are covered with patches of briars and sumacs and a lot of young walnut trees. Tobacco of an extraordinary quality was once grown here, and then the soil wore thin, and these places were given up for the more accessible ridges that were not so steep, where row cropping made better sense anyway. But now, under the thicket growth, a mat of bluegrass has grown to testify to the good nature of this ground. It was fine dirt that lay here once, and I am far from being able to say that I could have resisted the temptation to plow it. My understanding of what is best for it is the tragic understanding of hindsight, the awareness that I have been taught what was here to be lost by the loss of it.

We have lived by the assumption that what was good for us would be good for the world. And this has been based on the even flimsier assumption that we could know with any certainty what was good even for us. We have fulfilled the danger of this by making our personal pride and greed the standard of our behavior toward the world—to the incalculable disadvantage of the world and every living thing in it. And now, perhaps very close to too late, our great error has become clear. It is not only our own creativity—our own capacity for life—that is stifled by our arrogant assumption; the creation itself is stifled.

We have been wrong. We must change our lives, so that it will be possible to live by the contrary assumption that what is good for the world will be good for us. And that requires that we make the effort to *know* the world and to learn what is good for it. We must learn to co-operate in its processes, and to yield to its limits. But even more important, we must learn to acknowledge that the creation is full of mystery; we will never entirely understand it. We must abandon arrogance and stand in awe. We must recover the sense of the majesty of creation, and the ability to be worshipful in its presence. For I do not doubt that it is only on the condition of humility and reverence before the world that our species will be able to remain in it.

Standing in the presence of these worn and abandoned fields, where the creation has begun its healing without the hindrance or the help of man, with the voice of the stream in the air and the woods standing in silence on all the slopes around me, I am deep in the interior not only of my place in the world, but of my own life, its sources and searches and concerns. I first came into these places following the men to work when I was a child. I knew the men who took their lives from such fields as these, and their lives to a considerable extent made my life what it is. In what came to me from them there was both wealth and poverty, and I have been a long time discovering which was which.

It was in the woods here along Camp Branch that Bill White, my grandfather's Negro hired hand, taught me to hunt squirrels. Bill lived in a little tin-roofed house on up nearer the head of the hollow. And this was, I suppose more than any other place, his hunting ground. It was the place of his freedom, where he could move without subservience, without considering who he was or who anybody else was. On late summer mornings, when it was too wet to work, I would follow him into the woods. As soon as we stepped in under the trees he would become silent and absolutely attentive to the life of the place. He was a good teacher and an exacting one. The rule seemed to be that if I wanted to stay with him, I had to make it possible for him to forget I was there. I was to make no noise. If I did he would look back and make a downward emphatic gesture with his hand, as explicit as writing: Be quiet, or go home. He would see a squirrel crouched in a fork or lying along the top of a branch, and indicate with a grin and a small jerk of his head where I should look; and then wait, while I, conscious of being watched and demanded upon, searched it out for myself. He taught me to look and to listen and to be quiet. I wonder if he knew the value of such teaching or the rarity of such a teacher.

In the years that followed I hunted often here alone. And later in these same woods I experienced my first obscure dissatisfactions with hunting. Though I could not have put it into words then, the sense had come to me that hunting as I knew it—the eagerness to kill something I did not need to eat—was an artificial relation to the place, when what I was beginning to need, just as inarticulately then, was a relation that would be deeply natural and meaningful. That was a time of great uneasiness and restlessness for me. It would be the fall of the year, the leaves would be turning, and ahead of me would be another year of school. There would be confusions about girls and ambitions, the wordless hurried feeling that time and events and my own nature were pushing me toward what I was going to be—and I had no notion what it was, or how to prepare.

And then there were years when I did not come here at all—when these places and their history were in my mind, and part of me, in places thousands of miles away. And now I am here again, changed from what I was, and still changing. The future is no more certain to me now than it ever was, though its risks are clearer, and so are my own desires: I am the father of two young children whose lives are hostages given to the future. Because of them and because of events in the world, life seems more fearful and difficult to me now than ever before. But it is also more inviting, and I am

constantly aware of its nearness to joy. Much of the interest and excitement that I have in my life now has come from the deepening, in the years
since my return here, of my relation to this countryside that is my native
place. For in spite of all that has happened to me in other places, the great
change and the great possibility of change in my life has been in my sense
of this place. The major difference is perhaps only that I have grown able
to be wholeheartedly present here. I am able to sit and be quiet at the foot
of some tree here in this woods along Camp Branch, and feel a deep peace,
both in the place and in my awareness of it, that not too long ago I was
not conscious of the possibility of. This peace is partly in being free of the
suspicion that pursued me for most of my life, no matter where I was, that
there was perhaps another place I *should* be, or would be happier or better in; it is partly in the increasingly articulate consciousness of being here,
and of the significance and importance of being here.

After more than thirty years I have at last arrived at the candor necessary to stand on this part of the earth that is so full of my own history and
so much damaged by it, and ask: What *is* this place? What is in it? What
is its nature? How should men live in it? What must I do?

I have not found the answers, though I believe that in partial and frag-
mentary ways they have begun to come to me. But the questions are more
important than their answers. In the final sense they *have* no answers. They
are like the questions—they are perhaps the same questions—that were
the discipline of Job. They are a part of the necessary enactment of humility, teaching a man what his importance is, what his responsibility is,
and what his place is, both on the earth and in the order of things. And
though the answers must always come obscurely and in fragments, the
questions must be persistently asked. They are fertile questions. In their
implications and effects, they are moral and aesthetic and, in the best and
fullest sense, practical. They promise a relationship to the world that is
decent and preserving.

They are also, both in origin and effect, religious. I am uneasy with the
term, for such religion as has been openly practiced in this part of the world
has promoted and fed upon a destructive schism between body and soul,
heaven and earth. It has encouraged people to believe that the world is of
no importance, and that their only obligation in it is to submit to certain
churchly formulas in order to get to heaven. And so the people who might
have been expected to care most selflessly for the world have had their

minds turned elsewhere—to a pursuit of "salvation" that was really only another form of gluttony and self-love, the desire to perpetuate their own small lives beyond the life of the world. The heaven-bent have abused the earth thoughtlessly, by inattention, and their negligence has permitted and encouraged others to abuse it deliberately. Once the creator was removed from the creation, divinity became only a remote abstraction, a social weapon in the hands of the religious institutions. This split in public values produced or was accompanied by, as it was bound to be, an equally artificial and ugly division in people's lives, so that a man, while pursuing heaven with the sublime appetite he thought of as his soul, could turn his heart against his neighbors and his hands against the world. For these reasons, though I know that my questions *are* religious, I dislike having to *say* that they are.

But when I ask them my aim is not primarily to get to heaven. Though heaven is certainly more important than the earth if all they say about it is true, it is still morally incidental to it and dependent on it, and I can only imagine it and desire it in terms of what I know of the earth. And so my questions do not aspire beyond the earth. They aspire *toward* it and *into* it. Perhaps they aspire *through* it. They are religious because they are asked at the limit of what I know; they acknowledge mystery and honor its presence in the creation; they are spoken in reverence for the order and grace that I see, and that I trust beyond my power to see.

The stream has led me down to an old barn built deep in the hollow to house the tobacco once grown on those abandoned fields. Now it is surrounded by the trees that have come back on every side—a relic, a fragment of another time, strayed out of its meaning. This is the last of my historical landmarks. To here, my walk has had insistent overtones of memory and history. It has been a movement of consciousness through knowledge, eroding and shaping, adding and wearing away. I have descended like the water of the stream through what I know of myself, and now that I have there is a little more to know. But here at the barn, the old roads and the cow paths—the formal connections with civilization—come to an end.

I stoop between the strands of a barbed-wire fence, and in that movement I go out of time into timelessness. I come into a wild place. I walk along the foot of a slope that was once cut bare of trees, like all the slopes of this part of the country—but long ago; and now the woods is established again, the ground healed, the trees grown big, their trunks rising clean, free of undergrowth. The place has a serenity and dignity that one feels immediately; the creation is whole in it and unobstructed. It is free of the strivings and dissatisfactions, the partialities and imperfections of places under the mechanical dominance of men. Here, what to a house-keeper's eye might seem disorderly is nonetheless orderly and within or-der; what might seem arbitrary or accidental is included in the design of the whole as if by intention; what might seem evil or violent is a com-fortable member of the household. Where the creation is whole nothing is extraneous. The presence of the creation here makes this a holy place, and it is as a pilgrim that I have come—to give the homage of awe and love, to submit to mystification. It is the creation that has attracted me, its perfect interfusion of life and design. I have made myself its follower and its apprentice.

One early morning last spring, I came and found the woods floor strewn with bluebells. In the cool sunlight and the lacy shadows of the spring woods the blueness of those flowers, their elegant shape, their delicate fresh scent kept me standing and looking. I found a rich delight in them that I cannot describe and that I will never forget. Though I had been famil-iar for years with most of the spring woods flowers, I had never seen these and had not known they grew here. Looking at them, I felt a strange feel-ing of loss and sorrow that I had never seen them before. But I was also exultant that I saw them now—that they were here.

For me, in the thought of them will always be the sense of the joyful surprise with which I found them—the sense that came suddenly to me then that the world is blessed beyond my understanding, more abundantly than I will ever know. What lives are still ahead of me here to be discov-ered and exulted in, tomorrow, or in twenty years? What wonder will be found here on the morning after my death? Though as a man I inherit great evils and the possibility of great loss and suffering, I know that my life is blessed and graced by the yearly flowering of the bluebells. How per-fect they are! In their presence I am humble and joyful. If I were given all the learning and all the methods of my race I could not make one of them, or even imagine one. Solomon in all his glory was not arrayed like one of these. It is the privilege and the labor of the apprentice of creation to come with his imagination into the unimaginable, and with his speech into the unspeakable.

Scott Russell Sanders

SETTLING DOWN

Scott Russell Sanders lives in Bloomington, Indiana, where he teaches literature at Indiana University. He recently purchased eighteen acres in a narrow
valley outside of town. He is a novelist whose collections of essays include *Staying Put: Making a Home in a Restless World*. In "Settling Down," Sanders recalls
a family in his rural area of Ohio that insisted on remaining to rebuild despite
damage to their house from three tornadoes. For Sanders this exemplifies a
crucial human drive: to stay put. Though many human cultures have been nomadic
and we are naturally drawn to explore new places, we must balance our migratory sensibility with our need to settle down. By developing loyalty to a place and
aligning oneself with its character, we can begin the process of healing a restless
culture.

Two friends arrived at our house for supper one May evening along with
the first rumblings of thunder. As Ruth and I sat talking with them on
our front porch, we had to keep raising our voices a notch to make ourselves heard above the gathering storm. The birds, more discreet, had already hushed. The huge elm beside our door began to sway, limbs creak-
ing, leaves hissing. Black sponges of clouds blotted up the light, fooling
the street lamps into coming on early. Above the trees and rooftops, the
murky southern sky crackled with lightning. Now and again we heard the
pop of a transformer as a bolt struck the power lines in our neighborhood.
The pulses of thunder came faster and faster, until they merged into a continuous roar.

We gave up on talking. The four of us, all Midwesterners teethed on
thunderstorms, sat down there on the porch to our meal of lentil soup,
cheddar cheese, bread warm from the oven, sliced apples and strawberries. We were lifting the first spoonfuls to our mouths when a stroke of

lightning burst so nearby that it seemed to suck away the air, and the lights flickered out, plunging the whole street into darkness.

After we had caught our breath, we laughed—respectfully, as one might laugh at the joke of a giant. The sharp smell of ozone and the musty smell of damp earth mingled with the aroma of bread. A chill of pleasure ran up my spine. I lit a pair of candles on the table, and the flames rocked in the gusts of wind.

In the time it took for butter to melt on a slice of bread, the wind fell away, the elm stopped thrashing, the lightning let up, and the thunder ceased. The sudden stillness was more exciting than the earlier racket. A smoldering yellow light came into the sky, as though the humid air had caught fire. We gazed at one another over the steady candle flames and knew without exchanging a word what this eerie lull could mean.

"Maybe we should go into the basement," Ruth suggested.

"And leave this good meal?" one of our friends replied.

The wail of a siren broke the stillness—not the lesser cry of ambulance or fire engine or squad car, but the banshee howl of the civil defense siren at the park a few blocks away.

"They must have sighted one," I said.

"We could take the food down with us on a tray," Ruth told our guests.

"It's up to you," I told them. "We can go to the basement like sensible people, or we can sit here like fools and risk our necks."

"What do you want to do?" one of them asked me.

"You're the guests."

"You're the hosts."

"I'd like to stay here and see what comes," I told them.

Ruth frowned at me, but there we stayed, savoring our food and the sulphurous light. Eventually the siren quit. When my ears stopped ringing, I could hear the rushing of a great wind, like the whoosh of a waterfall. An utter calm stole over me. The hair on my neck bristled. My nostrils flared. Heat rose in my face as though the tip of a wing had raked over it.

Although I found myself, minutes later, still in the chair, the faces of my wife and friends gleaming in the candlelight, for a spell I rode the wind, dissolved into it, and there was only the great wind, rushing.

The tornado missed us by half a mile. It did not kill anyone in our vicinity, but it ripped off chimneys, toyed with cars, and plucked up a fat old maple by the roots.

Prudent folks would have gone to the basement. I do not recommend our decision; I merely report it. Why the others tarried on the porch I cannot say, but what kept me there was a mixture of curiosity and awe. I had never seen the whirling black funnel except in cautionary films, where it left a wake of havoc and tears. And now here was that tremendous power, paying us a visit. When a god comes calling, no matter how bad its reputation, would you go hide? If the siren had announced the sighting of a dragon, I would have sat there just the same, hoping to catch a glimpse of the spiked tail or fiery breath.

As a boy in Ohio I knew a farm family, the Millers, who not only saw but suffered from three tornadoes. The father, mother, and two sons were pulling into their driveway after church when the first tornado hoisted up their mobile home, spun it around, and carried it off. With the insurance money, they built a small frame house on the same spot. Several years later, a second tornado peeled off the roof, splintered the garage, and rustled two cows. The younger of the sons, who was in my class at school, told me that he had watched from the barn as the twister passed through, "And it never even mussed up my hair." The Millers rebuilt again, raising a new garage on the old foundation and adding another story to the house. That upper floor was reduced to kindling by a third tornado, which also pulled out half the apple trees and slurped water from the stock pond. Soon after that I left Ohio, snatched away by college as forcefully as by any cyclone. Last thing I heard, the family was preparing to rebuild yet again.

Why did the Millers refuse to budge? I knew them well enough to say they were neither stupid nor crazy. After the garage disappeared, the father hung a sign from the mailbox that read: TORNADO ALLEY. He figured the local terrain would coax future whirlwinds in their direction. Then why not move? Plain stubbornness was a factor. These were people who, once settled, might have remained at the foot of a volcano or on the bank of a flood-prone river or beside an earthquake fault. They had relatives nearby, helpful neighbors, jobs and stores and school within a short drive, and those were all good reasons to stay. But the main reason, I believe, was because the Millers had invested so much of their lives in the land, planting orchards and gardens, spreading manure on the fields, digging ponds, building sheds, seeding pastures. Out back of the house were groves of walnuts, hickories, and oaks, all started by hand from acorns and nuts.

Honeybees zipped out from a row of white hives to nuzzle clover in the pasture. April through October, perennial flowers in the yard pumped out a fountain of blossoms. This farm was not just so many acres of dirt, easily exchanged for an equal amount elsewhere; it was a particular place, intimately known, worked on, dreamed over, cherished.

Psychologists tell us that we answer trouble with one of two impulses, either fight or flight. I believe that the Millers' response to tornadoes and my own keen expectancy on the porch arose from a third instinct, that of staying put. When the pain of leaving behind what we know outweighs the pain of embracing it, or when the power we face is overwhelming and neither fight nor flight will save us, there may be salvation in sitting still. And if salvation is impossible, then at least before perishing we may gain a clearer vision of where we are. By sitting still I do not mean the paralysis of dread, like that of a rabbit frozen beneath the dive of a hawk. I mean something like reverence, a respectful waiting, a deep attentiveness to forces much greater than our own. If indulged only for a moment, as in my case on the porch, this reverent impulse may amount to little; but if sustained for months and years, as by the Millers on their farm, it may yield marvels. The Millers knew better than to fight a tornado, and they chose not to flee. Instead they devoted themselves, season after season, to patient labor. Instead of withdrawing, they gave themselves more fully. Their commitment to the place may have been foolhardy, but it was also grand. I suspect that most human achievements worth admiring are the result of such devotion.

These tornado memories dramatize a choice we are faced with constantly: whether to go or stay, whether to move to a situation that is safer, richer, easier, more attractive, or to stick where we are and make what we can of it. If the shine goes off our marriage, our house, our car, do we trade it for a new one? If the fertility leaches out of our soil, the creativity out of our job, the money out of our pocket, do we start over somewhere else? There are voices enough, both inner and outer, urging us to deal with difficulties by pulling up stakes and heading for new territory. I know them well, for they have been calling to me all my days. I wish to raise here a contrary voice, to say a few words on behalf of standing your ground, confronting the powers, going deeper.

In a poem written not long before he leapt from a bridge over the Mississippi River, John Berryman ridiculed those who asked about his "roots" ("as if I were a *plant*"), and he articulated something like a credo for the dogma of rootlessness:

> Exile is in our time like blood. Depend on
> interior journeys taken anywhere.
>
> I'd rather live in Venice or Kyoto,
> except for the languages, but
> O really I don't care where I live or have lived.
> Wherever I am, young Sir, my wits about me,
>
> memory blazing, I'll cope & make do.

It is a bold claim, but also a hazardous one. For all his wits, Berryman in the end failed to cope well enough to stave off suicide. The truth is, none of us can live by wits alone. For even the barest existence, we depend on the labors of other people, the fruits of the earth, the inherited goods of our given place. If our interior journeys are cut loose entirely from that place, then both we and the neighborhood will suffer.

Exile usually suggests banishment, a forced departure from one's homeland. Famines and tyrants and wars do indeed force entire populations to flee; but most people who move, especially within the industrialized world, do so by choice. Salman Rushdie chose to leave his native India for England, where he has written a series of brilliant books from the perspective of a cultural immigrant. Like many writers, he has taken his own condition to represent not merely a possibility but a norm. In the essays of *Imaginary Homelands* he celebrates "the migrant sensibility," whose development he regards as "one of the central themes of this century of displaced persons." Rushdie has also taken this condition to represent something novel in history:

> The effect of mass migrations has been the creation of radically new types of human being: people who root themselves in ideas rather than places, in memories as much as in material things; people who have been obliged to define themselves—because they are so defined by others—by their otherness; people in whose deepest selves strange fusions occur, unprecedented unions between what they were and where they find themselves.

In the history of America, that description applies just as well to the Pilgrims in Plymouth, say, or to Swiss homesteading in Indiana, to Chinese trading in California, to former slaves crowding into cities on the Great Lakes, or to Seminoles driven onto reservations a thousand miles from their traditional land. Displaced persons are abundant in our century, but hardly a novelty.

Claims for the virtues of shifting ground are familiar and seductive to Americans, this nation of restless movers. From the beginning, our heroes have been sailors, explorers, cowboys, prospectors, speculators, backwoods ramblers, rainbow-chasers, vagabonds of every stripe. Our Promised Land has always been over the next ridge or at the end of the trail, never under our feet. One hundred years after the official closing of the frontier, we have still not shaken off the romance of unlimited space. If we fish out a stream or wear out a field, or if the smoke from a neighbor's chimney begins to crowd the sky, why, off we go to a new stream, a fresh field, a clean sky. In our national mythology, the worst fate is to be trapped on a farm, in a village, in the sticks, in some dead-end job or unglamorous marriage or played-out game. Stand still, we are warned, and you die. Americans have dug the most canals, laid the most rails, built the most roads and airports of any nation. In the newspaper I read that, even though our sprawling system of interstate highways is crumbling, the president has decided that we should triple it in size, and all without raising our taxes a nickel. Only a populace drunk on driving, a populace infatuated with the myth of the open road, could hear such a proposal without hooting.

So Americans are likely to share Rushdie's enthusiasm for migration, for the "hybridity, impurity, intermingling, the transformation that comes of new and unexpected combinations of human beings, cultures, ideas, politics, movies, songs." Everything about us is mongrel, from race to language, and we are stronger for it. Yet we might respond more skeptically when Rushdie says that "to be a migrant is, perhaps, to be the only species of human being free of the shackles of nationalism (to say nothing of its ugly sister, patriotism)." Lord knows we could do with less nationalism (to say nothing of its ugly siblings, racism, religious sectarianism, or class snobbery). But who would pretend that a history of migration has immunized the United States against bigotry? And even if, by uprooting ourselves, we shed our chauvinism, is that all we lose?

In this hemisphere, many of the worst abuses—of land, forests, animals, and communities—have been carried out by "people who root themselves in ideas rather than places." Rushdie claims that "migrants must, of necessity, make a new imaginative relationship with the world, because of the loss of familiar habitats." But migrants often pack up their visions and values with the rest of their baggage and carry them along. The Spaniards devastated Central and South America by imposing on this New World the religion, economics, and politics of the Old. Colonists brought slavery with them to North America, along with smallpox and Norway rats. The Dust Bowl of the 1930s was caused not by drought but by the transfer onto the Great Plains of farming methods that were suitable to wetter regions. The habit of our industry and commerce has been to force identical schemes onto differing locales, as though the mind were a cookie-cutter and the land were dough.

I quarrel with Rushdie because he articulates as eloquently as anyone the orthodoxy that I wish to counter: the belief that movement is inherently good, staying put is bad; that uprooting brings tolerance, while rootedness breeds intolerance; that imaginary homelands are preferable to geographical ones; that to be modern, enlightened, fully of our time is to be displaced. Wholesale dis-placement may be inevitable; but we should not suppose that it occurs without disastrous consequences for the earth and for ourselves. People who root themselves in places are likelier to know and care for those places than are people who root themselves in ideas. When we cease to be migrants and become inhabitants, we might begin to pay enough heed and respect to where we are. By settling in, we have a chance of making a durable home for ourselves, our fellow creatures, and our descendants.

What are we up against, those of us who aspire to become inhabitants, who wish to commit ourselves to a place? How strong, how old, is the impulse we are resisting?

Although our machines enable us to move faster and farther, humans have been on the move for a long time. Within a few clicks on the evolutionary clock, our ancestors roamed out of their native valleys in Africa and spread over the Eurasian continent. They invaded the deserts, the swamps, the mountains and valleys, the jungle and tundra. Drifting on boats and rafts, they pushed on to island after island around the globe. When glaciers locked up enough sea water to expose a land bridge from Asia to North America, migrants crossed into this unknown region, and within a few thousand years their descendants had scattered from the Bering Strait to Tierra del Fuego.

The mythology of those first Americans often claimed that a tribe had been attached to a given spot since the beginning of time, and we in our craving for rootedness may be inclined to believe in this eternal bond between people and place; but archaeology suggests that ideas, goods, and populations were in motion for millennia before the first Europeans reached these shores, hunters and traders and whole tribes roving about, boundaries shifting, homelands changing hands. Even agricultural settlements, such as those associated with the mound-building cultures in the Mississippi and Ohio valleys, reveal a history of arrivals and departures, sites used for decades or centuries and then abandoned. By comparison to our own hectic movements, an association between people and place lasting decades or centuries may seem durable and enviable; but it is not eternal.

What I am saying is that we are a wandering species, and have been since we reared up on our hind legs and stared at the horizon. Our impulse to wander, to pick up and move when things no longer suit us in our present place, is not an ailment brought on suddenly by industrialization, by science, or by the European hegemony over dark-skinned peoples. It would be naive to think that Spanish horses corrupted the Plains Indians, tempting a sedentary people to rush about, or that snowmobiles corrupted the Inuit, or that Jeeps corrupted the Aborigines. It would be just as naive to say that the automobile gave rise to our own restlessness; on the contrary, our restlessness gave rise to the automobile, as it led to the bicycle, steamboat, and clipper ship, as it led to the taming of horses, lacing of snowshoes, and carving of dugout canoes. With each invention, a means of moving farther, faster, has answered to a desire that coils in our genes. Mobility is the rule in human history, rootedness the exception.

Our itch to wander was the great theme of the English writer Bruce Chatwin, who died in 1989 from a rare disease contracted in the course of his own incessant travels. For Chatwin, "the nature of human restlessness" was "the question of questions." One hundred pages of *The Songlines,* his best known work, are filled with notebook entries supporting the view that "man is a migratory species." In a posthumous collection of essays entitled *What Am I Doing Here,* he summed up his observations:

> [W]e should perhaps allow human nature an appetitive drive for movement in the widest sense. The act of journeying contributes towards a sense of physical and mental well-being, while the monotony of prolonged settlement or regular work weaves patterns in the brain that

engender fatigue and a sense of personal inadequacy. Much of what the ethologists have designated "aggression" is simply an angered response to the frustrations of confinement.

I am dubious about the psychology here, for I notice Chatwin's own frustrations in the passage, especially in that irritable phrase about "the monotony of prolonged settlement or regular work"; but I agree with his speculation that deep in us there is "an appetitive drive for movement."

The movement chronicled in *The Songlines*—the purposeful wandering of the Australian Aborigines—may suggest a way for us to harness our restlessness, a way to reconcile our need to rove with our need to settle down. As hunter-gatherers in a harsh continent, the Aborigines must know their land thoroughly and travel it widely in order to survive. According to their belief, the land and all living things were created in a mythic time called the Dreaming, and the creative spirits are still at work, sustaining the world. Humans keep the world in touch with the power of the Dreaming by telling stories and singing songs. The whole of Australia is crisscrossed by pathways known to the Aborigines, who must walk them at intervals, performing the songs that belong to each path. Every tribe is responsible for the tracks within its own territory, and for passing down the appropriate songs from generation to generation. "There was hardly a rock or creek in the country," Chatwin remarks, "that could not or had not been sung." The movement of the Aborigines is not random, therefore, but deliberate, guided by hunger and thirst, but also by the need to participate in the renewal of the world. The land supplies the necessities of life, and in return humans offer knowledge, memory, and voice.

The Aboriginal walkabout illustrates "the once universal concept," in Chatwin's words, "that wandering re-establishes the original harmony . . . between man and the universe." Unlike vagabonds, who use up place after place without returning on their tracks, the Aborigines wed themselves to one place, and range over it with gratitude and care. So that they might continue as residents, they become stewards. Like the rest of nature, they move in circles, walking again and again over sacred ground.

The Australian Aborigines are among the "inhabitory peoples" whom Gary Snyder has studied in his search for wisdom about living in place, a wisdom he described in *The Old Ways:*

People developed specific ways to *be* in each of those niches: plant knowledge, boats, dogs, traps, nets, fishing—the smaller animals, and smaller
tools. From steep jungle slopes of Southwest China to coral atolls to
barren arctic deserts—*a spirit of what it was to be there* evolved, that spoke
of a direct sense of relation to the "land"—which really means, the total-
ity of the local bio-region system, from cirrus clouds to leaf-mold.

Such knowledge does not come all at once; it accumulates bit by bit over
generations, each person adding to the common lore.

Even nomads, whose name implies motion, must be scholars of their
bioregion. As they follow herds from pasture to pasture through the cycle
of the year, they trace a loop that is dictated by what the land provides.
For inhabitory peoples, listening to the land is a spiritual discipline as well
as a practical one. The alertness that feeds the body also feeds the soul. In
Native American culture, "medicine" is understood not as a human invention, but as a channeling of the power by which all things live.
Whether you are a hunter-gatherer, a nomad, a farmer, or a suburbanite,
to be at home in the land is to be sane and whole.

The Aborigines worked out an accommodation with their land over forty
thousand years, no doubt through trial and error. They would not have
survived if their mythology had not soon come to terms with their ecology. Even so, their population was never more than about one-hundredth
as large as that of modern Australia. We who live in North America are engaged in our own trials and errors, which are greatly magnified by the size
of our population and the power of our technology. A man with a bulldozer can make a graver mistake in one day than a whole tribe with digging sticks can make in a year. In my home region, mistakes are being made
seven days a week—with machinery, chemicals, guns, plows, fountain pens,
bare hands. I suspect the same is true in every region. But who is keeping
track? Who speaks for the wordless creatures? Who supplies memory and
conscience for the land?

Half a century ago, in *A Sand County Almanac,* Aldo Leopold gave us
an ecological standard for judging our actions: "A thing is right when it
tends to preserve the integrity, stability, and beauty of the biotic community. It is wrong when it tends otherwise." We can only apply that standard
if, in every biotic community, there are residents who keep watch over what
is preserved and what is lost, who see the beauty that escapes the frame of

the tourist's windshield or the investor's spreadsheet. "The problem," Leopold observed, "is how to bring about a striving for harmony with land among a people many of whom have forgotten there is any such thing as land, among whom education and culture have become almost synonymous with landlessness."

The question is not whether land belongs to us, through titles registered in a courthouse, but whether we belong to the land, through our loyalty and awareness. In the preface to his *The Natural History and Antiquities of Selborne,* the eighteenth-century English vicar, Gilbert White, notes that a comprehensive survey of England might be compiled if only "stationary men would pay some attention to the districts on which they reside." Every township, every field and creek, every mountain and forest on earth would benefit from the attention of stationary men and women. No one has understood this need better than Gary Snyder:

> One of the key problems in American society now, it seems to me, is people's lack of commitment to any given place—which, again, is totally unnatural and outside of history. Neighborhoods are allowed to deteriorate, landscapes are allowed to be strip-mined, because there is nobody who will live there and take responsibility; they'll just move on. The reconstruction of a people and of a life in the United States depends in part on people, neighborhood by neighborhood, county by county, deciding to stick it out and make it work where they are, rather than flee.

We may not have forty years, let alone forty thousand, to reconcile our mythology with our ecology. If we are to reshape our way of thinking to fit the way of things, as the songs of the Aborigines follow their terrain, many more of us need to *know* our local ground, walk over it, care for it, fight for it, bear it steadily in mind.

But if you stick in one place, won't you become a stick-in-the-mud? If you stay put, won't you be narrow, backward, dull? You might. I have met ignorant people who never moved; and I have also met ignorant people who never stood still. Committing yourself to a place does not guarantee that you will become wise, but neither does it guarantee that you will become parochial. Who knows better the limitations of a province or a culture than the person who has bumped into them time and again? The history of settlement in my own district and the continuing abuse of land hereabouts provoke me to rage and grief. I know the human legacy here too well to glamorize it.

To become intimate with your home region, to know the territory as well as you can, to understand your life as woven into the local life does not prevent you from recognizing and honoring the diversity of other places, cultures, ways. On the contrary, how can you value other places if you do not have one of your own? If you are not yourself *placed,* then you wander the world like a sightseer, a collector of sensations, with no gauge for measuring what you see. Local knowledge is the grounding for global knowledge. Those who care about nothing beyond the confines of their parish are in truth parochial, and are at least mildly dangerous to their parish; on the other hand, those who *have* no parish, those who navigate ceaselessly among postal zones and area codes, those for whom the world is only a smear of highways and bank accounts and stores, are a danger not just to their parish but to the planet.

Since birth, my children have been surrounded by images of the earth as viewed from space, images that I first encountered when I was in my twenties. Those photographs show vividly what in our sanest moments we have always known—that the earth is a closed circle, lovely and rare. On the wall beside me as I write there is a poster of the big blue marble encased in its white swirl of clouds. That is one pole of my awareness; but the other pole is what I see through my window. I try to keep both in sight at once.

For all my convictions, I still have to wrestle with the fear—in myself, in my children, and in some of my neighbors—that our place is too remote from the action. This fear drives many people to pack their bags and move to some resort or burg they have seen on television, leaving behind what they learn to think of as the boondocks. I deal with my own unease by asking just what action I am remote *from*—a stock market? a debating chamber? a drive-in mortuary? The action that matters, the work of nature and community, goes on everywhere.

Since Copernicus we have known better than to see the earth as the center of the universe. Since Einstein, we have learned that there is no center; or alternatively, that any point is as good as any other for observing the world. I take this to be roughly what medieval theologians meant when they defined God as a circle whose circumference is nowhere and whose center is everywhere. I find a kindred lesson in the words of the Zen master, Thich Nhat Hanh: "This spot where you sit is your own spot. It is on this very spot and in this very moment that you can become enlightened. You don't have to sit beneath a special tree in a distant land." There are no privileged locations. If you stay put, your place may become a holy center, not because it gives you special access to the divine, but because in your stillness you hear what might be heard anywhere. All there is to see can be seen from anywhere in the universe, if you know how to look; and the influence of the entire universe converges on every spot.

Except for the rare patches of wilderness, every place on earth has been transformed by human presence. "Ecology becomes a more complex but far more interesting science," René Dubos observes in *The Wooing of Earth*, "when human aspirations are regarded as an integral part of the landscape." Through "long periods of intimate association between human beings and nature," Dubos argues, landscape may take on a "quality of blessedness." The intimacy is crucial: the understanding of how to dwell in a place arises out of a sustained conversation between people and land. When there is no conversation, when we act without listening, when we impose our desires without regard for the qualities or needs of our place, then landscape may be cursed rather than blessed by our presence.

If our fidelity to place is to help renew and preserve our neighborhoods, it will have to be informed by what Wendell Berry calls "an ecological intelligence: a sense of the impossibility of acting or living alone or solely in one's own behalf, and this rests in turn upon a sense of the order upon which any life depends and of the proprieties of place within that order." Proprieties of place: actions, words, and values that are *proper* to your home ground. I think of my home ground as a series of nested rings, with house and marriage and family at the center, surrounded by the wider and wider hoops of neighborhood and community, the bioregion within walking distance of my door, the wooded hills and karst landscape of southern Indiana, the watershed of the Ohio River, and so on outward—and inward—to the ultimate source.

The longing to become an inhabitant rather than a drifter sets me against the current of my culture, which nudges everyone into motion. Newton taught us that a body at rest tends to stay at rest, unless acted on by an outside force. We are acted on ceaselessly by outside forces—advertising, movies, magazines, speeches—and also by the inner force of biology. I am not immune to their pressure. Before settling in my present home, I lived in seven states and two countries, tugged from place to place in childhood by my father's work and in early adulthood by my own. This itinerant life is so common among the people I know that I have been slow to conceive of an alternative. Only by knocking against the golden calf of mobility, which looms so large and shines so brightly, have I come to realize that it is hollow. Like all idols, it distracts us from the true divinity.

The ecological argument for staying put may be easier for us to see than the spiritual one, worried as we are about saving our skins. Few of us worry about saving our souls, and fewer still imagine that the condition of our souls has anything to do with the condition of our neighborhoods. Talk about enlightenment makes us jittery because it implies that we pass our ordinary days in darkness. You recall the scene in *King Lear* when blind and wretched old Gloucester, wishing to commit suicide, begs a young man to lead him to the brink of a cliff. The young man is Gloucester's son, Edgar, who fools the old man into thinking they have come to a high bluff at the edge of the sea. Gloucester kneels, then tumbles forward onto the level ground; on landing, he is amazed to find himself alive. He is transformed by the fall. Blind, at last he is able to see his life clearly; despairing, he discovers hope. To be enlightened, he did not have to leap to someplace else; he only had to come hard against the ground where he already stood.

My friend Richard, who wears a white collar to his job, recently bought forty acres of land that had been worn out by the standard local regimen of chemicals and corn. Evenings and weekends, he has set about restoring the soil by spreading manure, planting clover and rye, and filling the eroded gullies with brush. His pond has gathered geese, his young orchard has tempted deer, and his nesting boxes have attracted swallows and bluebirds. Now he is preparing a field for the wildflowers and prairie grasses that once flourished here. Having contemplated this work since he was a boy, Richard will not be chased away by fashions or dollars or tornadoes. On a recent airplane trip he was distracted from the book he was reading by thoughts of renewing the land. So he sketched on the flyleaf a plan of labor for the next ten years. Most of us do not have forty acres to care for, but that should not keep us from sowing and tending local crops.

I think about Richard's ten-year vision when I read a report chronicling the habits of computer users who, apparently, grow impatient if they have to wait more than a second for their machine to respond. I use a computer, but I am wary of the haste it encourages. Few answers that matter will come to us in a second; some of the most vital answers will not come in a decade, or a century.

When the chiefs of the Iroquois nation sit in council, they are sworn to consider how their decisions will affect their descendants seven generations into the future. Seven generations! Imagine our politicians thinking beyond the next opinion poll, beyond the next election, beyond their own lifetimes, two centuries ahead. Imagine our bankers, our corporate executives, our advertising moguls weighing their judgments on that scale. Looking seven generations into the future, could a developer pave another farm? Could a farmer spray another pound of poison? Could the captain of an oil tanker flush his tanks at sea? Could you or I write checks and throw switches without a much greater concern for what is bought and sold, what is burned?

As I write this, I hear the snarl of earthmovers and chain saws a mile away destroying a farm to make way for another shopping strip. I would rather hear a tornado, whose damage can be undone. The elderly woman who owned the farm had it listed in the National Register, then willed it to her daughters on condition they preserve it. After her death, the daughters, who live out of state, had the will broken, so the land could be turned over to the chain saws and earthmovers. The machines work around the clock. Their noise wakes me at midnight, at three in the morning, at dawn. The roaring abrades my dreams. The sound is a reminder that we are living in the midst of a holocaust. I do not use the word lightly. The earth is being pillaged, and every one of us, willingly or grudgingly, is taking part. We ask how sensible, educated, supposedly moral people could have tolerated slavery or the slaughter of Jews. Similar questions will be asked about us by our descendants, to whom we bequeath an impoverished planet. They will demand to know how we could have been party to such waste and ruin. They will have good reason to curse our memory.

What does it mean to be alive in an era when the earth is being devoured, and in a country which has set the pattern for that devouring? What are we called to do? I think we are called to the work of healing, both inner and outer: healing of the mind through a change in con-

sciousness, healing of the earth through a change in our lives. We can begin that work by learning how to abide in a place. I am talking about an
active commitment, not a passive lingering. If you stay with a husband or
wife out of laziness rather than love, that is inertia, not marriage. If you
stay put through cowardice rather than conviction, you will have no
strength to act. Strength comes, healing comes, from aligning yourself with
the grain of your place and answering to its needs.

"The man who is often thinking that it is better to be somewhere else
than where he is excommunicates himself," we are cautioned by Thoreau,
that notorious stay-at-home. The metaphor is religious: to withhold yourself from where you are is to be cut off from communion with the source.
It has taken me half a lifetime of searching to realize that the likeliest path
to the ultimate ground leads through my local ground. I mean the land
itself, with its creeks and rivers, its weather, seasons, stone outcroppings,
and all the plants and animals that share it. I cannot have a spiritual center without having a geographical one; I cannot live a grounded life without being grounded in a *place*.

In belonging to a landscape, one feels a rightness, at-homeness, a knit-
ting of self and world. This condition of clarity and focus, this being fully
present, is akin to what the Buddhists call mindfulness, what Christian
contemplatives refer to as recollection, what Quakers call centering down.
I am suspicious of any philosophy that would separate this-worldly from
other-worldly commitment. There is only one world, and we participate
in it here and now, in our flesh and our place.

Gary Snyder

From

THE PLACE, THE REGION,
AND THE COMMONS

When you find your place where you are, practice occurs.

DŌGEN

Gary Snyder lives in the foothills of the Sierra Nevada in northern California. Growing up in a rural area outside of Seattle, he was exposed to the power of the Cascade Mountains, the continuing presence of Native American culture, and the compelling character of Asian culture. A few years after graduating from college, he journeyed to Japan to become a student of Zen Buddhism. His writings exhibit this double influence of American Indian and Buddhist religions, grounded in the physical work of living with the land. His inclusion of a penetrating social critique along with a deep ecological concern for wilderness reflects the radical social views that were also part of his youth, and he is active in local ecological and social issues with the Yuba Watershed Institute. His many volumes of poetry include *Turtle Island,* and he has written collections of essays and published an anthology of interviews.

Snyder is one of the major voices of bioregionalism, and the following essay (two excerpts from "The Place, the Region, and the Commons" in *The Practice of the Wild*) outlines some of the basic principles of that movement. A subtle awareness of the uniqueness of one's place and a commitment to stay put can enable one to listen to the spirits of the land. This ecological sensitivity is linked to criticism of nation-state politics and the international homogenization of culture. In addition, a cosmopolitan, planetary consciousness (rather than imperialistic global thinking) and a sweeping view of history that includes the Paleolithic is combined with attention to one's local region. As Snyder notes, bioregionalism also cultivates a sense of place in urban areas. Thus nature and culture, urban and rural, local and planetary are (to use Snyder's Buddhist terminology) nondual. Such a complex, integrated view allows one to be at home in the land.

The World Is Places

We experience slums, prairies, and wetlands all equally as "places." Like a mirror, a place can hold anything, on any scale. I want to talk about place as an experience and propose a model of what it meant to "live in place" for most of human time, presenting it initially in terms of the steps that a child takes growing into a natural community. (We have the terms *enculturation* and *acculturation,* but nothing to describe the process of becoming placed or re-placed.) In doing so we might get one more angle on what a "civilization of wildness" might require.

For most Americans, to reflect on "home place" would be an unfamiliar exercise. Few today can announce themselves as someone *from* somewhere. Almost nobody spends a lifetime in the same valley, working alongside the people they knew as children. Native people everywhere (the very term means "someone born there") and Old World farmers and city people share this experience of living in place. Still—and this is very important to remember—being inhabitory, being place-based, has never meant that one didn't travel from time to time, going on trading ventures or taking livestock to summer grazing. Such working wanderers have always known they had a home-base on earth, and could prove it at any campfire or party by singing their own songs.

The heart of a place is the home, and the heart of the home is the firepit, the hearth. All tentative explorations go outward from there, and it is back to the fireside that elders return. You grow up speaking a home language, a local vernacular. Your own household may have some specifics of phrase, of pronunciation, that are different from the *domus,* the *jia* or *ie* or *kum,* down the lane. You hear histories of the people who are your neighbors and tales involving rocks, streams, mountains, and trees that are all within your sight. The myths of world-creation tell you how *that mountain* was created and how *that peninsula* came to be there. As you grow bolder you explore your world outward from the firepit (which is the center of each universe) in little trips. The childhood landscape is learned on foot, and a map is inscribed in the mind—trails and pathways and groves—the mean dog, the cranky old man's house, the pasture with a bull in it—going out wider and farther. All of us carry within us a picture of the terrain that was learned roughly between the ages of six and nine. (It could as easily be an urban neighborhood as some rural scene.) You can almost totally recall the place you walked, played, biked, swam. Revisualizing that place with its smells and textures, walking through it again in your imagination, has a grounding and settling effect. As a contemporary thought we might also wonder how it is for those whose childhood landscape was being ripped up by bulldozers, or whose family moving about made it all a blur. I have a friend who still gets emotional when he recalls how the avocado orchards of his southern California youth landscape were transformed into hillside after hillside of suburbs.

Our place is part of what we are. Yet even a "place" has a kind of fluidity: it passes through space and time—"ceremonial time" in John Hanson Mitchell's phrase. A place will have been grasslands, then conifers, then beech and elm. It will have been half riverbed, it will have been scratched and plowed by ice. And then it will be cultivated, paved, sprayed, dammed, graded, built up. But each is only for a while, and that will be just another set of lines on the palimpsest. The whole earth is a great tablet holding the multiple overlaid new and ancient traces of the swirl of forces. Each place is its own place, forever (eventually) wild. A place on earth is a mosaic within larger mosaics—the land is all small places, all precise tiny realms replicating larger and smaller patterns. Children start out learning place by learning those little realms around the house, the settlement, and outward.

One's sense of the scale of a place expands as one learns the *region*. The young hear further stories and go for explorations which are also subsistence forays—firewood gathering, fishing, to fairs or to market. The outlines of the larger region become part of their awareness. (Thoreau says in "Walking" that an area twenty miles in diameter will be enough to occupy a lifetime of close exploration on foot—you will never exhaust its details.)

The total size of the region a group calls home depends on the land type. Every group is territorial, each moves within a given zone, even nomads stay within boundaries. A people living in a desert or grassland with great visible spaces that invite you to step forward and walk as far as you can see will range across tens of thousands of square miles. A deep old-growth forest may rarely be traveled at all. Foragers in gallery forests and grasslands will regularly move broadly, whereas people in a deep-soiled valley ideal for gardens might not go far beyond the top of the nearest ridge. The regional boundaries were roughly drawn by climate, which is what sets the plant-type zones—plus soil type and landforms. Desert wastes, mountain ridges, or big rivers set a broad edge to a region. We walk across or wade through the larger and smaller boundaries. Like children first learning our homeland we can stand at the edge of a big river, or on the crest of a major ridge, and observe that the other side is a different soil, a change of plants and animals, a new shape of barn roof, maybe less or more rain. The lines between natural regions are never simple or clear, but vary according to such criteria as biota, watersheds, landforms, elevation. (See Jim Dodge, 1981.) Still, we all know—at some point—that we are no longer in the Midwest, say, but in the West. Regions seen according to natural criteria are sometimes called bioregions.

(In pre-conquest America people covered great distances. It is said that the Mojave of the lower Colorado felt that everyone at least once in their lives should make foot journeys to the Hopi mesas to the east, the Gulf of California to the south, and to the Pacific.)

Every region has its wilderness. There is the fire in the kitchen, and there is the place less traveled. In most settled regions there used to be some combination of prime agricultural land, orchard and vine land, rough pasturage, woodlot, forest, and desert or mountain "waste." The de facto wilderness was the extreme backcountry part of all that. The parts less visited are "where the bears are." The wilderness is within walking distance—it may be three days or it may be ten. It is at the far high rough end, or the deep forest and swamp end, of the territory where most of you all live and work. People will go there for mountain herbs, for the trapline, or for solitude. They live between the poles of home and their own wild places.

Recollecting that we once lived in places is part of our contemporary self-rediscovery. It grounds what it means to be "human" (etymologically something like "earthling"). I have a friend who feels sometimes that the world is hostile to human life—he says it chills us and kills us. But how could we *be* were it not for this planet that provided our very shape? Two conditions—gravity and a livable temperature range between freezing and boiling—have given us fluids and flesh. The trees we climb and the ground we walk on have given us five fingers and toes. The "place" (from the root *plat,* broad, spreading, flat) gave us far-seeing eyes, the streams and breezes gave us versatile tongues and whorly ears. The land gave us a stride, and the lake a dive. The amazement gave us our kind of mind. We should be thankful for that, and take nature's stricter lessons with some grace.

Bioregional Perspectives

The Region is the elsewhere of civilization.
MAX CAFARD

The little nations of the past lived within territories that conformed to some set of natural criteria. The culture areas of the major native groups of North America overlapped, as one would expect, almost exactly with broadly defined major bioregions (Kroeber, 1947). That older human experience of a fluid, indistinct, but genuine home region was gradually replaced—across Eurasia—by the arbitrary and often violently imposed boundaries of emerging national states. These imposed borders sometimes cut across biotic areas and ethnic zones alike. Inhabitants lost ecological knowledge and community solidarity. In the old ways, the flora and fauna and landforms are *part of the culture.* The world of culture and nature, which is actual, is almost a shadow world now, and the insubstantial world of political jurisdictions and rarefied economies is what passes for reality. We live in a backwards time. We can regain some small sense of that old membership by discovering the original lineaments of our land and steering— at least in the home territory and in the mind—by those rather than the borders of arbitrary nations, states, and counties.

Regions are "interpenetrating bodies in semi-simultaneous spaces" (Cafard, 1989). Biota, watersheds, landforms, and elevations are just a few of the facets that define a region. Culture areas, in the same way, have subsets such as dialects, religions, sorts of arrow-release, types of tools, myth motifs, musical scales, art styles. One sort of regional outline would be floristic. The coastal Douglas Fir, as the definitive tree of the Pacific Northwest, is an example. (I knew it intimately as a boy growing up on a farm between Lake Washington and Puget Sound. The local people, the Snohomish, called it *lukta tciyats,* "wide needles.") Its northern limit is around the Skeena River in British Columbia. It is found west of the crest through Washington, Oregon, and northern California. The southern coastal limit of Douglas Fir is about the same as that of salmon, which do not run south of the Big Sur River. Inland it grows down the west slope of the Sierra as far south as the north fork of the San Joaquin River. That outline describes the boundary of a larger natural region that runs across three states and one international border.

The presence of this tree signifies a rainfall and a temperature range and will indicate what your agriculture might be, how steep the pitch of your roof, what raincoats you'd need. You don't have to know such details to get by in the modern cities of Portland or Bellingham. But if you do know what is taught by plants and weather, you are in on the gossip and can truly feel more at home. The sum of a field's forces becomes what we call very loosely the "spirit of the place." To know the spirit of a place is to realize that you are a part of a part and that the whole is made of parts, each of which is whole. You start with the part you are whole in.

As quixotic as these ideas may seem, they have a reservoir of strength and possibility behind them. The spring of 1984, a month after equinox, Gary Holthaus and I drove down from Anchorage to Haines, Alaska. We went around the upper edge of the basin of the Copper River, skirted some tributaries of the Yukon, and went over Haines Summit. It was White and Black Spruce taiga all the way, still frozen up. Dropping down from the pass to saltwater at Chilkat inlet we were immediately in forests of large Sitka Spruce, Skunk Cabbage poking out in the swamps, it was spring. That's a bioregional border leap. I was honored the next day by an invitation to Raven House to have coffee with Austin Hammond and a circle of other Tlingit elders and to hear some long and deeply entwined discourses on the responsibilities of people to their places. As we looked out his front window to hanging glaciers on the peaks beyond the saltwater, Hammond spoke of empires and civilizations in metaphors of glaciers. He described how great alien forces—industrial civilization in this case—advance and retreat, and how settled people can wait it out.

Sometime in the mid-seventies at a conference of Native American leaders and activists in Bozeman, Montana, I heard a Crow elder say something similar: "You know, I think if people stay somewhere long enough— even white people—the spirits will begin to speak to them. It's the power of the spirits coming up from the land. The spirits and the old powers aren't lost, they just need people to be around long enough and the spirits will begin to influence them."

Bioregional awareness teaches us in *specific* ways. It is not enough just to "love nature" or to want to "be in harmony with Gaia." Our relation to the natural world takes place in a *place,* and it must be grounded in information and experience. For example: "real people" have an easy familiarity with the local plants. This is so unexceptional a kind of knowledge that everyone in Europe, Asia, and Africa used to take it for granted. Many contemporary Americans don't even *know* that they don't "know the plants," which is indeed a measure of alienation. Knowing a bit about the flora we could enjoy questions like: where do Alaska and Mexico meet? It would be somewhere on the north coast of California, where Canada Jay and Sitka Spruce lace together with manzanita and Blue Oak.

But instead of "northern California" let's call it Shasta Bioregion. The present state of California (the old Alta California territory) falls into at least three natural divisions, and the northern third looks, as the Douglas Fir example shows, well to the north. The boundaries of this northern third would roughly run from the Klamath/Rogue River divide south to San Francisco Bay and up the delta where the Sacramento and San Joaquin rivers join. The line would then go east to the Sierra Crest and, taking that as a distinct border, follow it north to Susanville. The watershed divide then angles broadly northeastward along the edge of the Modoc Plateau to the Warner Range and Goose Lake.

East of the divide is the Great Basin, north of Shasta is the Cascadia/Columbia region, and then farther north is what we call Ish River country, the drainages of Puget Sound and the Straits of Georgia. Why should we do this kind of visualization? Again I will say: it prepares us to begin to be at home in this landscape. There are tens of millions of people in North America who were physically born here but who are not actually living here intellectually, imaginatively, or morally. Native Americans to be sure have a prior claim to the term native. But as they love this land they will welcome the conversion of the millions of immigrant psyches into fellow "Native Americans." For the non-Native American to become at home on this continent, he or she must be *born again* in this hemisphere, on this continent, properly called Turtle Island.

That is to say, we must consciously fully accept and recognize that this is where we live and grasp the fact that our descendants will be here for millennia to come. Then we must honor this land's great antiquity—its wildness—learn it—defend it—and work to hand it on to the children (of all beings) of the future with its biodiversity and health intact. Europe or Africa or Asia will then be seen as the place our ancestors came from, places we might want to know about and to visit, but not "home." Home—deeply, spiritually—must be here. Calling this place "America" is to name it after a stranger. "Turtle Island" is the name given this continent by Native Americans based on creation mythology (Snyder, 1974). The United States, Canada, Mexico, are passing political entities; they have their legitimacies, to be sure, but they will lose their mandate if they continue to abuse the land. "The State is destroyed, but the mountains and rivers remain."

But this work is not just for the newcomers of the Western Hemisphere, Australia, Africa, or Siberia. A worldwide purification of mind is called for: the exercise of seeing the surface of the planet for what it is—by nature. With this kind of consciousness people turn up at hearings and in front of trucks and bulldozers to defend the land or trees. Showing solidarity with a region! What an odd idea at first. Bioregionalism is the entry of place into the dialectic of history. Also we might say that there are "classes" which have so far been overlooked—the animals, rivers, rocks, and grasses—now entering history.

These ideas provoke predictable and usually uninformed reactions. People fear the small society and the critique of the State. It is difficult to see, when one has been raised under it, that it is the State itself which is inherently greedy, destabilizing, entropic, disorderly, and illegitimate. They cite parochialism, regional strife, "unacceptable" expressions of cultural diversity, and so forth. Our philosophies, world religions, and histories are biased toward uniformity, universality, and centralization—in a word, the ideology of monotheism. Certainly under specific conditions neighboring groups have wrangled for centuries—interminable memories and hostilities cooking away like radioactive waste. It's still at work in the Middle East. The ongoing ethnic and political miseries of parts of Europe and the Middle East sometimes go back as far as the Roman Empire. This is not something that can be attributed to the combativeness of "human nature" per se. Before the expansion of early empires the occasional strife of tribes and natural nations was almost familial. With the rise of the State, the scale of the destructiveness and malevolence of warfare makes a huge leap.

In the times when people did not have much accumulated surplus, there was no big temptation to move in on other regions. I'll give an example from my own part of the world. (I describe my location as: on the western slope of the northern Sierra Nevada, in the Yuba River watershed, north of the south fork at the three-thousand-foot elevation, in a community of Black Oak, Incense Cedar, Madrone, Douglas Fir, and Ponderosa Pine.) The western slope of the Sierra Nevada has winter rain and snowfall and a different set of plants from the dry eastern slope. In pre-white times, the native people living across the range had little temptation to venture over, because their skills were specific to their own area, and they could go hungry in an unfamiliar biome. It takes a long education to know the edible plants, where to find them, and how to prepare them. So the Washo of the Sierra east side traded their pine nuts and obsidian for the acorns, yew bows, and abalone shells of the Miwok and Maidu to the west. The two sides met and camped together for weeks in the summer Sierra meadows, their joint commons. (Dedicated raiding cultures, "barbarians," evolve as a response to nearby civilizations and their riches. Genghis Khan, at an audience in his yurt near Lake Baikal, was reported to have said: "Heaven is exasperated with the decadence and luxury of China.")

There are numerous examples of relatively peaceful small-culture coexistence all over the world. There have always been multilingual persons peacefully trading and traveling across large areas. Differences were often eased by shared spiritual perspectives or ceremonial institutions and by the multitude of myths and tales that cross language barriers. What about the deep divisions caused by religion? It must be said that most religious exclusiveness is the odd specialty of the Judeo/Christian/Islamic faith, which is a recent and (overall) minority development in the world. Asian religion, and the whole world of folk religion, animism, and shamanism, appreciates or at least tolerates diversity. (It seems that the really serious cultural disputes are caused by different tastes in food. When I was choker-setting in eastern Oregon, one of my crew was a Wasco man whose wife was a Chehalis woman from the west side. He told me that when they got in fights she would call him a "goddamn grasshopper eater" and he'd shout back "fish eater"!)

Cultural pluralism and multilingualism are the planetary norm. We seek the balance between cosmopolitan pluralism and deep local consciousness. We are asking how the whole human race can regain self-determination in place after centuries of having been disenfranchised by hierarchy and/or centralized power. Do not confuse this exercise with "nationalism," which is exactly the opposite, the impostor, the puppet of the State, the grinning ghost of the lost community.

So this is one sort of start. The bioregional movement is not just a rural program: it is as much for the restoration of urban neighborhood life and the greening of the cities. All of us are fluently moving in multiple realms that include irrigation districts, solid-waste management jurisdictions, long-distance area code zones, and such. Planet Drum Foundation, based in the San Francisco Bay Area, works with many other local groups for the regeneration of the city as a living place, with projects like the identification and restoration of urban creeks (Berg et al., 1989). There are groups worldwide working with Third and Fourth World people revisualizing territories and playfully finding appropriate names for their newly realized old regions (*Raise the Stakes,* 1987). Four bioregional congresses have been held on Turtle Island.

As sure as impermanence, the nations of the world will eventually be more sensitively defined and the lineaments of the blue earth will begin to reshape the politics. The requirements of sustainable economies, ecologically sensitive agriculture, strong and vivid community life, wild habitat—and the second law of thermodynamics—all lead this way. I also realize that right now this is a kind of theater as much as it is ecological politics. Not just street theater, but visionary mountain, field, and stream theater. As Jim Dodge says: "The chances of bioregionalism succeeding . . . are beside the point. If one person, or a few, or a community of people, live more fulfilling lives from bioregional practice, then it's successful." May it all speed the further deconstruction of the superpowers. As "The Surre(gion)alist Manifesto" says:

> Regional politics do not take place in Washington, Moscow, and other "seats of power." Regional power does not "sit"; it flows everywhere. Through watersheds and bloodstreams. Through nervous systems and food chains. The regions are everywhere & nowhere. We are all illegals. We are natives and we are restless. We have no country; we live in the country. We are off the Inter-State. The Region is against the Regime— any Regime. Regions are anarchic. (Cafard, 1989)

Thomas Berry

THE HUDSON RIVER VALLEY:
A Bioregional Story

Thomas Berry is a Passionist priest who has described himself as a "geologian." He studied in China and has written books on Asian religions as well as the theology of the earth and cosmos. His book *Dream of the Earth* has had enormous impact on ecological spirituality. He is the founder of the Riverdale Center for Religious Research in New York City and has taught at a number of universities. Now retired, he lives in his hometown of Greensboro, North Carolina. Berry is especially concerned about understanding the structure and processes of the earth and the human role in the dynamics of the universe. His sweeping and progressivist historical perspective is indebted to his close study of Teilhard de Chardin. Berry has stressed the importance of developing a new story of the earth, and this selection from *Dream of the Earth* offers a bioregional story—marked by both glory and tragedy—of the Hudson Valley, where he formerly lived.

Tell me a story. How often we said that as children. Tell me a story. Story illumined the world for us in childhood. Even now we might make the request: tell me a story. Tell me the story of the river and the valley and the streams and woodlands and wetlands, of the shellfish and finfish. Tell me a story. A story of where we are and how we got here and the characters and roles that we play. Tell me a story, a story that will be my story as well as the story of everyone and everything about me, the story that brings us together in a valley community, a story that brings together the human community with every living being in the valley, a story that brings us together under the arc of the great blue sky in the day and the starry heavens at night, a story that will drench us with rain and dry us in the wind, a story told by humans to one another that will also be the story that the wood thrush sings in the thicket, the story that the river recites in its downward journey, the story that Storm King Mountain images forth in the fullness of its grandeur.

It's a long story, a story that begins with the fracture across the eastern borders of the North American continent resulting from the clashing and rifting of tectonic plates, and it includes the molten intrusion whereby the Palisades emerged to terminate in those massive cracked columns to the west. The story of the great hydrological cycle that has drawn up from the Gulf and across from the Pacific and down from the Arctic and in from the Atlantic entire oceans of water and has poured them down in unending sequence over this region to give to the valley its shape, its fertility, and made of it a meeting place as the northern extreme of southern lifeforms and the southern extreme of northern lifeforms.

The story of the valley is the story of the glaciation that came down from the frigid north as recently as fifty thousand years ago to cover this area with ice more than a thousand feet in height, driving southward the multitude of living beings for some thousands of years and then returning northward some fifteen thousand years ago, leaving this region to take on its present shape and luxuriance of life, its trees and grasses and flowers, its singing birds and ambling bears, its red foxes, pheasants, wild turkeys, and bobolinks.

The story of the valley is also the story of the Indians who originally dwelled in this region. Even now, in the names of the area, we recognize the ghosts of the indigenous peoples: the Mahicans, the Wappinger, the Hackensack and the Raritan, the Kitawonks, the Tappans across the river, the Sinsinks of the Ossining area. These names of earlier tribes carry a mysterious abiding quality. As Chief Seattle once said of us and our cities: "When the last Red Man shall have perished, and the memory of my tribe shall have become a myth among the White Men, these shores will swarm with the invisible dead of my tribe, and when your children's children think themselves alone in the field, the store, the shop, upon the highway, or in the silence of the pathless woods, they will not be alone." Chief Seattle then continues with a profound insight into the enduring trauma being shaped in the psychic depths of the white man: "At night, when the streets of your cities and villages are silent and you think them deserted, they will throng with the returning hosts that once filled them and still love this beautiful land. The White Man will never be alone."

These voices are there in the wind, in the unconscious depths of our minds. These voices are there not primarily to indict us for our cruelties, but to identify the distortions in our relations with the land and its inhabitants, and also to guide us toward a mutually enhancing human-earth relationship in this beautiful valley.

The valley was at the height of its grandeur when one day the mainmast of a strange sailing vessel broke over the horizon. The sails unfurled to their full expanse as the *Half Moon* came into full view and sailed across the bar at Sandy Hook and on through the Narrows into the channel and eventually up into the valley, past this region, to the shores of Albany.

Never was the region more brilliant in its color, in the exuberance of its life expression, in the grandeur of its tall white pines, in its beaver population, in the abundance of its oysters and clams, in its shad and tomcod and striped bass. Never were the woodlands more resonant with their songbirds, never were the skies more often witness to the peregrine falcon, the red-tailed hawks, and the bald eagles. Nor was the water ever more refreshing as it came down from the Adirondacks to meet the sea water around what later became Poughkeepsie.

We need to recall all this as we tell the story of the valley, for the valley required heavenly as well as earthly forces to bring it into being. It was a poignant moment then, when the sails from the east appeared over the horizon, for never again would the region have quite the mysterious brooding of the natural world in its pre-European phase, or that special mode of human presence to the natural world as was given by the indigenous peoples of this continent. When the sails appeared, the entire continent might have shuddered.

In 1907 there were numerous celebrations throughout the valley commemorating the arrival of our European ancestors in this region. Our settlements, our cultural and industrial achievements, were seen as high moments in the story of the valley. As we look back on these celebrations now, they appear to have had a certain naiveté, an exaggerated pride, even a certain arrogance, witnessing to our human tendencies toward self-glorification, oblivious of the larger consequences of our actions. These earlier celebrations honored the human at the expense of every other living being in the valley.

The distinguishing aspect of our more recent celebrations is that we now honor this region in and for itself, while trying to discover how our human presence in the region can be an enhancement rather than a diminishment. In this sense our celebrations are the opposite of those earlier celebrations. We have looked back over the centuries since the first European vessel sailed into the river and found that while they have been a period of glory and conquest for ourselves, what have they been from the standpoint of the valley in its natural form.

What did it mean to the beaver that soon became extinct in much of the region? What did it mean to the millions of hemlock that were cut down simply for their bark for tanning hides? What did it mean for the great oyster beds and for the other shellfish that thrived so abundantly in the river? What did it mean to the organisms in the soil that later suffered from abusive agriculture? What did it forbode for the river that would receive the toxic runoff of chemical agriculture? What did it mean for the wetlands along the river that were filled in for trash heaps or to make way for railroads and highways? What did it mean for the river life when a nuclear generating station was set up at Indian Point? So we might ask ourselves those questions concerning the valley and the meaning of that moment when the mainmast of the *Half Moon* appeared above the Atlantic horizon.

As it came through the gap between Sandy Hook and the Rockaway Peninsula, through the Narrows into the upper bay, then into the river, the native peoples watching could have known nothing of their future or of the thoughts or intentions of the men in the great vessel. Nor could the men on the *Half Moon* have known fully their own minds nor the larger intentions of their political regimes nor the cultural ideals or economic forces that had brought them. Obscure forces were at work, driving an awesome transformation of this planet, ambivalent forces capable of both benign and deleterious consequences, forces with demonic intensity, forces ready to tear the North American continent to pieces in a stupendous effort to transcend the human condition in some serene millennial fulfillment.

We have all experienced these forces. A kind of possession seized us, and every being on this planet has felt its impact on a scale somewhat like those great geological upheavals or like the descent of a glacier. The valley and ourselves are both somewhat shattered. And yet the enormous creative forces deep in the reality of things are asserting themselves. Gratefully the valley before us has not been ruined so extensively as those valleys where a long sequence of dams has been built or where toxic wastes have completely ruined the aquatic life or where the water has been drained off into the fields for irrigation projects. We think of the Tennessee Valley, the Ohio, the Colorado, and the irreparable damage done to those and so many other regions over the years.

The Hudson River has not been dammed below the region of Troy. The abundant rainfall is sufficient for agricultural production. The river has, so far, been saved from exploitation of its fresh water because of the abundant water available from the Delaware Basin.

Even if the valley is more resilient than many other valleys of the North American continent and even if it has been saved from the devastation they have experienced, the river, the woodlands, and the soil have become seriously deteriorated over these past centuries, especially in this century, when the valley has been saturated with petrochemical residues in its air, its water and its soil. Every living species in the valley has experienced the deleterious influence of our human presence. Even now the increased occupation of the land for shopping malls, parking lots, roadways, corporate headquarters, industrial sites, and development projects is progressively eliminating habitat needed by various bird and animal as well as insect and plant species. Even now our chemical agriculture is damaging the soil and poisoning the streams; industrial waste products and city sewage are pouring through the valley. Realizing all this, we must ask, what has happened?

It would appear that we could not possibly have done all this or presently be doing this, for we see now that it is all self-destructive. We must have been in a trance state—caught up in our illusory world of wires and wheels and concrete and steel and roadways—where we race back and forth in unending frenzy.

The world of life, of spontaneity, the world of dawn and sunset and starlight, the world of soil and sunshine, of meadow and woodland, of hickory and oak and maple and hemlock and pineland forests, of wildlife dwelling around us, of the river and its well-being—all of this some of us are discovering for the first time as the integral community in which we live. Here we experience the reality and the values that evoke in us our deepest moments of reflection, our revelatory experience of the ultimate mystery of things. Here, in this intimate presence to the valley in all its vitality, we receive those larger intuitions that lead us to dance and sing, intuitions that activate our imaginative powers in their most creative functions. This, too, is what inspires our weddings, our home life, and our joy in our children. Even our deepest human sensitivities emerge from our region, our place, our specific habitat, for the earth does not give itself to us in a global sameness. It gives itself to us in arctic and tropical regions, in seashore and desert, in prairie-lands and woodlands, in mountains and valleys. Out of each a unique shaping of life takes place, a community, an integral community of all the geological as well as the biological and the human components. Each region is a single community so intimately related that any benefit or any injury is immediately experienced throughout the entire community.

So it is also with ourselves. We who live here in the Hudson River Valley constitute a single organic community with the river and the lowlands and the surrounding hills, with the sunlight and the rain, with the grasses and the trees and all the living creatures about us. We are all in some manner needed by one another. We may disdain the insects and the lowly plankton in the river, we may resent the heat of summer or the ice of winter, we may try to impose our mechanistic patterns on the biological rhythms of the region, but as soon as any one of these natural functions is disturbed in its proper expression, we are in trouble, and there is no further support to which we can appeal.

The natural world has produced its present variety, its abundance, and the creative interaction of all its components through billions of experiments. To shatter all this in the belief that we can gain by thwarting nature in its basic spontaneities is a brash and foolish thing, as is amply demonstrated by many of our past activities. If we do not alter our attitude and our activities, our children and grandchildren will live not only amid the ruins of the industrial world, but also amid the ruins of the natural world itself. That this will not happen, that the valley will be healed where it is damaged, preserved in its present integrity and renewed in its creative possibilities, is the hope that is before us.

Just now we are, as it were, returning to the valley, finding our place once again after a long period of alienation. At such a moment in our own history, as well as in the history of the region, we need first of all an extreme sensitivity to the needs of all the various components of the valley community—the needs of the river, the soil, the air; the needs of the various living forms that inhabit the valley; and the special needs of the human community dwelling here in the valley. We need to know how these relate to one another. Prior to our coming from abroad, all of these components of the region had worked out a mutually enhancing relationship. The valley was flourishing.

When we arrived we brought with us an attitude that the region was here for our exploitation. Even though we broke our treaties with the Indian tribes, we did recognize their rights and made treaties with them. It never entered our minds that we should also have made treaties with the river and with the land and with the region as a whole. In this we failed to do what even God did after the flood: "I set my rainbow in the cloud and it shall be a sign of the covenant between me and the earth. When I bring clouds over the earth and the rainbow is seen in the clouds, I will remember my covenant which is between me and you and every living creature of all flesh; and the waters shall never again become a flood to destroy all flesh."

Such a treaty, or some such spiritual bond, between ourselves and the natural world, is needed, a bonding based on the principle of mutual enhancement. The river and its valley are neither our enemy to be conquered, nor our servant to be controlled, nor our mistress to be seduced. The river is a pervasive presence beyond all these. It is the ultimate psychic as well as the physical context out of which we emerge into being and by which we are nourished, guided, healed, and fulfilled. As the gulls soaring above the river in its estuary region, as the blossoms along its banks, the fish within its waters, so, too, the river is a celebration of existence, of life lived in intimate association with the sky, the winds from every direction, the sunlight. The river is the binding presence throughout the valley community. We do not live primarily in Poughkeepsie or Peekskill, Newburgh or Yonkers. We live primarily along the river or in the valley. We are river people and valley people. That fact determines more than anything else the way we live, the foods we eat, the clothes we wear, how we travel. It also provides the content and context for celebrating life in its most sublime meaning.

We celebrate the valley not in some generalized planetary context, but in the specific setting that we have indicated. It is a celebration of our place, but our place as story, for we need only look about us to appreciate the grandeur of these surroundings. The grandeur of the valley is expressed most fully in its story.

The story, as we have seen, is a poignant one, a story with its glory, but not without its tragedy. Now the story begins to express the greatest change in the valley since the modern story of the valley began in 1609. This is the moment of change from a sense of the valley as subservient to human exploitation to a sense of the valley as an integral natural community which is itself the basic reality and the basic value, and of the human as having its true glory as a functioning member, rather than as a conquering invader, of this community. Our role is to be the instrument whereby the valley celebrates itself. The valley is both the object and the subject of the celebration. It is our high privilege to articulate this celebration in the stories we tell and in the songs we sing.

NATIVE CULTURES AND THE SEARCH FOR PLACE

Melissa Nelson

BECOMING MÉTIS

Melissa Nelson was born and raised in the San Francisco Bay Area and she is currently in the doctorate program in cultural ecology at the University of California, Davis. Of Ojibwe, Nordic, and French heritage, she serves as the president of The Cultural Conservancy, a native non-profit group committed to preserving traditional cultures and their lands. In this essay she speaks to the challenge of integrating different cultural traditions in her life and worldview. Influenced earlier by Asian mysticism and deep ecology, she now highlights the interplay of nature and culture found in Native American traditions. By "decolonizing the mind," she brings together Indian wisdom and the best of European rationality. Ultimately, traditional knowledge is found in deep self-knowledge within a broad ecocultural context. Drawing both on received teachings and on individual creativity, we can work toward honoring the place where we live.

Growing up in America, most of us are challenged with integrating different parts of our lives, as most of us represent a mix of cultures, backgrounds, traditions, and worldviews. My particular challenge has been to find my authentic voice as a mixed-blood person who has both Native American and European ancestry. I am Métis, or "Michef," as they call us at my home reservation at the Turtle Mountain Chippewa community in North Dakota. I am blessed with inheriting one of the rich, land-based cultural traditions of North America. I have also inherited the blood of my Nordic and French ancestors who, two centuries ago, fled from the injustices of their homelands to seek a better life in a new land. Through the St. Lawrence River, travelers, voyageurs, fur traders entered the Great Lakes region. On the forested shorelines, they found beaver and birch bark and met the Anishinabe dreamers in their woodland homes. Greeting each other in their respective tongues—"bonjour," "boohzhoo"—some of the French and Ojibwe united, coevolved, became Métis.

The reservation my mother was born and raised on is called the Turtle Mountain Band of Chippewa Indians. The word "Chippewa" is a French interpretation of the name my ancestors called themselves, "Ojibwe," which refers to the type of moccasin they wore. The older, original name for my people, "Anishinabe," describes a larger group of Native Americans in the Great Lakes region. This name goes back to the creation stories and is usually interpreted to mean "original or spontaneous being."

Today, I am concerned with learning how to honor all parts of myself: the spiritual traditions of my Ojibwe ancestors as well as the traditional knowledge of my European ancestors. I keep asking, how do I simultaneously honor the past and transcend the past in order to live in the present? I am also looking for that place in myself, independent of my heritage, that is completely new and different each moment, the part that is constantly revealing itself.

Not having grown up on the land my indigenous ancestors called home and being the most recent offspring from a long line of "half-breeds" on my mother's side, I was not raised within my Anishinabe tradition. My mother remembered some of her Anishinabemowin, her native tongue, but even that was mixed with Cree and Canadian French. When she was sent away to Catholic boarding school she was forbidden to speak this strange "Michef" language. My father remembered some Norwegian, but his parents discouraged him from continuing to speak it. Emerging from the fifties, both my parents were swayed by the dominant culture to "become Americans—drop that past nonsense." For my mom, this "choice" was reinforced by the implementation of federal relocation and assimilation policies. After she returned to her reservation and completed high school, she was selected to be a part of the relocation program that sent reservation Indians into major urban centers around the country. My mother was given a one-way train ticket to California and ended up in downtown Oakland, close to where I was later born.

Neither of my parents fully took in the strict Catholic and Lutheran religions they were immersed in as children, nor did they put any pressure on me or my brother to conform to the rigors of those religions. My imagination was free to wander through the many possible explanations and descriptions of the eternal mysteries. Not feeling connected enough to my indigenous heritage to claim an Indian identity and spiritual path, I wandered, like so many other young people, through the books and lectures and ashrams of the many branches of Buddhism, Taoism, Christian mysticism, and the meditations of classic and contemporary nature writers and philosophers such as Robinson Jeffers, Arne Naess, Gary Snyder, Carolyn Merchant, and Theodore Roszak.

The deep ecology perspective offered me some very satisfying ideas about the connection between humans and the natural world. It explicitly emphasized the intrinsic value of nonhuman nature, and the peace found in "wilderness." Part of my interest in deep ecology also stemmed from the fact that it was articulated by an old Norwegian man, Arne Naess, who closely resembled my father and his uncles. Something in the slate blue eyes, those charming eye folds that evolved to protect us from the glaring snow, the high, brooding forehead, and the adamant sense that being "outside" in the open air was so much better than being indoors. I was joyfully surprised to discover such an environmentally sensitive philosophy coming from Norway.

But where was my Native American family in the deep ecology philosophy? Haven't these ideas been a part of traditional cultures for thousands of years? Yes and no. Within the deep ecology movement people often make a distinction between an anthropocentric worldview and a "biocentric" one. This distinction can support a "people versus nature" type of thinking that has very little meaning for indigenous peoples. A friend, native restoration ecologist Dennis Martinez, has said, "We need to move beyond the anthropocentric-biocentric dichotomy and see that we are really kin-centric"; meaning we must recognize the reality of our extended family—the rock people, the plant people, the bird people, the water people—and human beings' humble place in this web of kin.

I learned, too, that even in the deep ecology movement there are those who share the racist and colonial assumptions implicit in a lot of mainstream environmentalism. Many deep ecologists adhere to a myth of pristine wilderness and consider Indians anti-environmental because they want to "use" the "untouched" wildlands. Yet more and more people are finally realizing that the precontact North American landscape was well cared for and highly managed by its original inhabitants. Many conservationists I've talked with still believe the stereotype of the "lazy, dirty Indian," and consequently, do not consider local Native Americans valuable contributors to discussions about how to manage resources. The more I got involved with traditional native ceremonies and indigenous resource management practices, the less interested I became in deep ecology.

To indigenous peoples, the basic tenets of deep ecology are just a reinvention of very ancient principles that they have been living by for millennia before their ways were disrupted, and in many cases destroyed, by colonial forces. To learn who I am today, on this land I live on, I've had to recover that heritage and realize a multicultural self.

In exploring what a multicultural self is, I found myself swimming through a sea of racial beliefs—pure, full-blood Indian, pure, full-blood European; tainted mixed-blood, diluted soul. This internal division parallels other prevalent dichotomies—mind and body, civilized and savage, rational and impulsive, science and folklore. It is difficult not to fall into the "either-or" pattern and to integrate all of these differences. By studying the process others have gone through to embrace the cultural richness of diverse backgrounds, I have come to understand the importance of decolonizing my mind.

Decolonizing the mind is not disregarding rationality or European heritage. It is transcending the self-centered, ethnocentric, and exploitive patterns of Western hegemony. It is explicitly questioning the so-called objectivity and universal character of the Western scientific paradigm. Decolonizing the mind allows other, more diverse and mysterious ways of knowing the world to enter the field of perception. For example, intuition and imagination are part of the creativity necessary to decolonize the mind. To facilitate my own creativity, I write poetry and have started to play the seljeflute, a Norwegian folk instrument. I was fascinated to discover that seljeflutes are often made out of birch bark, the same subarctic tree so sacred to the Ojibwe. Birch trees and their bark have become a living symbol of my heritage.

Another powerful way I have found to decolonize my mind is by simply questioning my certainty about things and asking, where do my thoughts and ideas come from? Because colonization is based on the belief in Manifest Destiny, i.e., the spreading of so-called universal truths, I also began to ask, are there really any universal truths? On the other end of the spectrum is the perspective of cultural relativism, which assumes that any cultural differences, be it genital mutilation or human sacrifice, are justified in the name of culture. How far can cultural relativism be taken? Where do ethics step in? Whose ethics?

Such questions helped me to see that, contrary to the popular opinion of wannabes, there are no special spiritual "goodies" in being part Native American. Traditional knowledge is really a deeper knowledge of the self within a wider ecocultural context. It comes with patience, hard work, and sacrifice. As I have learned from many elders and teachers, if someone is interested in Native American spirituality, they must also learn about the colonial history of North America and be aware of contemporary Indian issues such as treaty rights and land claims, poverty and health problems, and efforts to gain federal recognition and revitalize tribal sovereignty. They must learn to honor the local, the distinctive, in the place where they live.

For example, because I live in central coastal California, which is primarily Ohlone territory, I support and work together with some Ohlone people and other California Indians who are working to protect the diversity and quality of all life in this region: endangered species, languages, habitats, songs, stories, and the free flow of rivers. Managing a native non-profit organization dedicated to these native land protection goals, I have spent many nights and weekends faxing letters to Congress, writing letters of support for tribes and communities, grant writing, compiling and sending out educational and technical information packets, and responding to various requests. This activism has been a part of my commitment to my own native heritage. I am learning to take care of our Mother by honoring the traditional way local native people have lived on and loved their homelands, be it harvesting certain plants and using fire at particular times, or conducting world renewal ceremonies. Giving something back to the earth, through ceremony, is one of the most important parts of Ojibwe and other native spiritual traditions. Ceremony is a unique blend of tradition and innovation. Ultimately, ceremony is creativity, where our own imaginations unfold and become part of the divine creative force of life. Vine Deloria, Jr., has written, "The underlying theme of ceremony is one of gratitude expressed by human beings on behalf of all forms of life, and they complete the largest possible cycle of life, ultimately representing the cosmos in its specific realizations, becoming thankfully aware of itself."

We all have earth-based spiritual traditions in our past and we should work to uncover our heritage. But we also have our own individual creativity, imagination, and distinct relationship with what we call the sacred. Our own heart-minds in this very moment of life can show us how to pray, praise, worship, give thanks and blessings. I have been deeply inspired by the teachings of the east Indian educator and philosopher Jiddu Krishnamurti, who has written, "To sing we must have a song in our heart, but having lost our song, we pursue, instead, the singer." We often sacrifice our own song, our individual connection to the sacred source within, by seeking wisdom outside of ourselves. But we don't need an endorsement from any priest, guru, or medicine person. In fact, these teachers' greatest gift to us is to show us that we have our own unique relationship to life and that no one but ourselves can facilitate that connection to the source of creation.

I am sitting outside with an Ojibwe elder and some other people, mixedbloods like myself—urban Métis and Mestizo, a few Lakota visiting from South Dakota, some non-native Berkeley students, a Sami woman from Norway, a Yurok California Indian man. We are facing what the Bay Miwok call "the mountain where the little animals play." Before entering the lodge, we get oriented, literally and metaphorically. We find our place in the cosmos. First we pray to the four sacred directions. Some tobacco is given to each orientation. We then honor the sky above, the earth below, our Mother. Then the final orientation is acknowledged, within ourselves, the inner origin. In silence, under the valley oaks and sycamore, individually and as a group, we embrace the mystery of which we are a part.

Terry Tempest Williams

A SPRIG OF SAGE

Terry Tempest Williams lives with her husband in the mountains outside Salt Lake City. She is naturalist-in-residence at the Utah Museum of Natural History. Her books include *Refuge: An Unnatural History of Family and Place* and *Pieces of White Shell: A Journey to Navajoland,* for which this essay serves as a prologue. With exquisite subtlety, Williams considers the complexity of being a Mormon and a devout student of Navajo culture. Differences between the cultures are fundamental, yet similarities and a sense of sharing nature are also real. The Navajo, and their culture, are her neighbors. Images of travel dominate: she migrates into Navajoland, with their stories as a guide. As with other contributors to this volume, stories play a critical role in her relation to the land, which speaks through them.

Out of my pouch falls a sprig of sage. I can crush its leaves between my fingers and remember who I am. I belong to the Great Basin. I feel most at home in the sagebrush plains of Utah. But I haven't always been able to say this. I hated sagebrush as a child. On every family vacation, whether we drove to the California coast or to the Tetons in Wyoming, we stared hour after hour out the window at sage. Nothing seemed to move. The color seldom varied. It made me feel very ordinary.

There was another side to sage. Wood ticks loved it and so did rattlesnakes. Parents warned their children and children warned their friends. Since sagebrush covered our foothills like fur, I had encounters with both tick and snake. After a while, you just learned to put them out of your mind. Pretty soon, sagebrush didn't even exist.

Things change. Sometimes you have to disclaim your country and inhabit another before you can return to your own. Now, there is nothing as dear to me as the smell of silver sage after a rainstorm.

Pieces of White Shell is a journey into one culture, Navajo, and back out again to my own, Mormon. I am reminded by a Shoshone friend that I come to the Navajo as a migrating bird, lighting for only brief periods of time. This is true. But it is also true that the lessons I learn come from similar places. No one culture has dominion over birdsong. We all share the same sky.

The path I travel is the path where my ancestors' bones lie: in the four corners of Utah, Colorado, New Mexico, and Arizona. Navajoland stretches thousands of miles across this region, encompassing over sixteen million acres in all. We are neighbors.

We are both relative newcomers to the land. Navajo migration patterns appear from the late 1300s to the 1500s, with Athabaskan ancestors coming into the American Southwest from an original homeland in western Canada and Alaska. My people's genesis is in the early 1800s, with pilgrimages from New York to Nauvoo, to Utah.

As a result of our histories, we both have a strong sense of locale. The Navajo's world emerged with each living thing bearing record of the next: All were relatives, the land their Mother. Brigham Young in 1847 stood on the threshold of the Salt Lake Valley and spoke four words: "This is the place."

There are problems. Navajos find themselves caught between modernization and tradition. So do Mormons. People question us. There are tensions. Self-preservation fosters naivete and shrewdness.

We are a spiritual people, Mormon and Navajo. We believe in a power that moves us, directs us, cares for us. We are taught to listen. The Navajo have their sacred mountains and we have our sacred groves and temples. Family ties are extended and strong. These are not exclusive characteristics. I merely highlight similarities of background.

But there are major differences, primarily in the stories we tell and the way in which we walk upon the earth. It is here that I am most aware of leaving my own culture and entering another. I take off my shoes and walk barefoot. There are risks, I know. My feet have been cut many times, but I am learning to pay attention.

Of the Navajo Way, Gladys Reichard says in *Navaho Religion,* "It must be considered as a design in harmony, a striving for rapport between man and every phase of nature, the earth and the waters under the earth, the sky and the land beyond the sky, and, of course, the earth and everything on and in it."

Navajo stories have been my guides across the desert. I have trusted them because I could find no others. They are rooted in native soil. To these people they are sacred. Truth. To me, they are beacons in a nation suspicious of nature.

A story grows from the inside out and the inside of Navajoland is something I know little of. But I do know myself and if I begin traveling with an awareness of my own ignorance, trusting my instincts, I can look for my own stories embedded in the landscapes I travel through.

A story allows us to envision the possibility of things. It draws on the powers of memory and imagination. It awakens us to our surroundings. I can follow an owl into a cottonwood grove or listen for Kokopeli's flute.* I can sit in the crepuscular hours of a day or imagine a snake uncoiling from a basket. It is here, by our own participation in nature, that we pick up clues to an awareness of what a story is. Story making comes out of our life experiences. And there are many, many layers we can penetrate.

Storytelling is the oldest form of education. It is the power of image making. Among Native Americans the oral tradition of a tribe is its most important vehicle for teaching and passing on sacred knowledge and practices of the people. Luther Standing Bear, a Lakota, recalls:

> Lakota children, like all others, asked questions and were answered to the best ability of our elders. We wondered, as do all young, inquisitive minds, about the stars, moon, sky, rainbows, darkness, and all other phenomena of nature. I can recall lying on the earth and wondering what it was all about. The stars were a beautiful mystery and so was the place where the eagle went when he soared out of sight. Many of these questions were answered in story form by the older people. How we got our pipestone, where corn came from, and why lightning flashed in the sky were all answered in stories.

Maria Chona, a Papago woman, explains how a child learned among her people:

> My father went on talking to me in a very low voice. This is how our people always talk to their children, so low and quiet, the child thinks he is dreaming. But he never forgets.

---

* Kokopeli is a mythic figure of a humpbacked flute player found as petroglyphs in the Southwest. *Ed.*

And then I asked Harold Drake of Navajo Mountain why stories are told.

"I will tell you this: They are for the children generation after generation."

I am not suggesting we emulate Native Peoples—in this case, the Navajo. We can't. We are not Navajo. Besides, their traditional stories don't work for us. It's like drinking another man's medicine. Their stories hold meaning for us only as examples. They can teach us what is possible. We must create and find our own stories, our own myths, with symbols that will bind us to the world as we see it today. In so doing, we will better know how to live our lives in the midst of change.

We have a tradition in our family that centers around the Christmas tree. It began with the birth of the first grandchild.

In 1955, my grandmother placed an angel with gossamer wings on top of a tiny tree. Other angels were hung on lower branches, along with a menagerie of beaded animals and a red bird made of ash. She hung the little bird on an outside limb to give it the appearance of flight. These were the "original" ornaments.

As the family grew, the tree grew. In the next few years, other grandchildren were born—seven boys and a girl. To accompany the angels and animals, my grandmother introduced clowns, elves, harlequins, and varieties of Santa Claus. The tree slowly became animated, so much so that the children would often ask each other if they had ever seen it move.

Each year new ornaments were added—picked for a particular child or event. Crocheted pandas were placed on the tree to symbolize endangered species, an alligator was sent from Florida by a grandchild who was living there, and gold bells hung on the branches to celebrate our grandparents' fiftieth wedding anniversary. Wooden stars, satin moons, sawwhet owls, skiers, a llama from Bolivia, and angels from every country—all held special significance. Other ornaments represented the darker side of life. As my grandmother would explain, there must always be two poles. And so every year we would look for the new "voodoo" as well as the "saint."

The Sunday following Thanksgiving weekend, that magical day, is "the day the tree goes up." As each ornament is taken out of its box and unwrapped it is like seeing an old friend. The women sit on the couches and talk, fixing broken treasures and supplying hooks for objects that need them. The men stretch out on the floor and sleep, occasionally opening their eyes to see how things are progressing while we children hang our personal histories on the tree.

After the last angel is placed, the boys stand back and throw ribbon-birds (blue, pink, and purple; green, orange, and yellow) onto the tree—the reckless, spontaneous finish.

Today the tree is an internal tree as well, our family tree. It continues to grow as we grow. My grandparents are in their seventies now. Last year, I asked my grandmother if she would write the saga of the tree, what story each ornament told. "We could do it together," I said. She smiled and said, "Yes, let's do." But I knew that behind her twinkling eyes she had other thoughts.

In 1982 the tree went up just as it had done for almost thirty years. The candles were lit. The fire was burning and Leontyne Price sang "Ave Maria." As we nestled into our chairs, my grandmother began to tell her story.

"You see, this tree is alive. . . ."

And she went into the layers of memories. I could feel the heat of the fire massaging my back. I marveled at her animation.

While my grandmother spoke of blue-eyed zebras and quail, I thought I heard the fluttering of wings. I didn't pay much attention until I heard them for the second time. I interrupted to ask if anyone else had heard the sound. Everyone just laughed, saying, "You always hear wings." My grandmother went on. "So you see why we think this tree is alive—"

Just then, a small bird flew down from the chimney, through the flames of the fire, and onto a branch of the tree. It was a weaver finch. No one could speak. A living ornament. He stood on the bough as though it were his favorite perch in the forest. He then circled the tree three times, flew over to the corner of the living room, hit the copper chimes, and landed back underneath the tree with all the animals.

By this time, we had acknowledged the bird's presence and were concerned about getting him back outside. Instinctively, I knelt under the tree with cupped hands and coaxed the bird into them. My fingers wrapped around him and I could feel the rapid heartbeat moving his feathers. There were several quick chirps but no singed wings. I forget who opened the door. The next thing I remember is crouching barefoot in the snow with the finch underneath a yew bush. I waited for some time, softly speaking to the little bird. And then he flew. The night was crystalline. As I walked back into the warm house, my grandmother put her arms around me as my grandfather quietly said, "The story's been written."

I offer you a sampling of the Navajo voice, of my voice, and the voice of the land that moves us. We are told a story and then we tell our own. Each of us harbors a homeland. The stories that are rooted there push themselves up like native grasses and crack the sidewalks.

A few years ago, my cousin Lynne Ann moved to Boston. She could hardly wait to leave Utah and plunge into city life. I told her, "One day you will miss these foothills." We laughed. That Christmas I received a card from her. It read: "Please send me some sage—"

Richard K. Nelson

THE GIFTS OF DEER

Richard K. Nelson lives in coastal Alaska with his family. A cultural anthropolo-
gist who has lived with Athapaskan Indian and Inuit communities, he has written
several anthropological studies, including *Make Prayers to the Raven,* which presents an account of Koyukon beliefs and practices. He has been profoundly
influenced by Native American culture, and his recent writings have focused
on deer as a point of connection between humans and nature. The following
selection is the last chapter of *The Island Within,* personal reflections on his relationship with nature and cultures. He hunts deer on an island near his home and,
in doing so, struggles over his cultural location. He has learned much from tribal
people such as the Koyukon Indians and is drawn deeply to their ways, yet he remains a European-American. In examining this personal situation with insight, honesty, and humility, he helps other whites to consider their relation not only to the
land but also to the native peoples who can serve as models for the cultivation of
a sense of place.

Cold, clear, and calm in the pale blue morning. Snow on the high peaks
brightening to amber. The bay a sheet of gray glass beneath a faint haze of
steam. A November sun rises with the same fierce, chill stare of an owl's eye.

I stand at the window watching the slow dawn, and my mind fixes on
the island. Nita comes softly down the stairs as I pack gear and complain
that I've slept too late for these short winter days. A few minutes later,
Ethan trudges out onto the cold kitchen floor, barefoot and half asleep.
We make no direct mention of hunting, to avoid acting proud or giving
offense to the animals. I say only that I'll go to the island and look around;
Ethan says only that he would rather stay at home with Nita. I wish he
would come along so I could teach him things, but know it will be quieter
in the woods with just Shungnak.

They both wave from the window as I ease the skiff away from shore, crunching through cakes of fresh-water ice the tide has carried in from Salmon River. It's a quick run through Windy Channel and out onto the freedom of Haida Strait, where the slopes of Kluksa Mountain bite into a frozen sky. The air stings against my face, but the rest of me is warm inside thick layers of clothes. Shungnak whines, paces, and looks over the gunwale toward the still-distant island.

Broad swells lying in from the Pacific alternately lift the boat and drop it between smooth-walled canyons of water. Midway across the strait a dark line of chop descends swiftly from the north, and within minutes we're surrounded by whitecaps. There are two choices: either beat straight up into them or cut an easier angle across the waves and take the spray. I vacillate for a while, then choose the icy spray over the intense pounding. Koyukon elders often told me it's wrong to curse the wind or complain about the cold, but this morning I do it anyway.

A kittiwake sweeps over the water in great, vaulting arcs, its wings flexed against the surge and billow of the air. As it tilts its head passing over the boat, I think how clumsy we must look. The island's shore lifts slowly in dark walls of rock and timber that loom above the apron of snow-covered beach. Approaching the shelter of Sea Lion Point, the chop fades and the swell diminishes. I turn up along the lee, running between the kelp beds and the surf, straining to see if any deer are grazing on seaweed at the tide's edge.

Near the end of the point is a gut that opens into a tight, shallow anchorage. I ease the boat between the rocks, with lines of surf breaking close on either side. The waves rise and darken, their edges sparkle in the sun, then long manes of spray whirl back as they turn inside out and pitch onto the reef. The anchor slips through ten feet of crystal water to settle among the kelp fronds and urchin-covered rocks. On a strong ebb the boat would go dry here, but today's tide range is only six feet. Before launching the punt, I pull the binoculars from my pack and warm them inside my coat so the lenses won't fog. Then I spend a few minutes scrutinizing the broad, rocky shore and the sprawls of brown grass along the timber's edge. A bunch of rock sandpipers flashes up from the shingle and an otter loops along the windrows of drift logs, but there are no signs of deer.

I can't help feeling a little anxious, because the season is drawing short and our year's supply of meat is not yet in. During the past few weeks, deer have been unusually wary, haunting the underbrush and slipping away at the least disturbance. I've come near a few, but these were young ones I stalked only for the luxury of seeing them from close range. Now that the rutting season has begun, there's a good chance of finding larger deer, and they'll be distracted by the search for mates.

A bald eagle watches from a tall hemlock as we bob ashore in the punt. Finally the bird lurches out, scoops its wings full of dense, cold air, and soars away beyond the line of trees. While I trudge up with the punt, Shungnak prances back and forth hunting for smells. The upper reaches are layered and slabbed with ice; slick cobbles shine like steel; frozen grass crackles underfoot. I lean the punt on a snow-covered log, pick up my rifle and small pack, and slip through the leafless alders into the forest.

My eyes adjust to the darkness, the deep green of boughs, and the somber, shadowy trunks. I feel safe and hidden here. The forest floor is covered with deep moss that should sponge gently underfoot. But today the softness is gone: frozen moss crunches with each step and brittle twigs snap, ringing out in the crisp air like strangers' voices. It takes a while to get used to this harshness in a forest that's usually wet and velvety and silent. I listen to the clicking of gusts in the high branches and think that winter has come upon us like a fist.

At the base of a spruce tree is a familiar white patch—a scatter of deer bones: ribs, legs, vertebrae, two pelvis bones, and two skulls with half-bleached antlers. I put them here last winter, saying they were for the other animals, to make clear they were not being thoughtlessly wasted. The scavengers soon picked them clean, the deer mice have gnawed them, and eventually they'll be absorbed into the forest again. Koyukon elders say it shows respect, returning animal bones to a clean, wild place instead of throwing them away with trash or discarding them in a garbage dump.

The long, quiet, methodical process of the hunt begins. I move deeper into the forest, ever mindful of treading the edge between protracted, eventless watching and the startling intensity of coming upon an animal, the always unexpected meeting of eyes. A deer could show itself at this moment, in an hour, in several hours, or not at all. Most of hunting is like this—an exercise in patient, isometric endurance and keen, hypnotic concentration. I lift my foot, step ahead, ease it down, wait, step again. Shungnak follows closely, as we work our way through a maze of windfallen trees, across the clear disks of frozen ponds, and around patches of snow beneath openings in the forest canopy. I remind myself there is probably a doe or a buck somewhere in this stretch of woods, perhaps close enough to hear a branch snap or a bough scratch against my clothes. Deep snow has forced the deer off Kluksa Mountain and Crescent Peak, so they're sure to be haunting these lowlands.

We climb a high, steep scarp that levels to a wooded terrace. After pausing to catch my breath, I stand atop a log and peer into the semi-open understory of twiggy bushes, probing each space with my eyes. A downy woodpecker's call sparks from a nearby tree. Several minutes pass. Then a huckleberry branch moves, barely shivers, without the slightest noise, not far ahead.

Amid the scramble of brush where I saw nothing a few minutes ago, a dim shape materializes, as if its own motion had created it. A doe steps into an open space, deep brown in her winter coat, soft and striking and lovely, dwarfed among the great trees, lifting her nose, looking right toward me. For perhaps a minute we're motionless in each other's gaze; then her head jerks to the left, her ears shift back and forth, her tail flicks up, and she turns away in the stylized gait deer always use when alarmed.

Quick as a breath, quiet as a whisper, the doe glides off into the forest. Sometimes when I see a deer this way I know it's real at the moment, but afterward it seems like a daydream.

As we move farther into the woods, I hope for another look at her and think a buck might have been following nearby. Any deer is legal game and I could almost certainly have taken her, but I'd rather wait for a larger buck and let the doe bring on next year's young. Shungnak savors the ghost of her scent that hangs in the still air, but she has vanished.

Farther on, the snow deepens to a continuous cover beneath smaller trees, and we cross several sets of deer tracks, including some big prints with long toe drags. I poke my fingers into one track and feel its edges: still soft and fluffy, with no hint of the crustiness that develops in a few hours when snow is disturbed in cold weather. The powder helps to muffle our steps, but it's hard to see very far because the bushes are heavily loaded. The thicket becomes a lattice of white on black, every branch spangled in a thick fur of jeweled flakes. We move through it like eagles cleaving between tumbled columns of cloud. New siftings occasionally drift down when the treetops are touched by the breeze.

I stop for a while, not to watch for deer so much as to catch my balance in this feathery mosaic of snow, with its distracting beauty and dizzying absence of relief. A Koyukon word keeps running through my mind: *duh-nooyh,* "clumps of powdery snow clinging on branches." In the old days, pregnant women drank water melted from this snow, so their children would grow up to be nimble and light-footed. For the same reason, I heard people advise the young boys to drink water melted from surface powder, not from the dense, granular snow, called *tliyh,* which forms underneath during the course of winter. Koyukon elders sometimes told riddles to help teach their children these words, to test their cleverness, and to sharpen their attention to details of the natural world:

> Wait, I see something: We are sitting all puffed up across from each other, in coats of mountain sheep skin.
> Answer: *duhnooyh.*

Slots between the trunks ahead shiver with blue where a muskeg opens. I angle toward it, feeling no need to hurry, picking every footstep carefully, stopping often to stare into the jumbled crannies, listening for any splinter of sound, keeping my senses tight and concentrated. A raven calls from high above the forest, and as I catch a glimpse of it the same old questions run through my mind. It lofts and plays on the wind, then folds up and rolls halfway over, a strong sign of hunting luck. Never mind the issue of knowing; I'll assume the power is here and let myself be moved by it.

I turn to look at Shungnak, taking advantage of her sharper hearing and magical sense of smell. She lifts her nose to the fresh but nebulous scent of deer who must have come through here this morning. I watch her little radar ears, waiting for her to focus in one direction and hold it, hoping to see her body tense as it does when something moves nearby. But she only hears the twitching of red squirrels on dry bark. Shungnak and I have a very different opinion of the squirrels. They excite her more than any other animal because she believes she'll catch one someday. But for a hunter, they make distracting spurts of movement and sound, and their sputtering alarm calls alert the deer.

We approach a low, abrupt rise, covered with obscuring brush and curtained with snow. A lift of wind hisses in the high trees, then drops away and leaves us in near-complete silence. I pause to choose a path through a scramble of blueberry bushes and little windfalls ahead, then glance back at Shungnak. She has her eyes and ears fixed toward our left, directly across the current of breeze. She stands very stiff, quivering slightly, leaning forward as if she has already started to run but cannot release her muscles. I shake my finger and look sternly into her eyes as a warning to stay.

I listen as closely as possible, but hear nothing. I work my eyes into every dark crevice and slot among the snowy branches, but see nothing. I stand perfectly still and wait, then look again at Shungnak. Her head turns so slowly I can barely detect the movement, until finally she's looking straight ahead. Perhaps it's just another squirrel. I consider taking a few steps for a better view.

Then I see it.

A long, dark body appears among the bushes, moving up into the wind, so close I can scarcely believe I didn't see it earlier. Without looking away, I gently slide the breech closed and raise the rifle to my shoulder, almost certain that a deer this size will be a buck. Shungnak, now forgotten behind me, must be contorted with the suppressed urge to give chase.

The deer walks silently, determinedly along the little rise, never looking our way. Then he turns straight toward us. Thick tines of his antlers curve over the place where I have the rifle aimed. I remember the Koyukon elders saying that animals come to those who have shown them respect, allowing themselves to be taken, in what is both a physical and spiritual passage. At a moment like this, it's easy to sense that despite my abiding doubt there is an invisible world beyond this one, a world filled with power and awareness, a world that demands recognition and exacts a price from those who ignore it.

It is a very large buck. He comes so quickly that I have no chance to shoot, and then he is so close I haven't the heart to do it. Fifty feet away, the deer lowers his head almost to the ground and lifts a slender branch that blocks his path. Snow shakes onto his neck and clings to the fur of his shoulders as he slips underneath. Then he half lifts his head and keeps coming. I ease the rifle down to watch, wondering how much closer he'll get. Just now he makes a long, soft rutting call, like the bleating of a sheep, except lower pitched and more hollow. His hooves tick against dry twigs hidden by the snow. I can almost feel the breeze blowing against his fur, the chill winnowing down through close-set hairs and touching his skin.

In the middle of a step he raises his head all the way up, and he sees me standing there—a stain against the pure white of the forest, a deadly interloper, the one utterly incongruous thing he has met here in all his life. He reaches his muzzle forward and draws in the affliction of our smell. A sudden spasm stuns him, so sharp and intense it's as if his fright spills out into the forest and tingles inside me like electricity. His front legs jerk apart and he freezes all askew, head high, nostrils flared, coiled and hard. I stare at him and wait, my mind snarled with irreconcilable emotions. Here is a perfect buck deer. In the Koyukon way, he has come to me; but in my own he has come too close. I am as congealed and transfixed as he is, as devoid of conscious thought. It's as if my mind has ceased to function and only my senses remain.

But the buck has no choice. He instantly unwinds in a burst of ignited energy, springs straight up from the snow, turns in midflight, stabs the frozen earth again, and makes four great bounds off to the left. His thick body seems to float, relieved of its own weight, as if a deer has the power to unbind itself from gravity.

The same deeper impulse that governs the flight of a deer governs the predator's impulse to pursue it. I watch the first leaps without moving a muscle. Then, not pausing for an instant of deliberation, I raise the rifle back to my shoulder, follow the movement of the deer's fleeing form, and wait until he stops to stare back. Almost at that moment, still moving without conscious thought, freed of the ambiguities that held me before, now no less animal than the animal I watch, my hands warm and steady and certain, acting from a more elemental sense than the ones that brought me to this meeting, I carefully align the sights and let go the sudden power.

The gift of the deer falls like a feather in the snow. And the rifle's sound has rolled off through the timber before I hear it.

I walk to the deer, now shaking a bit as accumulated emotions pour through me. Shungnak is already next to it, whining and smelling, racing from one side to the other, stuffing her nose down in snow full of scent. She looks off into the brush, searching back and forth, as if the deer that ran is somewhere else, still running. She tries to lick at the blood that trickles down, but I stop her out of respect for the animal. Then, I suppose to consummate her own frustrated predatory energy, she takes a hard nip at its shoulder, shuns quickly away, and looks back as if she expects it to leap to its feet again.

I whisper thanks to the animal, hoping I might be worthy of it, worthy of carrying on the life it has given, worthy of sharing in the larger life of which the deer and I are a part. Incompatible emotions clash inside me—elation and remorse, excitement and sorrow, gratitude and shame. It's always this way: the sudden encounter with death, the shock that overrides the cushioning of the intellect. I force away the sadness and remember that death is the spark that keeps life itself aflame: these deer we eat from, and the fish, and the plants that die to feed us.

It takes a few minutes before I settle down enough to begin the other work. Then, I tie a length of rope onto the forelegs, run it over a low branch, back down through a loop in the rope, and up over the branch again like a double pulley, so I can raise the animal above the ground. This done, I cut the dark, pungent scent glands from its hind legs, to prevent their secretions from tainting the meat. Next, I make a small incision through the belly skin, insert my hand to shield the knife blade from the distended stomach, and slice upward to make an opening about a foot long. Reaching inside, I loosen the stomach and intestines, then work them out through the incision, pulling carefully to avoid tearing the thin membranes and spilling stomach contents into the body cavity. The deer's inward parts feel very hot, slippery, and wet, as I suppose my own would if I could ever touch them. Finally the viscera slide out onto the ground: soft, bladder-like stomach and flaccid ribbons of intestine; a gray, shining mound, webbed with networks of veins and lacy fat, steaming into the cold, saturating the air with a rich odor of plant mulch and body fluids.

Next, I roll up my jacket sleeve and thrust my arm deep inside the deer, until I feel the diaphragm, a sheet of muscle that separates the abdomen from the chest. When I slice through it, a thick, hot rush of blood flows down my arm and sloshes into the vacant belly. There is a hollow, tearing sound as I pull the lungs free; and reaching up inside the chest, I can feel the firm, softball-sized muscle of the heart. The lungs are marbled creamy-pink and feel like soft, airy sponge. As I lay them beside the other organs, I whisper that these parts are left here as food for the animals. Shungnak wants to take some for herself but I make her stay away. Koyukon elders say the sensitivity and awareness leave an animal's remains slowly, and there are rules about what should be eaten by a dog. Shungnak will have her share of the scraps later on, when more of the life is gone.

The inside of the deer is now empty, except for the heart and the dark-purple liver, which I've left attached. I tie a short piece of cord around the end of the lower intestine to keep the remaining blood from flowing out when I carry the animal on my back. Then I poke a series of holes in the hide along either side of the belly incision and lace it shut with another cord. After lowering the deer onto the ground, I cut through the "knee" joints of the forelegs, leaving them attached by a stout tendon, then slice a hole in the hock—a space between the bone and tendon of the hind leg—and I toggle the forelegs through these openings. This way I can put my arms through the joined legs and carry the deer like a pack—not a trick to be used if there is the slightest chance another hunter might be around and mistake my burden for a live animal.

I barely have enough strength to lift the buck and trudge along, but there is plenty of time to work back toward the beach, stopping occasionally to rest and cool down. During one of these breaks, I hear two ravens in an agitated exchange of croaks and gurgles, and I wonder if those black eyes have already spotted the remnants. No pure philanthropist, if Raven gave this luck to me, it was only to create luck for himself. I remember how difficult it was, at first, to accept the idea of a sanctified creature having such a contradictory personality. The Raven described by elders like Grandpa William was both good and evil, sage and fool, benefactor and thief—embodiment of the human paradox. When Joe Stevens described an American president of dubious character, he said, "Just like Raven."

Half an hour later, sweating and exhausted, I push through the low boughs of the beachside trees, lay the animal down, and find a comfortable seat on the driftwood. Afternoon sun throbs off the water, but the north wind takes every hint of warmth out of it. Little gusts splay dark patterns across the anchorage; the boat paces on its mooring line; the strait races with whitecaps. I take a good rest, watching a fox sparrow flit among the alders and a bunch of crows hassle over some bit of food near the water's edge. At this low tide, Sea Lion Point has expanded to a flat sill of rock reaching out several hundred yards from the island's shore. The point has such scant relief that higher tides reduce it to a fraction of this size. The anchorage is nothing more than a gouge in the rocks, closely rimmed with breakers and jagged boulders, so it's only accessible to small skiffs whose pilots are either reckless or foolish. Despite its barren appearance, Sea Lion Point has extensive tide flats, ponds, and beds of estuarine grass that attract congregations of birds, especially during the spring and fall migrations.

Today, hundreds of gulls have gathered on the outer reaches of the point, all sitting with their beaks into the wind. They appear sluggish and languid, as if their sole purpose is to huddle together against the chill. But they're also keeping watch. When the breeze slacks to a momentary calm, a black foil sweeps out from the forest's edge. The eagle leans sharply down, half folds its wings, banks toward the gulls, and builds speed, falling and blurred and sinister. Gulls and crows swirl up like a handful of salt and pepper thrown into the wind. Clusters of ducks spray off the water in opposite directions. Shorebirds dazzle over the tangled skeins of kelp. A close formation of oystercatchers babbles across the anchorage in front of us.

The eagle shears through the scattering swarm, looking ponderous and clumsy, oddly outclassed by its darting prey. Carried into a steep climb by its momentum, the eagle swings around and drops again, legs dangling, unsheathed talons gaping in the frosted air. But the birds have whirled away, leaving an empty void like the eye of a storm. Its voice mingles with the cries and wails of the gulls, a shrill complaint amid easy laughter. Finally the eagle flaps off to a high perch. Swaying back and forth, jerking and flexing its wings for balance, it watches the crows dwindle away over the rocks, the gulls float down onto the flats again. All of the birds seem calm and unhurried, as if nothing of significance has happened, as if the whole thing has been only a game. The hoary quiet of winter returns, and the wait begins once more.

Though I feel satisfied, grateful, and contented sitting here, much remains to be done, and at this time of year the daylight ebbs quickly. Hunters are allowed more than one deer, so I'll stay on the island and take another look around tomorrow. As we idle from the anchorage, we pass within a few yards of lovely surf peeling across a smooth, triangular reef. If I had a surfboard and wetsuit it would be impossible to resist, no matter how frigid the air and water might be. I stop to watch a few waves pour over the shoals like liquid silver; then I follow the shore toward Bear Creek. By the time I've anchored and unloaded the boat, the wind has diminished and a growing winter chill sinks down in the pitched, hard shadow of Kluksa Mountain.

Bear Creek cabin is situated in a thicket well back from shore, hidden in summer but easily seen once the leaves have fallen. I split some half-dry wood, which hisses and sputters in the rusty stove, then reluctantly gives way to flames. After the fire starts crackling, I walk down to the creek. Dipping a bucket into a clear pool, I notice a few salmon bones scattered among the rocks and pebbles. I'm surprised to see them, but also surprised that so little would remain from the hordes of fish I watched here this fall. I had a similar feeling recently, when I went looking for the sperm whale carcass that beached last summer near Tsandaku Point. At first it seemed the storm swells had washed it away, but then I found a bare vertebra and a rib among the rocks. Eventually, I came across the skull—about ten feet long and weighing hundreds of pounds—half buried in the driftwood. Six months after the whale came ashore, scavengers and decay had taken every bit of flesh, gnawed or carried off the smaller bones, and left only a few fragments to wash in the surge.

After fetching water, I carry the deer inside the cabin and hang it from a low beam. Better to work on it now than wait, in case tomorrow brings more luck. The animal is dimly lit by a kerosene lantern and a blush of daylight through the windows. I feel strange in its presence, as if it still watches, still glows with something of its life, still demands that nothing be done carelessly and no offensive words be spoken in its presence. Grandpa William told me that a hunter should never let himself be deluded by pride or a false sense of dominance. It's not through his own power that a person takes life in nature, but through the power of nature that life is given to him.

After sharpening the knife, I slit the deer's skin along the whole length of its underside and down each leg to the hoof. Then I peel the soft hide away, using the blade to separate it from the muscles underneath, gradually revealing the inner perfection of the deer's body. When the skinning is finished, I follow an orderly sequence, cutting through crisp cartilage, severing the leg joints, brisket, ribs, vertebrae, and pelvis, following the body's own design to disarticulate bone from bone. Everything comes apart smoothly and easily, as deer becomes meat, animal becomes food, the most vital and fundamental transformation in all of living existence. There is no ugliness in it, only hands moving in concert with the beauty of an animal's shape. While I work with the deer, it's as if something has already begun to flow into me. I couldn't have understood this when I was younger and had yet to experience the process of one life being passed on to another.

Before I lived with the Eskimo people, I had never hunted and had never seen how game is prepared. But I was immediately fascinated by their skill at taking an animal into its component parts. The Eskimos always watched me closely and found my mistakes entertaining. If I did something uncharacteristically well, someone was likely to look bemused and declare: "Accident." They were passionate hunters and incredibly hard workers. When they hunted walrus, it took only a short while to stalk the animals but many hours to butcher them. As we pulled the skin-covered boat onto the ice, someone was sure to say, "Well, the excitement's over. Now it's time for the real work." But somehow, it never seemed like work to me, this deeply engaged process of learning about animals from the inside and out, of binding my own existence more closely to the lives that sustained me.

By the time I went to live with Koyukon people, I could skin and butcher animals; but I knew little about the delicate matter of keeping a right mind while working with them. Sarah and Joe Stevens were especially scrupulous about treating each animal as a sentient being and butchering it according to the traditional pattern, which was not only a technique but also a ritual of respect. They made certain that no usable part was wasted or tossed carelessly aside, that the meat was covered to keep dogs and scavengers away, and that it was well cached so nothing would spoil. Once, I met Sarah carrying a platter of meat to her neighbor's house, with a piece of cloth over it. She explained, "It wouldn't be right to leave this open to the air, like it doesn't mean anything." In this and other ways, she treated meat as a sacred substance, a medium of interchange between herself and the empowered world in which she lived. It seemed that everything she did in relationship to nature was both an activity and a prayer.

When I've finished with the deer, I put two slices from the hindquarter in a pan atop the stove. Scraps of meat and fat boil in a separate pot for Shungnak. She whines impatiently, perhaps remembering her sled dog days, when she lived mostly on meat and fish and bones. As soon as she's been fed, I sit on a sawed log and eat venison straight from the pan. No meal could be simpler, more satisfying, or more directly a part of the living process. I also savor a deep feeling of security in having this meat, bringing it home to freeze or can for the year ahead—pure food, taken from a clean, wild place, and prepared by our own efforts. There is a special intimacy in living directly from nature, nourishing my body from the same wildness that so elevates my spirit.

I wish Ethan were here to share this meal, so I could explain to him again that when we eat the deer, its flesh becomes our flesh. Each time we eat we should remember the deer and feel gratitude for what it has given us. And each time, we should carry a thought like a prayer inside: "Thanks to the animal and to all that made it—the island and the forest, the air, and the rain . . ." I would tell Ethan that in the course of things, he and Nita and I are all generations of deer and of the life that feeds us. Like the deer, we also come from the island, and from the earth that sustains us and gives us breath.

Later, perched atop rocks near the mouth of Bear Creek, Shungnak and I look out over Haida Strait to the sea beyond. A distant winter sun sprawls against the horizon, thins to a mound of shivering flame, and drowns itself in the cold Pacific. The sky fades to violet, darkens, and relaxes, like a face losing expression at the edge of sleep. Silence hovers in the brittle woods.

A great blue heron glides down into the anchorage cove and stands motionless in the shallows, like the shadow of a pterodactyl against the Mesozoic sky. Every few minutes I notice the bird's stance and position have changed, but invisibly, like a clock's hands, so that I never actually see its legs move. Then I notice its head slowly lowering, its body tilting, its neck stretching forward. Suddenly it flashes out and draws back, and a fish wriggles on the dripping spear of its beak. The recoiling heron stands erect, flips the fish lengthwise, gulps it, and resumes hunting. Over the next few minutes, the bulge of the fish gradually moves down its serpentine neck.

I've watched herons many times before, admiring them as elegantly plumed, primeval works of art. But I never thought about their impeccable skill and patience as hunters. This event gives me a better sense of the way they live—the measured and timeless stalks, the penetrating eyes fixed at the water's edge, the shadows of prey moving below, the saber beak striking down, the sudden consummation of predatory impulse. Given a choice of birds, I would be a heron, or an owl, a falcon, an eagle. I love these quick, canny animals, perhaps because they seem closest to my own kind. To feel otherwise about predators would be like shrinking from the face in the mirror.

Dusk settles on the waters of Haida Strait, swallows the far peaks and inlets, drifts down through the surrounding forest, takes the island inside itself, and joins it with the sky. Sitting in the darkness, I feel overcome with gratitude and wish for a way to express it. Words seem frail and empty; offerings seem foreign and artificial. Perhaps just being here is enough, becoming wholly engaged with this place, touching it, eating from it, winding my life as tightly as possible into it. The island and I, turning ourselves ever more inside out.

Warm in my sleeping bag, I let the fire ebb to coals. The lamp is out. The cabin roof creaks in the growing chill. I drift toward sleep, pleased that there is no moon, so the deer will wait until dawn to feed. On the floor beside me, Shungnak jerks and whimpers in her dog's dreams.

Dawn. The cold fire of winter sun climbs a pallid wall of sky. Mountains stand out as sharp and clear as the sound of shattering glass. Clouds of steam rise above the open riffles of Bear Creek. The silver calm of Haida Strait is splotched with dark blue where an uncertain breeze touches down against it. Three goldeneye ducks drift in the anchorage, like smudges on a sheet of polished iron.

The temperature is twenty degrees, perhaps much colder back away from shore. Although it rarely drops to zero along this coast, sea humidity and gusty winds often intensify the chill. But even so, our winter is a far cry from that of Koyukon country, where temperatures average below zero for five months of the year and may hover at forty to sixty below for weeks. Not surprisingly, Koyukon elders treat cold weather as a conscious thing, with a potent and irritable spirit. They warn the younger ones to speak carefully about cold, lest they incite its frigid wrath. In the old days, children were even told not to throw snowballs, because the frivolity or annoyance could bring on bitter weather.

When Shungnak was born it was so cold that one of her littermates froze stiff. Thawed out behind the wood stove, he survived, although his tail eventually fell off. Perhaps because she grew up in that climate, and because the frozen landscape meant freedom and adventure for a sled dog, Shungnak still loves winter weather. As we walk back to the cabin, she prances around me, full of excited energy, anxious to get started with the day.

An hour later, I anchor the boat at Sea Lion Point. After paddling the punt ashore, I follow Shungnak to where our tracks from yesterday enter the woods. Just beyond the place of the buck, a pair of does drifts at the edge of sight and disappears. For an hour we angle north, then come slowly back deeper into the woods, moving crosswise to a growing easterly breeze. In two places, deer snort and pound away, invisible beyond a shroud of brush. Otherwise there is nothing.

We keep on in the same direction, probing first through snowy thickets, then through heavy forest with bare, frozen moss underneath. In a dense maze of young spruce, I come face to face with a red squirrel, clinging to the trunk of a dead tree. Luckily, Shungnak has lagged a few yards behind. And instead of scurrying to a high branch, the squirrel stays put, bold, curious and confident, apparently unconcerned about my intentions. I inch ahead, wait, then move again, until he's so close I could ruffle his fur if I blew hard enough.

The squirrel twitches this way and that on his skinny white tree, first head up, then head down, leaning out as if to get a closer look at me. He sticks effortlessly to the smooth wood, or actually hangs from it by the tips of his curved claws. Never satisfied to simply observe, I wonder how his claws can possibly be so sharp, and what keeps them from getting dull? The squirrel spends a long minute checking me out, constantly in motion, scratching up the tree and back down again, jerking from one angle to another, stitching his little feet, shaking his frizzy tail, shivering his long black whiskers. Then he jumps to a spruce just as close but with a slightly different angle. I can see the crenulations of his nose, the fine hairs on his snout, the quick pumping of his ribs, and my face reflecting on his bright indigo eye. When he's seen enough, he turns and jitters to a place above my head. I can tell he's ready to burst into a chatter, as squirrels often do after some deliberation, so I edge past and leave him alone.

A short while later we follow a familiar stretch of trail through a copse of shore pines and cedars. I kneel down to examine a bunch of deer bones in the snowless patch under a tree. Darkened by age and half covered with moss, they're hardly visible any more. I first came across them several years ago, when they still had a blanched white color, with bits of clinging skin, cartilage, and tufts of fur. It looked as if the deer had died only a few months before, and because the nearby tree trunk was heavily clawed, I guessed a bear had either killed the animal or scavenged its carcass. I always looked at the bones when I passed by, but never touched them because I wanted to see how long it took an animal's remains to vanish from the forest floor. Each year, a few more bones were missing or were cloaked over by the moss.

Last summer, I walked through here with a friend and showed him the bones. He touched several of them and pulled one out from the moss. Both of us were stunned by what he found: a hind-leg bone that had been fractured in several places while the deer was alive. It was so badly shattered that a piece the thickness of my index finger had stuck out almost two inches from the wound, as indicated by a line where healing flesh had closed around it. The deer must have lived a long time after its terrible injury. Long enough so the fragments knitted themselves together, as if liquid bone had seeped into the wound and solidified as a porous, bulging, convoluted mass. Though gnarled and misshapen, the fused bone seemed almost as strong as a healthy one. But the deer's leg was considerably shortened and had a hollow ivory splinter piercing out from it. As we turned the bone in our hands, I marveled at the determination of living things, and of life itself, to carry on, to mend, and to become whole again after being torn apart.

What could have caused such a wound? It might have been a bad fall, an unskilled hunter's bullet, or a bear. Hardest of all to imagine was the agony this deer went through, the days and weeks of unrelievable pain, endured in solitude, through nights of rain and storm, burdened by the omnipresent danger of being discovered by a bear. Of course, it might have been another bear that eventually killed the animal. After my friend and I left the bones, the forest seemed less beautiful for a while, less a place of shelter than of violence and tragedy. At that same moment, some other animal was probably suffering toward death not far away—perhaps severed by an eagle's beak or broken by a bear, perhaps old and weakened, perhaps riven with disease—biting the moss in torment and fear. I thought, there is little mercy in nature, little to relieve the pain or loneliness of death. Many of the tragedies found in the human world are also found here. Then I realized that loving nature meant loving it all, accepting nature exactly as it is, not idealizing it or ignoring the hard truths, not reducing it to an imaginary world of peace and perfection. How could I crave the beauty of the flame without accepting the heat that made it?

Shortly after noon we come into a narrow muskeg with scattered shore pines and a ragged edge of brushy, low-growing cedar. I squint against the sharp glare of snow. It has that peculiar look of old powder, a bit settled and touched by wind, very lovely but without the airy magic of a fresh fall. I gaze up the muskeg's easy slope. Above the encroaching wall of timber, seamed against the deep blue sky, is the peak of Kluksa Mountain, with a great plume of snow streaming off in what must be a shuddering gale. It has a contradictory look of absoluteness and unreality about it, like a Himalayan summit suspended in midair over the saddle of a low ridge.

I move slowly up the muskeg's east side, away from the breeze and in the sun's full warmth. Deer tracks crisscross the opening, but none of the animals stopped here to feed. Next to the bordering trees, the tracks join as a single, hard-packed trail, showing the deer's preference for cover. Shungnak keeps her nose to the thickly scented snow. We come across a pine sapling that a buck has assaulted with his antlers, scattering twigs and flakes of bark all around. But his tracks are hardened, frosted, and lack sharpness, indicating they're at least a day old.

We slip through a point of trees, then follow the edge again, pausing long moments between footsteps. A mixed tinkle of crossbills and siskins moves through the high timber, and a squirrel rattles from deep in the woods, too far off to be scolding us. Shungnak picks up a strong ribbon of scent, but she hears nothing. I stop for a few minutes to study the muskeg's raveled fringe, the tangle of shade and thicket, the glaze of mantled boughs.

Then my eye barely catches a fleck of movement up ahead, near the ground and almost hidden behind the trunk of a leaning pine—perhaps a squirrel's tail or a bird. I slowly lift my hand to shade the sun, stand dead still, and wait to see if something is there. Finally it moves again.

At the very edge of the trees, almost out of sight in a little swale, small and furry and bright-tinged, turning one direction and then another, is the funnel of a single ear. Having seen this, I soon make out the other ear and the slope of a doe's forehead. Her neck is behind the leaning pine, but on the other side I can barely see the soft, dark curve of her back above the snow. She is comfortably bedded, gazing placidly into the distance, chewing her cud.

Shungnak has stopped twenty yards behind me in the point of trees and has no idea about the deer. I shake my finger at her until she lays her ears back and sits. Then I watch the doe again. She is fifty yards ahead, ten yards beyond the leaning tree, and still looking off at an angle. Her left eye is visible and she refuses to turn her head away, so it might be impossible to get closer. Perhaps I should just wait here, in case a buck is attending her nearby. But however improbable it might be under these circumstances, a thought is lodged in my mind: I can get near her.

My first step sinks down softly, but the second makes a loud budging sound, like stepping on a piece of toast. She snaps my way, stops chewing, and stares for several minutes. It seems hopeless, especially out here in an open field of crispy snow with only the narrow tree trunk for a screen. But she turns away and starts to chew again. I move just enough so the tree blocks her eye and the rest of her head, but I can still see her ears. Every time she chews they shake just a bit, so I watch them and step when her hearing is obscured by the sound of her own jaws.

Either this works or the deer has decided to ignore me, because after a while I've come close enough so the noise of my feet has to reach her easily. She should have jumped up and run long ago, but instead she lies there in serene repose. I deliberate on every step, try for the softest snow, wait long minutes before the next move, stalking like a cat toward ambush. I watch beyond her, into the surrounding shadows and across to the muskeg's farther edge, for the shape of a buck deer; but there is nothing. I feel ponderous, clumsy-footed, out of place, inimical. I should turn and run away, take fear on the deer's behalf, flee the mirrored image in my mind. But I clutch the cold rifle at my side and creep closer.

The wind refuses to blow and my footsteps seem like thunder in the still sunshine. But the doe only turns once to look my way, without even pointing her ears toward me, then stares off and begins to chew again.

I am ten feet from the leaning tree. My heart pounds so hard I think those enchanted ears should hear the blood rushing in my temples. Yet a strange assurance has come into me, a quite unmystical confidence. Perhaps she has decided I am another deer, a buck attracted by her musk or a doe feeding gradually toward her. My slow pace and lapses of stillness would not seem human. For myself, I have lost awareness of time; I have no feeling of patience or impatience. It's as if the deer has moved slowly toward me on a cloud of snow, and I am adrift in the pure motion of experience.

I take the last step to the trunk of the leaning pine. It's bare of branches, scarcely wider than my outstretched hand, but perfectly placed to break my odd profile. There is no hope of getting any closer, so I slowly poke my head out to watch. She has an ideal spot: screened from the wind, warmed by the sun, and with a clear view of the muskeg. I can see muscles working beneath the close fur of her jaw, the rise and fall of her side each time she breathes, the shining edge of her ebony eye.

I hold absolutely still, but her body begins to stiffen, she lifts her head higher, and her ears twitch anxiously. Then instead of looking at me she turns her face to the woods, shifting her ears toward a sound I cannot hear.

A few seconds later, the unmistakable voice of a buck drifts up, strangely disembodied, as if it comes from somewhere underneath the snow. I huddle as close to the tree as I can, press against the hard dry bark, and peek around its edge.

There is a gentle rise behind the doe, scattered with sapling pines and bushy juniper. A rhythmic crunching of snow comes invisibly from the slope, then a bough shakes . . . and a buck walks easily into the open sunshine.

Focusing completely on the doe, he comes straight to her and never sees my intrusive shape just beyond. He slips through a patch of small trees, stops a few feet from where she lies, lowers his head and stretches it toward her, then holds this odd pose for a long moment. She reaches her muzzle to one side, trying to find his scent. When he moves up behind her she stands quickly, bends her body into a strange sideways arc, and stares back at him. A moment later she walks off a bit, lifts her tail, and puts droppings in her tracks. The buck moves to the warm ground of her bed and lowers his nose to the place where her female scent is strongest.

Inching like a reptile on a cold rock, I have stepped out from the tree and let my whole menacing profile become visible. The deer are thirty feet away and stand well apart, so they can both see me easily. I am a hunter hovering near his prey and a watcher craving inhuman love, torn between the deepest impulses, hot and shallow-breathed and seething with unreconciled intent, hidden from opened eyes that look into the nimbus of sun and see nothing but the shadow they have chosen for themselves. In this shadow now, the hunter has vanished and only the watcher remains.

Drawn by the honey of the doe's scent, the buck steps quickly toward her. And now the most extraordinary thing happens. The doe turns away from him and walks straight for me. There is no hesitation, only a wild deer coming along the trail of hardened snow where the other deer have passed, the trail in which I stand at this moment. She raises her head, looks at me, and steps without pausing.

My existence is reduced to a pair of eyes; a rush of unbearable heat flushes through my cheeks; and a sense of absolute certainty fuses in my mind.

The snow blazes so brightly that my head aches. The deer is a dark form growing larger. I look up at the buck, half embarrassed, as if to apologize that she's chosen me over him. He stares at her for a moment, turns to follow, then stops and watches anxiously. I am struck by how gently her hooves touch the trail, how little sound they make as she steps, how thick the fur is on her flank and shoulder, how unfathomable her eyes look. I am consumed with a sense of her perfect elegance in the brilliant light. And then I am lost again in the whirling intensity of experience.

The doe is now ten feet from me. She never pauses or looks away. Her feet punch down mechanically into the snow, coming closer and closer, until they are less than a yard from my own. Then she stops, stretches her neck calmly toward me, and lifts her nose.

There is not the slightest question in my mind, as if this was sure to happen and I have known all along exactly what to do. I slowly raise my hand and reach out.

And my fingers touch the soft, dry, gently needling fur on top of the deer's head, and press down to the living warmth of flesh underneath.

She makes no move and shows no fear, but I can feel the flaming strength and tension that flow in her wild body as in no other animal I have touched. Time expands and I am suspended in the clear reality of the moment.

Then, by the flawed conditioning of a lifetime among fearless domesticated things, I instinctively drop my hand and let the deer smell it. Her black nose, wet and shining, touches gently against my skin at the exact instant I realize the absoluteness of my error. And a tremor runs through her entire body as she realizes hers. Her muscles seize and harden; she seems to wrench her eyes away from me but her body remains, rigid and paralyzed. Having been deceived by her other senses, she keeps her nose tight against my hand for one more moment.

Then all the energy inside her triggers in a series of exquisite bounds. She flings out over the hummocks of snow-covered moss, suspended in effortless flight like fog blown over the muskeg in a gale. Her body leaps with such power that the muscles should twang aloud like a bowstring; the earth should shudder and drum; but I hear no sound. In the center of the muskeg she stops to look back, as if to confirm what must seem impossible. The buck follows in more earthbound undulations; they dance away together; and I am left in the meeting place alone.

There is a blur of rushing feet behind me. No longer able to restrain herself, Shungnak dashes past, buries her nose in the soft tracks, and then looks back to ask if we can run after them. I had completely forgotten her, sitting near enough to watch the whole encounter, somehow resisting what must have been a prodigious urge to explode in chase. When I reach out to hug her, she smells the hand that touched the deer. And it seems as if it happened long ago.

I walk slowly from the spot, letting the whole event roll through my mind again and again, remembering the dream that began many months ago, that I might someday touch a deer. After trying and failing with the naive little fawn earlier this fall, I'd begun to think the idea was farfetched, perhaps even foolish. But now, totally unexpected and in a strange way, it has happened. Was the deer caught by some reckless twinge of curiosity? Had she never encountered a human on this wild island? Did she yield to some odd amorous confusion? Then I realize I truly do not care. I would rather accept this as pure experience and not give in to a notion that everything should be explained.

Koyukon elders simply accept what comes to them. They teach that everything in the natural world has its own spirit and awareness, and they give themselves to that other world, without expecting voices, without waiting for visions, without seeking admission to the hidden realms.

I am reminded of something that happened the last time I hunted with Grandpa William. While we sat talking at the edge of a meadow, an unusual bird started singing and chattering in a nearby treetop. At first it looked like a small hawk, but there was something different about its color and shape. When I asked what it was, he listened closely to its calls, then took my binoculars and watched it for a long while, intrigued and perplexed. "I don't know," he muttered, mostly to himself; then he suggested a difficult Koyukon name I'd never heard before. Shortly, his interest darkened to concern: was the arrival of this strange bird a sign, an omen?

Suddenly he began addressing the bird at length in the Koyukon language, speaking in a soft, gentle voice. "Who are you," he wondered, "and what are you saying to us?" He walked out into the meadow, still talking, still trying to establish that the loquacious bird was something ordinary, not an ominous stranger. "Wish us good luck, whoever you are," he said. "Wish us well, and surround us—your grandchildren—within a circle of protection." By this time I'd lost interest in identifying the bird, and my whole attention was focused on Grandpa William: a man imploring mercy and protection from a bird, addressing a feathered emissary in a treetop.

Those moments epitomized everything I had learned from Koyukon people, everything they had tried to tell me about living in a natural world filled with spirit and power. I've had few experiences that so moved me.

For how many thousand generations, I wondered, have people spoken and prayed to the natural beings around them, as a customary part of daily life? At any other time in human history, this event would be as ordinary as talking to another person. To me, Grandpa William represented the universal man beseeching the powers that pervade his living world, powers so recently forgotten among my own people. More than anything else, I wished it had seemed quite unremarkable for me, wished my ancestors hadn't forsaken what Grandpa William still understood.

Neither Grandpa William nor I ever knew what that bird was, though I later concluded it must be a young northern shrike. And if the bird did carry an omen, who was it for?

I stop in the shadows along the muskeg's upper edge, and think back over the years with Koyukon people. What stands out for me at this moment is a special wisdom of their tradition—to expect nothing of nature, but to humbly receive its mystery, beauty, food, and life. In return, Koyukon people show the same respect toward nature that is shown toward humans, acknowledging that spirit and sacredness pervade all things. If I understand correctly, their behavior toward nature is ordered around a few simple principles: Move slowly, stay quiet, watch carefully, be ever humble, show no hint of arrogance or disrespect. And if they follow one overarching commandment, it is to approach all life, of which humans are a part, with humility and restraint. All things are among the chosen.

As I reflect on the experiences of yesterday and today, I find an important lesson in them, viewed in the light of wisdom taken from the earth and shaped by generations of elders. Two deer came and gave the choices to me. One deer I took and we will now share a single body. The other deer I touched and we will now share that moment. These events could be seen as opposites, but perhaps they are identical. Both are founded on the same principles, the same relationship, the same reciprocity. Both are the same kind of gift.

Koyukon elders would explain, in words quite different from my own, that I moved into two moments of grace, or what they would call luck. This is the source of success for a hunter or a watcher; not skill, not cleverness, not guile. Something is only given in nature, never taken.

Well soaked and shivering from a rough trip across the Strait, we pull into the dark waters of Anchor Bay. Sunset burns on the spindled peak of Antler

Mountain. The little house is warm with lights that shimmer on the calm near shore. I see Nita looking from the window and Ethan dashes out to wait by the tide, pitching rocks at the mooring buoy. He strains to see inside the boat, knowing that a hunter who tells his news aloud might offend the animals by sounding boastful. But when he sees the deer his excited voice seems to roll up and down the mountainside.

He runs for the house with Shungnak, carrying a load of gear, and I know he'll burst inside with the news. Ethan, joyous and alive, boy made of deer.

Part Two

PLACES TO LIVE

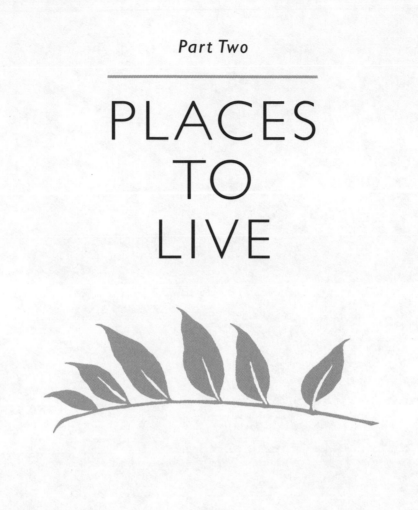

HOMESTEADING

John Haines

From

THE WRITER AS ALASKAN
Beginnings and Reflections

In this excerpt from an essay that appeared in the book *Living Off the Country*, John Haines recounts his life of homesteading in Alaska. Poetry and imagination are tied closely to the difficulties of such a life and the details of the land. In that linkage, the earth comes alive and place becomes an active force that molds the people who inhabit it. Intimate contact with nature and the richness of dreams helps one enter what Haines calls "the first morning of existence." But such experience always includes the "dangers and choices" that are part of living in place.

As a poet I was born in a particular place, a hillside overlooking the Tanana River in central Alaska, where I built a house and lived for the better part of twenty-two years. It was there, in the winter of 1947–48, that I began writing poems seriously, and there many years later that I wrote my first mature poems. Many things went into the making of those poems and the others I've written since: the air of the place, its rocks, soil, and water; snow and ice; human history, birds, animals, and insects. Other things, surely, not directly related to the place: the words of other poets learned once, forgotten, and remembered again. Old stories from childhood, voices out of dreams. Images, a way of seeing learned partly from several years' study as a painter and sculptor. And human relationship, life shared with another person whose existence mingled with my own, so that we saw the world as one person. But it was finally the place itself that provided the means of unifying all of these into a single experience.

I must have carried in myself from an early age some vague design of such a place and such a life. I grew up more or less homeless, moved from place to place, and came, I think, to regard all residence and all relationships as only temporary. It would naturally follow that I nourished in myself a great wish for something more permanent. What I got from that early life was a good sense of geography, but also great insecurity and uncertainty about who I was. I think I knew then that I would have to find a specific place and be born over again as my own person.

Why I chose that particular place rather than another probably can't be answered completely. I might have gone elsewhere and become a very different poet and person. But there was, most likely, no other region where I might have had that original experience of the North American wilderness. Unlike other "wilderness" areas, Alaska in those days seemed open-ended. I could walk north from my homestead at Richardson all the way to the Arctic Ocean and never cross a road nor encounter a village. This kind of freedom may no longer be available, but at that time it gave to the country a limitlessness and mystery hard to find now on this planet.

From the first day I set foot in interior Alaska, and more specifically on Richardson Hill, I knew I was home. Something in me identified with that landscape. I had come, let's say, to the dream place. Not exactly, of course, for there never was an exact place, but here was something so close to it that I could accept it at once. I think such a recognition must be rare, and I was extremely fortunate to have it happen in the way that it did. Such a purity of feeling, of joy and of being in the right place, I have not often felt since.

What that experience meant to me, in terms of self-discovery and the sort of work I was to do, could be told at great length, but I will try only to suggest in this essay some of the most important features of its personal significance.

There was, first of all, the experience of the wilderness itself, of finding life on more basic terms than those given me without thought as a child. This may seem like a strange thing to say, but perhaps it will make better sense if I link it to a more general theme. At times it becomes necessary for people to turn away from their cultural origins and return for a while to an older and simpler existence. One of the consequences of having a language and a culture is that these begin to exist for themselves in place of the original things we once lived by. Words become abstract, institutions and customs become unrelated to anything necessary or authentic.

And they begin subtly to sap vitality from us; we begin to live falsely, and after a while we find it necessary to turn away from them and find ourselves once more in the hard, irreducible world of natural things—of rock and water, fire and wood, flesh and blood.

So here, on a steep hillside, seventy miles from Fairbanks, was a place to begin. It was for me the beginning of what I have come to understand as the myth-journey of humankind. This life of food gathering, of making for ourselves out of what we can find around us, this is what we have come from and will return to. The Scottish poet, Edwin Muir, speaks in terms of the biblical Fall from Paradise, and he may be right. Think of what we have done to the earth and to ourselves—this fallen kingdom, the landscapes we make everywhere, devoid of beauty and grandeur. I can still remember the intensity of my feeling, of actual pain and outrage, seeing the landscape of southern California once more after twelve years in the wilderness. I saw it slowly, as I drove south from Alaska, through Canada—the accumulating ruin of the North American landscape.

I had when younger a habit of mind, of dreaminess, a vague drifting through the world. I was naturally observant, but unfocused. Living as I did there at Richardson, limited by circumstances to a small area, I found it necessary to learn more and more about it in order to get a living from it. I was forced to pay attention, to learn in detail many things of a kind I could not have learned if I had stayed only briefly in the country or had lived there in easier circumstances. I learned quickly, because it was an adventure for me, a young person from the city unused to knowing any place intimately, to distinguish actual things, particular and exact, from the vague and general character of the world. Words began to fasten themselves to what I saw. I learned the names of the things to be found there, characteristic of the subarctic the world over: the forest trees and shrubs, their kinds and uses, what made good building material or fuel, and what did not; what could be eaten, preserved, and put up for later use. I began for the first time to make things for myself, to build shelters, to weave nets, to make sleds and harness, and to train animals for work. I learned to hunt, to watch, and to listen, to think like a moose, if need be, or a marten, or a lynx. I watched the river, and saw in its gray and swirling water, heavy with silt, the probable trace of salmon, and knew where to set my nets. I read the snow and what was written there. I became familiar with the forms of frost, the seeding of the grasses, the early swelling of the birch leaves. I

watched a tree, no bigger than my wrist when I first built there, grow ten-
fold over the years, until I had to cut away its branches from the rain gut-
ters of the house.

Digging in the soil, picking away the rock, uprooting stumps, I became
in time a grower of things sufficient to feed myself and another. Slowly
finding my way into the skills of hunter and trapper, I understood what
blood and bone, hide and muscle, marrow and sinew really are; not as
things read about, but as things touched and handled until they became
as familiar to me as my own skin. Land itself came alive for me as it never
had before, more alive sometimes than the people who moved about on
it. I learned that it is land, *place,* that makes people, provides for them the
possibilities they will have of becoming something more than mere lumps
of sucking matter. We today who live so much from the inheritance of
land and culture do not understand this as well as we need to. Few of us
these days are really residents anywhere, in the deep sense of that term.
We live off the surface of things and places, the culture as well as the land;
ours is a derivative life: we take what we find without thought, without
regard for origin or consequences, unaware for the most part that the resources, both natural and cultural, are fast diminishing.

These were big lessons, basic things, and I was a long time assimilating
them and understanding their significance. Never really privileged in
youth, I was never in actual want, either. Like most people in our society,
I did not know what it was to be hungry, to look for food and find myself short when I needed it most. That old life, unchanged for centuries,
in time with the seasons, the rising and setting of the sun, the coming and
going of birds and animals, the sources of food and light, became for me
not a passage in a book of histories, but a matter of daily occurrence, a
way still vital and full of meaning. I grew to feel that if civilization failed,
I could still make my way, and in general, thrive. I still feel that way, though
I am old enough to know that it would not be as easy for me now as it
was twenty or thirty years ago.

The place in which I settled, Richardson, which included Banner Creek
and the nearby Tenderfoot area, had been a thriving gold rush camp from
around 1905 until the late years of the First World War. As with many such
settlements, conditions rapidly changed; the easy gold was mined, and
people left for another camp, another strike. By the time I came there in
1947, only six or eight of the older residents still lived along the creeks, or
in the hills above the Tanana. Most of the old buildings were gone, and it

was only by listening to what the residents told me that I learned something of the history of Richardson. And what I learned seemed to confirm what Thomas Hardy said once in respect to local life, long residence in a certain place, and the changes he had witnessed in his own lifetime.

> The change at the root of this has been the recent supplanting of the class of stationary cottagers, who carried on the local traditions and humours, by a population of more or less migratory labourers, which has led to a break of continuity in local history, more fatal than any other thing to the preservation of legend, folk-lore, close inter-social relations, and eccentric individualities. For these the indispensible conditions of existence are attachment to the soil of one particular spot by generation after generation. [Preface to *Far from the Madding Crowd*].

What I found at Richardson was a late beginning of just that local condition of which Hardy is speaking. The few gold rush survivors, men and women, could not have been living in the area for more than fifty years, but in their memories and the stories they told, full of humor and spite, already the place had begun to acquire the dimensions of myth. Each of the persons I came to know before the last of them died in the late 1960s had a clarity of outline, a distinctiveness of temperament that only simplicity and a certain isolation allow human character. For the first time in my life I became aware of individuals, in all their quirkiness and singularity. I was fortunate indeed, for what I found has by now nearly vanished from American life, and in its place all life takes on the same bland mediocrity one finds so plentiful in the suburbs. It may be true, as I sometimes find reason to believe, that this change has been more than just a sign of deterioration in social life. In order for a new form of life to occupy a place, another must die. When our imaginations have grown enough, perhaps we will understand that for us the local must one day include the continent, and finally the planet itself. It seems likely that nothing else will allow us to thrive as a species. But it is also true that meanwhile we are painfully aware that an honored and durable way of life has disappeared, leaving an empty place in our lives.

It would be easy to say that something of the cold and clarity of the land, and much of the rest I have been talking about, just somehow got into the poems I wrote while I lived there. In a way this is true, but there is more to it. It was an awakening, profound and disturbing. Everything was so new to me that it was like finding myself for the first time with my feet on the earth. To the extent that it was possible for me, I entered the original mystery of things, the great past out of which we came. I saw the midwinter sun sink in a cleft of the mountains to the south, and I felt I had learned a great secret. The winter solstice was an actual event, and it came on with a menace and a grandeur much older than a date on the Christian calendar.

But most important, as I have already suggested, was the meeting of place and dream. Without my being entirely conscious of it, this place and this life were what I had wanted more than any other thing. All doors seemed to open there; things hidden away, brooded upon for years, came to life: the owls I sketched as a child, the grass flowing on the hillside, the lynx track in the snow. When I was a small boy, five or six years old, my father read to me on winter evenings from Kipling's *Jungle Books*. Something took shape then and there in my mind: the wolf in the mouth of the cave, ready for the night's hunting, the forest coming awake, and far away the village of men. Thirty years went by, and that shape surfaced in a poem, "Book of the Jungle," from *Winter News*.

> The animal, rising at dusk
> from its bed in the trampled
> grass—
>   this is how it all began.
>
> Far off the shaggy tribesmen
> listened and fed their fires
> with thorns.
>
> Secret paths of the forest,
> when did your children walk
> unarmed, clothed only
> with the shadows of leaves?
>
> We are still kneeling
> and listening,
> as from the edge of a field
> there rises sometimes at evening
> the snort of a rutting bull.

Poetry seems to have been a natural response to my living there. My first winter in the cabin at Richardson, unable for some reason to paint, I began attempting poems in which I could express some of my feeling for this place I was coming to know, amazed at all I was seeing and learning. The poems were not, of course, very good. They were hardly poems at all. I had a lot to learn, about writing and about myself. To really know the place, I had to live there, build there, become intimate with it and know it for a long time, before I could say anything about it that would be personal and distinctive. It was nearly ten years before I wrote anything that satisfied me.

On that hillside, remote from many distractions, it was possible for me to see things, all things, more clearly, and to think in a quiet that is hard to come by these days. The events of my life seemed to reach into both past and future. Sometimes on a fall evening, looking out on that great valley, the route of migrations, I saw, or in some way felt, a future invasion of the continent—some force out of Asia, as in the not-so-remote past. In a poem called "Foreboding" I tried to convey something of the essence of this feeling, call it a vision if you like: a suggestion of an event still to come.

> Something immense and lonely
> divides the earth at evening.
>
> For nine long years I have watched
> from an inner doorway:
> as in a confused vision,
> manlike figures approach, cover
> their faces, and pass on,
> heavy with iron and distance.
>
> There is no sound but the wind
> crossing the road, filling
> the ruts with a dust as fine as chalk.
>
> Like the closing of an inner door,
> the day begins its dark
> journey, across nine bridges
> wrecked one by one.

I hope it will be clearer from this brief description how much and in what ways those years at Richardson formed me as a person and as a poet. There is one part of it I have hardly mentioned, and that concerns the two women who lived there with me much of the time, and one in particular. It seems only honest in an account of this sort not to have it appear that I was alone all the time, or that whatever was done I did all by myself. Without that companionship and support, physical and emotional, it seems unlikely that I would have gotten through those years, deprived as in some ways they were; and it seems to me not the least of things that I did finally learn to live with another human being.

It is still a place I go back to, in mind and in spirit, though it seems I cannot return to it fully in fact. The material it gave me is still part of my life, and I go back to it in poems and in prose, trying to understand as well as I can the significance of what happened to me there. The experience was so powerful that it has influenced everything else I have done. Probably I measure everything else against it. Of all things I have and am, it is something I do not lose. While writing parts of this essay I could see on a table before me a broken sandstone seed mortar that I dug up from a field in California a few years ago. When I found it I was out early in the morning, looking at some Indian rock paintings not far from where I was camped with my wife and a group of schoolchildren. Such things, and the landscapes of which they are part, would not have for me the significance they do if I had not explored for myself during those years in Alaska something of the original life of the continent.

But I no longer live at Richardson. In more ways than one, perhaps, that life is gone. Place for me has shifted from the north country wilderness to a house in suburban California; from there to some rocks in the arid California foothills, to the rainy outlines of a city in the Northwest, and to a windy street in Missoula, Montana. These places have added to the sum of what I have been; and then, returning to some enduring stillness in my life, I find myself once more in a familiar setting of broad river and sunlit hill. Behind all I write there is a landscape, partly idealized, perhaps, upon which the human figure, my own or another's, acts out a part of its life. That original place still sustains me. It gave me a way of perceiving the world that I might not have acquired otherwise, and not least, a solitude in which I could learn to listen to my own voice. But as I have tried to show, I do not think that place, outer place, alone can account for this. There must be another place, and that is within the person himself. When that interior place, formed out of dream and fantasy, and by intense imagination, finds its counterpart in a physical landscape, then some genuine human reality can be created.

The homestead at Richardson provided a place of departure from which I might go out into the world forearmed. On the evidence of my own experience, I believe that one of the most important metaphors of our time is the journey out of wilderness into culture, into the forms of our complicated and divided age, with its intense confusions and deceptions. The eventual disintegration of these cultural forms returns us once more to the wilderness. This journey can be seen both as fall and as reconciliation. And place, once again, means actual place, but also a state of mind, of consciousness. Once that place is established, we carry it with us, as we do a sense of ourselves.

RANCHING

Sharon Butala

THE SUBTLETY OF THE LAND

Sharon Butala lives in southwest Saskatchewan, which, she notes, is best understood as part of the vast Great Plains of North America extending down into Texas. She was born in another part of rural Canada, but went to the city for her education and completed a graduate degree. At thirty-six she married a cattle rancher and left a promising teaching job at a university to live once again in the country. At first, life on the ranch was a struggle for her, but with time she began to feel "congruent," at home in her body and in her land. Her mystical experiences in nature and in dreams became the basis for her successful career as a novelist. *Perfection of the Morning: An Apprenticeship in Nature* is her spiritual and artistic autobiography. It is filled with depictions of painful isolation, the tie between the feminine and the natural world, and the healing power of nature. In this selection, she meditates on truly being a part of such country, with nature shaping people rather than the other way around.

Some years later, when I was an established author, I said to a Toronto reporter who had asked me a question about him, "My husband is a true rural man."

"What does that mean?" the reporter asked, his voice full of skepticism.

"It means," I said, "that he understands the world in terms of wild things." I was a little surprised myself at my answer, having been called upon to explain something that until that moment had seemed self-evident, and realizing that, caught off guard, I had hit on the heart of the matter.

The reporter's pencil stopped moving, his eyes shifted away from me, he reflected, his eyes shifted back to me, and without writing anything down he changed the subject. When I told this story to a writer-naturalist friend, he said, laughing, that for the reporter my answer "does not compute."

A true rural person must be somebody born and raised on the land, outside of towns, and far from most other people. That being a given, then it follows that such life experience must result in an intrinsic understanding of the world different from that of someone raised in the cement, asphalt, glass and crowds of the city. Peter's thinking about the world was different from mine in ways that went beyond our different sexes or our different lifestyles. Where I had been trained to understand human nature from Freud and pop psychology, and the functioning of the world from classes in political economy and in history, that is, from formal education, Peter's starting point was what he had all his life lived in the midst of—it was Nature.

As years on the ranch passed, though, I began to learn from Nature too; I began to catch a glimpse of the world as he saw it through my own life in Nature. When that began to happen, a new understanding slowly, very slowly, began to dawn on me about what a life in Nature teaches one. I began to see that there might be more at the root of this difference in understanding of how the world works than I had guessed at, thinking it had to do only with simple, surface matters, like understanding cattle behavior well enough to predict their next move, or knowing the habits of antelope, or reading the sky with accuracy. I didn't yet have any idea what this deeper knowledge might be, but I watched Peter closely and tried to see what he saw.

While he was doing the spring irrigation at the hay farm, he would sometimes come across fawns only a few days old lying in the hay where they'd been left by their mothers who had gone off to forage. More than once he came to the house to get me so I could see the little spotted creature for myself.

"Watch," he would say. "When they're this young they don't even move when you come near them." Then he would bend down, pick up the trusting fawn in his arms, carry it to the closest grass-covered dike, and place it gently down where the irrigation water couldn't reach it. I worried about the mother locating her baby, but he said, with the confidence born of experience, "Don't worry. It won't take her a minute to find him." When we went back hours later the fawn would always be gone. These and other incidents reminded me over and over again that Peter, and other rural people who knew no other landscape, had formed his attitude to the prairie and his understanding of its weather, its growth patterns and its animals by a lifetime of immersion in it.

In my reading and occasionally in conversation with urban visitors, I read or hear people either saying directly or implying indirectly that *true rural* people don't notice or appreciate the beauty in which they live. Although I don't say so, the arrogance and ignorance of such remarks always makes me angry, implying as it does that rural people lack humanity, are somehow an inferior branch of the human species, that beauty is beyond their ken. It is one thing to come from the city and be overwhelmed by the beauty of Nature and to speak of it, and another thing entirely to have lived in it so long that it has seeped into your bones and your blood and is inseparable from your own being, so that it is part of you and requires no mention or hymns of praise.

Peter preferred to do our annual spring and fall cattle drives on horseback, a trek which took three days. Bringing the cattle down to the valley around Christmastime could be very unpleasant and then it was often hard to get help, so that we sometimes made that move with only Peter, me and one other person. But three days out on the prairie during a warm spring were paradise; we never had any trouble rounding up enough riders then. If the spring move was usually a joy, the best part of it was the eight to ten miles of unbroken prairie without even any true roads through it that we used to cross each time.

I knew the first time Peter took me across those miles of prairie that I loved to be there far from towns or even houses, on native shortgrass that had never been broken, where the grass hadn't been overgrazed and was full of birds' nests in the spring, and long-eared jackrabbits as big as small dogs, antelope in the distance, and coyotes that often followed us singing all the way.

Of course, unless she's a dyed-in-the-wool, bona fide horse-and-cattle-woman herself, when it's time to move cattle, and especially if there are adolescent sons on the place, the rancher's wife usually gets stuck driving the truck. The rancher is the one with the understanding of the cattle, knowledge of the route, and the cattle-management skills. As boss and owner, he has to ride. If there are adolescents along, it's taken for granted that they'll ride because they have to learn, which has a high priority on Saskatchewan ranches, and because it's so much fun and nobody wants to deprive kids of a little harmless fun.

The rancher's wife packs the meals, stows them in the truck, serves them when the time comes and packs up after. She carries drinking water and coffee and the extra jackets or the ones taken off when the day gets too warm. She carries tack, fencing pliers and other tools, and sometimes, if the move is just before calving begins, she'll have a newborn in the back of the truck and often several of them, each one marked in some way—maybe a colored string around its neck—so it can be returned to the right mother every few hours. As the drive wears on, she's likely to have exhausted adolescents in the cab with her, while their horses are either driven ahead or led by one of the men from his own horse. Usually, at some point, somebody will take pity on her and spell her off for an hour or so, so that she can get out into the fresh air and ride a little herself.

When you move cattle you move, depending on the weather, at the leisurely pace of about two miles an hour. For long stretches you don't need to speak at all, and you can ride a mile or more away from any other rider if you want to. As you ride, the prairie slowly seeps into you. I have never felt such pure, unadulterated joy in simple existence as I have felt at moments out on the prairie during the spring move.

Ordinarily I wouldn't get to ride until we were close to the ranch and our helpers went home. Then Peter and I changed our headquarters from the hay farm to the ranch house and we'd ride horses out to the cattle to bring them the rest of the way home. Occasionally, he'd have someone along who didn't ride and who would drive the truck so that I could ride. Most of the time, though, I reluctantly drove the truck and kept my fingers crossed for a chance either to ride or, as I sometimes did, to walk leading Peter's horse—for me to ride him was unthinkable, the very thought making my stomach turn over and my knees quake—while Peter spelled me off in the driver's seat.

Nowadays we calve at the hay farm instead of at the ranch, mostly because it's easier to keep an eye on the cows, but also because there's shelter for them here during the inevitable calf-killing spring storms. Often, too, in spring there is no water in the ditches or fields along the way and, of course, the cattle must have water each day, moving or not. If we calve at the hay farm—Peter not being a believer in early calving—by the time we're ready to move in late April most of the farmers along the route have seeded their crops. The traditional mistrust between farmers and ranchers being what it is, it would be dangerous if one cow strayed one foot from the road allowances, those which, usually without bothering to get permission from the municipality, farmers haven't plowed up and seeded to wheat. And cows being what they are, you never know when one might take it into her head to head out, calf at her side, racing for Alaska or Mexico across a newly seeded field with a couple of cowboys in hot pursuit. Guns have been pointed on such occasions. Nowadays, it hardly seems worth the risk.

During one of the last spring moves we made, Peter had had more people along than he'd expected and before we'd gone very far he'd given one of the kids my horse, which he'd been leading, to ride. Not long after that, he'd given my saddle—the only one with stirrups that could be shortened enough for small people—to another teenager to use. I had reconciled myself to not being able to ride on this move. I could still look at the landscape, I could roll down the window and smell the sweet air and feel the breeze and the sun on my face, and occasionally I could stop, get out, and stroll around a bit in the grass.

We always made it a practice to stop for a meal when we reached that stretch of pure unbroken prairie. The riders would dismount and hobble their horses or tie them to the fence, I'd park the truck, Peter would throw down a couple of hay bales for a table or for people to sit on, and I'd put out the lunch. We'd sit in the sun and eat sandwiches, and his mother's baked beans, the pot wrapped in layers of newspapers to keep it warm, and drink coffee from thermoses. Long before we reached there I'd have begun to look forward to that moment.

I discovered what the annual day spent crossing these acres of prairie meant to me when, as we were about to begin that part of the trip, a circumstance arose—I don't even remember what it was—that meant somebody had to drive one of the men the twenty or so miles around the fields, down the roads and wait with him there at the corrals for the riders and cattle to arrive. Since Peter could hardly order anybody else to do it, and nobody volunteered, it was taken for granted that as his wife I would leave the drive and take this man where he needed to go.

I wanted to protest, but I couldn't bring myself to do it in front of so many people, especially since arguing or complaining are just not done on a trip like that. It would be a little like a sailor telling the captain of a ship that he didn't feel like taking the watch that night. My true feelings were too private to speak out loud, and I couldn't come up with any practical reason why I shouldn't have to that didn't hint of adolescent pique or, not knowing how the others felt about the prairie—but the fact that nobody volunteered to go should have given me a hint—that I could be sure anybody but Peter would understand. And everyone else was a volunteer; I was official staff. I knew I wouldn't be able to go back and catch up with the drive, either. For me, for that year, the drive was over.

I got back in the truck and started driving, trying to smile, trying to make conversation, while all the time I was fighting back tears. I wanted so badly to spend that last few hours on the prairie, the only time we ever went through those fields, that I had an actual pain in my chest as I drove away and that stayed with me till I went to bed that night.

I said about that incident much later to a friend, "If everything happens to teach you something, why was that taken away from me? What was I supposed to learn from that?" and answered myself, "To teach me how much the wild prairie means to me." Years later, I was able to go further: to understand how precious it is, how unique, how deeply it might affect one, changing even one's understanding of life.

Sometimes I think I'm still not over that loss. Especially since, during the good times, farmers bought all that land the rest of the gang traveled over on horseback that day, and plowed it up to turn it into a farm. Now, ten years later, the farming operation is failing, but you can't turn plowed-up short-grass prairie back into the original terrain. It's gone forever, or given a human life span, as good as forever, along with the wildlife that lived on it.

It occurs to me now to wonder if perhaps the very real—and surprising even to me—sorrow I felt that day as I drove away, and all the rest of the day and for days afterward, wasn't perhaps intuitive, if perhaps a part of me knew that I would never again experience the sweetness of that air, the sun warm on my face and hands, the view so vast the soul felt free, because by the next spring or the spring after that it would be gone forever.

As the years passed, I felt more and more that the best comfort I had was in being in the landscape. I was only mildly curious about how the prairie was formed, and when and how it was evolving, and I certainly had none of the interests of ecologists or environmentalists. I was merely looking at the prairie as a human being, savoring it for its beauty which engaged all the senses and brought with it a feeling of well-being, contentment and often even joy.

My approach was to simply wander in it with no particular destination, to lie in the sun and bury my nose in the sweet-smelling grasses and forbs such as sage, to admire the colors and textures of the sedges, shrubs and succulents which make up the mixed grass prairie, or to sit on a slope looking out across miles of prairie to the horizon, watching the shifting of shadows and light across it, thinking no thoughts that, a moment later, I would remember. I was there only to enjoy the prairie. I asked for nothing more, not thinking there was anything more.

I had only the most cursory interest in the names of the plants, although Peter's mother taught me a few of those which flowered: scarlet mallow, three-flowered avens, gumbo primrose, golden bean, which she called "buffalo bean," and which someone else told me she knew as the wild sweet pea. I could hardly miss the wild rose or the prairie sunflower, and I knew a few others such as the wild licorice and the wild morning glory and anemones which grow along the riverbank, from my childhood in the north. Peter showed me the greasewood, badger bush and club moss and pointed out the two species of cactus—the prickly pear and the pincushion—and much later I learned from a rancher's wife (herself a rancher and also a poet) that if you had the patience to gather the berries, you could make cactus-berry jelly. I taught myself a few: the many types of cinquefoil and sage, and milkweed, and the Canada thistle with its purple flower that a saddle horse—"Watch this," Peter said—would clip tidily off with its bared teeth, never touching a barb. I longed to see a field of wild prairie lilies as I had in my childhood in the north, but I never have, not even a single flower growing wild in the grass.

Because we had a hay farm, I learned to identify a number of grasses—timothy, bromegrass, foxtail—and legumes—clover, alfalfa—which I saw every day, some of which were imported species, crested wheat grass, Russian wild rye, and many of which, like reed canary grass, were very beautiful. I attended three day-long range schools with Peter, one in the Bears Paw Mountains of Montana, but I did so chiefly for the adventure and to spend an entire day on the prairie instead of only a few hours. At these schools I learned to identify death camas when I saw it, and a few of the many native species of grass—needle-and-thread grass, June grass, blue grama or buffalo grass—and a forb or two.

Other seasons brought different pleasures. All one snowy winter I walked a mile down the riverbed every morning with the dog trotting ahead, flushing out cattle from the banks or far back around the last curve where the fenceline crossed and stopped them, then chasing them up to the feedgrounds where Peter and his hired man were throwing out hay, grain bales and grain itself. For two winters the snow was so deep that it muffled sound so that the cattle which had sought shelter in these snug places couldn't hear the tractor and didn't come out for feed. Or sometimes, looking back, I think Peter came and got me each morning to make that walk out of understanding that I needed to feel useful, a part of the operation, and that if I spent all of each day inside that tiny log house I would soon be "bushed," develop cabin fever, be impossible to live with—that I might leave.

I remember those walks each morning as among the best of my life. I would head down the riverbed, following in the tracks of the cattle where the snow was too deep to walk comfortably in. The banks of the river are high and steep, and the winds had pushed the snow into deep banks that overhung the edges of the cliffsides in fat lips of snow that looked like waves on the ocean and from which long icicles sometimes hung. Looking up from the snowy riverbed, I saw white walls of snow and then the snowy billows and beyond them the brilliant sky. I saw the places where partridges snuggled up for the night to keep warm and followed the tracks of coyotes and foxes and animals whose tracks I didn't recognize. I was picking up knowledge, hardly even noticing that was what I was doing. Running to cut off a cow, I fell headlong in the snow and, with no one watching me, lay there laughing, blinking up at the sky, losing myself in its blue depths.

For most people the worse the weather is, the more likely they are to stay indoors; not so for old-fashioned ranchers—for them the worse the weather, the more likely the rancher is to be out in it, in the midst of blizzards searching for cattle out on the prairie and chasing them down into the shelter of deep coulees, or home to the windbreaks and corrals. On such days I went along with Peter and learned again that the human limits of endurance are much greater than day-to-day life has us believe; that is, I became less afraid of the weather at the same time as I became a good deal more respectful of it.

One of the first Christmas gifts Peter gave me was a pair of cross-country skis, and as long as there was enough snow, which there usually isn't in this desert country, I'd be out on the prairie in the winter, too, skiing. I began to take my skis and go out into the hills during storms, having discovered that I liked storms for the way they changed the appearance of familiar places and for the sense of mystery they brought to them.

Memories of my childhood came back to me: playing in the bush with my friends, with my sisters and cousins in our grandmother's garden, skating on frozen sloughs in winter till the pain from the cold became so bad even we kids couldn't stand it anymore and went home, the winter we had built a snow fort that lasted for months as we added on and made it more and more substantial so that it stood well into spring. I felt like a child again, had fleeting moments when I remembered how wonderful the world itself had once seemed, and how it was to be cared for, worry-free, and living in the body again and not just the mind.

And I was recreating myself as a writer. I not only was meditative by nature, this having been developed in me as the result of being an extremely shy and retiring child in a big family, I had also developed in me the seeds of the observer. It was a lucky thing, although I'd never have admitted it then, to have arrived a stranger in a strange land, when I was no longer young, with a touch of the observer's cold eye already in my makeup.

I found myself observing the very people with whom I seemed to have so little in common. I saw the people of my new community as different from those of the rest of the province, and I was surprised to discover that they themselves seemed to define themselves as different, although nobody ever explicitly said so, in that they often had closer links both in terms of lifestyle and in family ties to Alberta and to Montana than they did to Saskatchewan. Many of the families had begun as Americans and had close relatives on the farms and ranches over the border and in Alberta, and when young people went off to higher education or trades schools or to jobs, when I first came here, they were much more likely to go to Alberta than to Saskatoon or even Regina. As a group they seemed to me often to think more like western Americans or like Albertans, with that essentially conservative, independent cast of mind, than they did like the good-old-Tommy-Douglas-prairie-socialist school of thought to which I belonged and which had always seemed to me to define Saskatchewan.

I soon discovered, in my attempt to tell the story of these people and this place, that my fund of facts, of precise knowledge, was inadequate to the task I'd set myself. Each story, each book, each play would become an exercise in information gathering. When Peter couldn't answer my questions I turned to books. Peter took me to meet old people, old men who'd pioneered in the area, and I listened to their stories and made notes, and where it was possible, which was practically never, I tried to match their memories to the scant written history I could find.

I carried a notebook everywhere. Chasing cows home on bitter winter days, I'd stop the truck, get out, draw a little diagram of the way an animal had pushed away the snow from a sage bush, write a description of the bush and the snow and the droppings the animal had left, the colors, the place where the sun was in the sky on that day at that time and how the cattle looked. I wrote the last few pages of *The Gates of the Sun* sitting on a straw bale in the back of the pickup in a neighbor's field while I waited for Peter to finish baling the straw, pausing in my scribbling only to ask questions of Peter and the neighbor, when they stopped for coffee, about what was a native species, whether bird, animal or plant, and what wasn't. It constantly amazed me how much the men knew.

With every story and every book I was forced to search out new information. My fund of information, of facts, obtained in all these ways—my own observations, Peter's answers to my incessant questions, the stories of old people, books—was growing. Without intending to or even really wanting to, I was becoming knowledgeable about the history of the area and its plant and animal life. Although I will never know all there is to know—Peter still knows a thousand times more than I do—having begun by being transported by its beauty, and then being overwhelmed by my sense of loneliness and purposelessness, I was at last starting to feel at home in the terrain, at home in the landscape. Of course, I didn't see this as it was happening, but by learning to name things in my new environment, by discovering the scheme of the place and the way the parts fit together, I was making them my own, and by this I was slowly healing myself.

Years later when I was the expert instead of the neophyte, a friend and I were out walking in the rain. In this semiarid country where rain is rare and precious, walking in it is exhilarating, imbued even with a touch of magic. We came to a place where a pair of great horned owls sat watching us, and as my friend went closer to see them better, I sat in the grass in my leaky boots and a borrowed yellow rain jacket which came to my knees, not minding the wet, looking out over the misty fields, noticing how everything smelled different because of the moisture, how colors had changed and intensified.

I thought of how my friend and I had moved over the wet ground, where we had gone and not gone, what we had found ourselves doing, and suddenly I realized that it was the land—Nature—that had guided our steps, made our choices for us, and not the other way around. That is, because we were friends and rambling in the countryside for the pleasure of each other's company and for the pleasure of being out-of-doors, having no set plan or goal, we had gone where the shape of the land had suggested itself to us; we had done what the land had made available to us. If it was too muddy or wet in one place, we went somewhere else; if a hill was too steep, we went around; there was no way to cross the river without swimming and it was too cold to swim, so we followed its course instead and sat on its bank.

I thought, then said, "This land makes Crees of us all." By this, I meant that it appeared to me that the Crees, for example, developed the culture they developed because it was the best fit between themselves and the land. And it was the *land* that taught them that. They adapted to the land, and not the other way around as we Europeans so stupidly did, trying to force this arid western land to be, as government propaganda had for seventy-five years and more put it, "the breadbasket of the world."

I began to think about the ways in which land affects the individual, or at least this particular landscape, the Great Plains of North America. I began to see that in our human arrogance we assume we can affect the land but it can't affect us—except in practical ways: hurricanes, floods, drought—when there are plenty of ways we might find that the land—Nature—is affecting us without our being aware of it. In considering the differences between Peter and myself, I had not imagined or considered the possibility that he had been shaped by the land, by Nature, that in subtle ways we've never identified nor even really talked about, his psyche itself had been shaped by Nature not merely by *his* observations of *it* but by its subtle, never described or even consciously realized, influence on *him*.

The Great Plains landscape is an elemental one. There is little natural water in the form of lakes or rivers or even ponds, no forests, no mountains—just miles and miles of land and a sky across which weather visibly, majestically passes. One winter visitor to this place said it reminded him of the high Arctic where he had once lived, and several others, Wallace Stegner included, spoke of the plains of Africa. The landscape is so huge that our imaginations can't contain it or outstrip it, and the climate is concomitantly arbitrary and severe.

It is geology stripped bare, leaving behind only a vast sky and land stretched out in long, sweeping lines that blend into the distant horizon with a line that is sometimes so clear and sharp it is surreal, and sometimes exists at the edge of metaphysics, oscillating in heat waves or, summer or winter, blending into mirages and the realm of dreams and visions which wavers just the other side of the horizon. The Great Plains are for visionaries, they induce visions, they are themselves visions, the line between fact and dream is so blurred. What other landscape around the world produces the mystic psyche so powerfully? Sky and land, that is all, and grass, and what Nature leaves bare the human psyche fills.

It was not until I moved into the country to live that my significant dreaming really began. I did not think about this fact, but if I had, I am sure I would have explained it as a by-product of the radical change in my way of life. Eventually it was suggested to me by an eminent western Canadian writer in whom I had confided that perhaps living in this ancient, skeletal landscape had brought on these dreams. At the time I reserved judgment, but a few years later, in another context, another western Canadian writer told me how she had, after years of living in the city where she didn't believe she had dreamt at all, moved out into the country and suddenly began having vivid, meaningful dreams. She attributed these to the influence of the landscape in which she now made her home.

In the context of these remarks it seems to me very significant that dreams have always held an important place in Aboriginal cultures of the Great Plains of North America, as they have in many other such cultures around the world. Aboriginal people take the content of their dreams as simply another source of information about the world, a guide for action, and as prophecy, either in their individual lives or as directives to their communities. In these cultures it is considered extremely foolish, a great insult, even a sin, to ignore an important dream.

Prophetic dreams are accepted at face value and are used as a basis for action. A South Dakota writer living near Rapid City told me that a few years ago Chief Crazy Horse—whose name I'm told should more accurately be translated as "Enchanted Horse," or "Vision Horse"—appeared in dreams to the elders of his nation to warn them about an imminent flood on a branch of the Cheyenne River. The flood did occur and it killed more than a hundred of his people who lived along its banks. Hugh Brody, in *Maps and Dreams,* describes a hunting culture, the Beaver Indians of northeastern British Columbia, where the best hunters are guided by dreams to their kill; the very best hunter-dreamers have even dreamt the way to heaven and then, awaking, have drawn the map.

Although I sometimes go for long stretches without any dreams that seem important to me, a few years ago I began to have the occasional prophetic dream myself. I dreamt the San Francisco earthquake a couple of weeks before it happened. Since I'd never been to San Francisco, I thought the city in the dream was Vancouver and the broken bridge, the Lions' Gate. Although it was a powerful enough dream to tell people about it, I certainly never took it as prophecy until I saw the broken span of the bridge on television. It was identical to the one in my dream where it had been the main icon. I dreamt of the Japanese airplane that lost its rudder and, after weaving drunkenly through the air for half an hour, crashed into a mountain. I was in bed dreaming it as it was happening. When I got up the first thing Peter did was to tell me about this terrible event that had just happened in Japan. I even dreamt of the death of one of the Russian Communist leaders a few days before he died. It may be that I've had more prophetic dreams than I know but simply haven't remembered. Actually I think this may be true of everyone, but most people don't record their dreams as I usually do, and so forget them.

I have described the dream I had in which a giant eagle and a giant owl appeared to me. It became for me a life-dream, a significant dream that launched me on a journey through comparative religion, mythology, the study of dreams, psychoanalysis, and finally into the study of the nature of the female. At an archetypal level, it is a dream about masculine power, symbolized by the soaring eagle, and feminine power, symbolized by the owl standing near me on the ground. In beauty and power they are exactly equal, but I, a woman, had spent my life to this point following the eagle—that is, accepting masculine interpretations of life in general and, of my own life, accepting masculine goals and taking masculine desires for my own—instead of cleaving to the owl, searching out and coming to terms with my own feminine soul.

My search for understanding of the dream led me into and through my novel *Luna*—the story of the lives of contemporary ranch and farm women and how they live, feel about, and understand their rural, agricultural, traditional lives—and from there into my short story collection *Fever*, a much more personal and urbanized study of the same issues. It's been a good dozen years since I had that dream and I still run across further ways to interpret it. Not only have I accepted it as guidance in the direction my life has taken, it is, to a degree, the foundation on which I have built the rest of my life.

I think that significant dreaming is one way in which Nature influences and changes the individual, developing in her/him an awareness of Nature as more than mere locale, or a setting, a context, as more than beauty, as more than something that is merely Other.

It was in Joseph Campbell's *Primitive Mythology* that I first heard of Aboriginal dreamtime, and, not long after, in a much more firsthand and compelling way in *The Lost World of the Kalahari* by Laurens van der Post. All peoples of the earth have creation stories of one kind or another. The stories of prescientific peoples tell variously of a time when the world was in the process of being created along with the creatures on it. This was a timeless time, a time before time, when animals, plants and people could become one another and the formations of the earth were taking shape. It is called, in mythologies around the world, dreamtime, and out of it springs stories and legends about archetypal creatures, sometimes gods, whose manifestations remain now in the fallen time.

It seems, too, that on some level this timeless time still exists in another realm, and those people peculiarly blessed—including, but never exclusively, shamans—may still go there. In this realm many strange things can happen: animals can converse with humans and vice versa; the dead may appear and speak, or creatures from the dreamtime thought by some of us to be merely metaphoric. The earth becomes more beautiful, approaches, even achieves, perfection, and everything in it and on it is imbued with meaning. And especially the sense of the ticking of time vanishes.

I believe that since Aboriginal people around the world have nontechnological cultures and live in and by Nature—or at least, once did when their cultures were developing—and these cultures had developed the concept of dreamtime and took dreaming very seriously whether in New Zealand, Australia, the Kalahari Desert of Africa, or the Great Plains of

North America, that surely it was Nature which, whether with will and intention or not, taught, allowed, gave them dreams as an instrument of knowledge.

I began to see from my own experience living in it that the land and the wild creatures who live in it and on it, and the turning of the earth, the rising and setting of the sun and the moon, and the constant passing of weather across its surface—that is, Nature—influenced rural people to make them what they are, more than even they knew.

Close proximity to a natural environment—being in Nature—alters all of us in ways which remain pretty much unexplored, even undescribed in our culture. I am suggesting that these ways in which such a closeness affects us, from dreams to more subtle and less describable phenomena, are real, and that we should stop thinking, with our inflated human egos, that all the influence is the other way around. We might try to shift our thinking in this direction so that we stop blithely improving the natural world around us, and begin to learn, as Aboriginal people have, what Nature in her subtle but powerful manner has to teach us about how to live.

More and more I am coming to believe that our alienation from the natural world is at the root of much that has gone so wrong in the modern world, and that if Nature has anything to teach us at all, her first lesson is in humility.

Gretel Ehrlich

A STORM, THE
CORNFIELD, AND ELK

Gretel Ehrlich has written memorably of her life on a cattle ranch in the Big
Horn Mountains of Wyoming. She now lives in her home state of California.
Her nature books include *The Solace of Open Spaces* and *Questions of Heaven:
The Chinese Journeys of an American Buddhist.* Ehrlich is a practicing Buddhist,
and Asian religion and aesthetics have influenced her writing. Her essays are
marked by rich and striking imagery that creates unforgettable portraits of
nature's beauty. She also draws full-bodied portraits of ranchers and cowhands.
In these two selections from *The Solace of Open Spaces,* she depicts the painful
difficulties of a place where nature works in extremes. A sense of closeness to
the land is paralleled by the struggle for survival. But living with nature's adversi-
ties helps deepen human community and sharpen the interplay of consciousness
with the natural world.

Last week a bank of clouds lowered itself down summer's green ladder and
let loose with a storm. A heavy snow can act like fists: trees are pummeled,
hay- and grainfields are flattened, splayed out like deer beds; field corn,
jackknifed and bleached blond by the freeze, is bedraggled by the brawl.
All night we heard groans and crashes of cottonwood trunks snapping. "I
slept under the damned kitchen table," one rancher told me. "I've already
had one of them trees come through my roof." Along the highway electric lines were looped to the ground like dropped reins.

As the storm blows east toward the Dakotas, the blue of the sky in-
tensifies. It inks dry washes and broad grasslands with quiet. In their most
complete gesture of restraint, cottonwoods, willows, and wild rose en-
gorge themselves with every hue of ruddiness—russet, puce, umber, gold,

musteline—whose spectral repletion we know also to be an agony, riding oncoming waves of cold.

The French call the autumn leaf *feuille morte*. When the leaves are finally corrupted by frost they rain down into themselves until the tree, disowning itself, goes bald.

All through autumn we hear a double voice: one says everything is ripe; the other says everything is dying. The paradox is exquisite. We feel what the Japanese call "aware"—an almost untranslatable word meaning something like "beauty tinged with sadness." Some days we have to shoulder against a marauding melancholy. Dreams have a hallucinatory effect: in one, a man who is dying watches from inside a huge cocoon while stud colts run through deep mud, their balls bursting open, their seed spilling onto the black ground. My reading brings me this thought from the mad Zen priest Ikkyu: "Remember that under the skin you fondle lie the bones, waiting to reveal themselves." But another day, I ride in the mountains. Against rimrock, tall aspens have the graceful bearing of giraffes, and another small grove, not yet turned, gives off a virginal limelight that transpierces everything heavy.

Fall is the end of a rancher's year. Third and fourth cuttings of hay are stacked; cattle and sheep are gathered, weaned, and shipped; yearling bulls and horse colts are sold. "We always like this time of year, but it's a lot more fun when the cattle prices are up!" a third-generation rancher tells me.

This week I help round up their cows and calves on the Big Horns. The storm system that brought three feet of snow at the beginning of the month now brings intense and continual rain. Riding for cows resembles a wild game of touch football played on skis: cows and cowboys bang into each other, or else, as the calves run back, the horse just slides. Twice today my buckskin falls with me, crushing my leg against a steep sidehill, but the mud and snow, now trampled into a gruel, is so deep it's almost impossible to get bruised.

When the cattle are finally gathered, we wean the calves from the cows in portable corrals by the road. Here, black mud reaches our shins. The stock dogs have to swim in order to move. Once, while trying to dodge a cow, my feet stuck, and losing both boots in the effort to get out of the way, I had to climb the fence barefooted. Weaning is noisy; cows don't hide their grief. As calves are loaded into semis and stock trucks, their mothers—

five or six hundred of them at a time—crowd around the sorting alleys with outstretched necks, their squared-off faces all opened in a collective bellowing.

On the way home a neighboring rancher who trails his steers down the mountain highway loses one as they ride through town. There's a high-speed chase across lawns and flower beds, around the general store and the fire station. Going at a full lope, the steer ducks behind the fire truck just as Mike tries to rope him. "Missing something?" a friend yells out her window as the second loop sails like a burning hoop to the ground.

"That's nothing," one onlooker remarks. "When we brought our cattle through Kaycee one year, the minister opened the church door to see what all the noise was about and one old cow just ran in past him. He had a hell of a time getting her out."

In the valley, harvest is on but it's soggy. The pinto bean crops are sprouting, and the sugar beets are balled up with mud so that one is indistinguishable from the other. Now I can only think of mud as being sweet. At night the moon makes a brief appearance between storms and laces mud with a confectionary light. Farmers whose last cutting of hay is still on the ground turn windrows to dry as if they were limp, bedridden bodies. The hay that has already been baled is damp, and after four inches of rain (in a county where there's never more than eight inches a year) mold eats its way to the top again.

The morning sky looks like cheese. Its cobalt wheel has been cut down and all the richness of the season is at our feet. The quick-blanch of frost stings autumn's rouge into a skin that is tawny. At dawn, mowed hay meadows are the color of pumpkins, and the willows, leafless now, are pink and silver batons conducting inaudible river music. When I dress for the day, my body, white and suddenly numb, looks like dead coral.

After breakfast there are autumn chores to finish. We grease head gates on irrigation ditches, roll up tarp dams, pull horseshoes, and truck horses to their winter pasture. The harvest moon gives way to the hunter's moon. Elk, deer, and moose hunters repopulate the mountains now that the livestock is gone. One young hunting guide has already been hurt. While he was alone at camp, his horse kicked him in the spleen. Immobilized, he scratched an SOS with the sharp point of a bullet on a piece of leather he cut from his chaps. "Hurt bad. In pain. Bring doctor with painkiller," it read. Then he tied the note to the horse's halter and threw rocks at the horse until it trotted out of camp. When the horse wandered into a ranch yard down the mountain, the note was quickly discovered and a doctor was helicoptered to camp. Amid orgiastic gunfire, sometimes lives are saved.

October lifts over our heads whatever river noise is left. Long carrier waves of clouds seem to emanate from hidden reefs. There's a logjam of them around the mountains, and the horizon appears to drop seven thousand feet. Though the rain has stopped, the road ruts are filled to the brim. I saw a frog jump cheerfully into one of them. Once in a while the mist clears and we can see the dark edge of a canyon or an island of vertical rimrock in the white bulk of snow. Up there, bull elk have been fighting all fall over harems. They charge with antlered heads, scraping the last of the life-giving velvet off, until one bull wins and trots into the private timber to mount his prize, standing almost humanly erect on hind legs while holding a cow elk's hips with his hooves.

In the fall, my life, too, is timbered, an unaccountably libidinous place: damp, overripe, and fading. The sky's congestion allows the eye's iris to open wider. The cornfield in front of me is torn parchment paper, as brittle as bougainvillea leaves whose tropical color has somehow climbed these northern stalks. I zigzag through the rows as if they were city streets. Now I want to lie down in the muddy furrows, under the frictional sawing of stalks, under corncobs which look like erections, and out of whose loose husks sprays of bronze silk dangle down.

Autumn teaches us that fruition is also death; that ripeness is a form of decay. The willows, having stood for so long near water, begin to rust. Leaves are verbs that conjugate the seasons.

Today the sky is a wafer. Placed on my tongue, it is a wholeness that has already disintegrated; placed under the tongue, it makes my heart beat strongly enough to stretch myself over the winter brilliances to come. Now I feel the tenderness to which this season rots. Its defenselessness can no longer be corrupted. Death is its purity, its sweet mud. The string of storms that came across Wyoming like elephants tied tail to trunk falters now and bleeds into a stillness.

There is neither sun, nor wind, nor snow falling. The hunters are gone; snow geese waddle in grainfields. Already, the elk have started moving out of the mountains toward sheltered feed-grounds. Their great antlers will soon fall off like chandeliers shaken from ballroom ceilings. With them the light of these autumn days, bathed in what Tennyson called "a mockery of sunshine," will go completely out.

Gretel Ehrlich

THE SMOOTH
SKULL OF WINTER

Winter looks like a fictional place, an elaborate simplicity, a Nabokovian invention of rarefied detail. Winds howl all night and day, pushing litters of storm fronts from the Beartooth to the Big Horn Mountains. When it lets up, the mountains disappear. The hayfield that runs east from my house ends in a curl of clouds that have fallen like sails luffing from sky to ground. Snow returns across the field to me, and the cows, dusted with white, look like snowcapped continents drifting.

The poet Seamus Heaney said that landscape is sacramental, to be read as text. Earth is instinct: perfect, irrational, semiotic. If I read winter right, it is a scroll—the white growing wider and wider like the sweep of an arm— and from it we gain a peripheral vision, a capacity for what Nabokov calls "those asides of spirit, those footnotes in the volume of life by which we know life and find it to be good."

Not unlike emotional transitions—the loss of a friend or the beginning of new work—the passage of seasons is often so belabored and quixotic as to deserve separate names so the year might be divided eight ways instead of four.

This fall ducks flew across the sky in great "V"s as if that one letter were defecting from the alphabet, and when the songbirds climbed to the memorized pathways that route them to winter quarters, they lifted off in a confusion, like paper scraps blown from my writing room.

A Wyoming winter laminates the earth with white, then hardens the lacquer work with wind. Storms come announced by what old-timers call "mare's tails"—long wisps that lash out from a snow cloud's body. Jack Davis, a packer who used to trail his mules all the way from Wyoming to southern Arizona when the first snows came, said, "The first snowball that hits you is God's fault; the second one is yours."

Every three days or so white pastures glide overhead and drop themselves like skeins of hair to earth. The Chinese call snow that has drifted "white jade mountains," but winter looks oceanic to me. Snow swells, drops back, and hits the hulls of our lives with a course-bending sound. Tides of white are overtaken by tides of blue, and the logs in the woodstove, like sister ships, tick toward oblivion.

On the winter solstice it is thirty-four degrees below zero and there is very little in the way of daylight. The deep ache of this audacious Arctic air is also the ache in our lives made physical. Patches of frostbite show up on our noses, toes, and ears. Skin blisters as if cold were a kind of radiation to which we've been exposed. It strips what is ornamental in us. Part of the ache we feel is also a softness growing. Our connections with neighbors—whether strong or tenuous, as lovers or friends—become too urgent to disregard. We rub the frozen toes of a stranger whose pickup has veered off the road; we open water gaps with a tamping bar and an ax; we splice a friend's frozen water pipe; we take mittens and blankets to the men who herd sheep. Twenty or thirty below makes the breath we exchange visible: all of mine for all of yours. It is the tacit way we express the intimacy no one talks about.

One of our recent winters is sure to make the history books because of not the depth of snow but, rather, the depth of cold. For a month the mercury never rose above zero and at night it was fifty below. Cows and sheep froze in place and an oil field worker who tried taking a shortcut home was found next spring two hundred yards from his back door. To say you were snowed in didn't express the problem. You were either "froze in," "froze up," or "froze out," depending on where your pickup or legs stopped working. The day I helped tend sheep camp we drove through a five-mile tunnel of snow. The herder had marked his location for us by deliberately cutting his finger and writing a big "X" on the ice with his blood.

When it's fifty below, the mercury bottoms out and jiggles there as if laughing at those of us still above ground. Once I caught myself on tiptoes, peering down into the thermometer as if there were an extension inside inscribed with higher and higher declarations of physical misery: ninety below to the power of ten and so on.

Winter sets up curious oppositions in us. Where a wall of snow can seem threatening, it also protects our staggering psyches. All this cold has an anesthetizing effect: the pulse lowers and blankets of snow induce sleep. Though the rancher's workload is lightened in winter because of the short days, the work that does need to be done requires an exhausting patience. And while earth's sudden frigidity can seem to dispossess us, the teamwork on cold nights during calving, for instance, creates a profound camaraderie—one that's laced with dark humor, an effervescent lunacy, and unexpected fits of anger and tears. To offset Wyoming's Arctic seascape, a nightly flush of Northern Lights dances above the Big Horns, irradiating winter's pallor and reminding us that even though at this time of year we veer toward our various nests and seclusions, nature expresses itself as a bright fuse, irrepressible and orgasmic.

Winter is smooth-skulled, and all our skids on black ice are cerebral. When we begin to feel cabin-feverish, the brain pistons thump against bone and mind irrupts—literally invading itself—unable to get fresh air. With the songbirds gone only scavengers are left: magpies, crows, eagles. As they pick on road-killed deer we humans are apt to practice the small cruelties on each other.

We suffer from snow blindness, selecting what we see and feel while our pain whites itself out. But where there is suffocation and self-imposed ignorance, there is also refreshment—snow on flushed cheeks and a pristine kind of thinking. All winter we skate the small ponds—places that in summer are water holes for cattle and sheep—and here a reflection of mind appears, sharp, vigilant, precise. Thoughts, bright as frostfall, skate through our brains. In winter, consciousness looks like an etching.

FARMING

David Mas Masumoto

LEARNING TO FAIL

David Mas Masumoto is a third-generation Japanese-American who grows peaches and grapes on his farm in California. He is a farm activist as well as a freelance writer. In his book *Epitaph for a Peach: Four Seasons on My Family Farm,* Masumoto recounts his attempt to develop a style of farming that eschews the values of industrial agriculture. He adopts organic methods and continues to raise an older type of peach known for its delicious flavor but condemned by merchants for its poor cosmetic value. In this excerpt from that book, he walks through his orchard seeking both answers to practical problems and a revitalized vision of nature. On this family farm begun by his grandfather, his eight-year-old daughter tries to grow her own little garden, and she helps her father learn how to fail. As family past, present, and future intersect with nature, he begins to develop the ability to listen to his farm.

Shovel of Earth

The blade slices into the soil. My muscles tense and push the shovel into the moist ground. Dark and damp, the sweet warm smell of wet earth. The tool eases through a mat of weeds, the ground flush with activity. The metal face slides partially in, the soil is heavy and gently resists. Roots extend deep into an underground tangled mass beyond my sight.

I can't count the thousands of shovelfuls of earth I have moved in my life. But I like to think of the thousands that lie in my future, if I am fortunate.

Spring irrigation brings life to the orchards and vineyards. Peaches ripen and the scent of bloom lingers in the air. The vine buds push and the pale green of fresh growth emerges pure and delicate. My shovel blade pierces the earth again and again. I guide the water into my fields in an act of renewal, a confirmation of one more season.

The work frees my mind. Each shovel of the heavy, dank earth nurtures my soul with meaning about this place. My thoughts wander—to images of work to feed the soil, of harvests to feed the thousands. My labor renews the spirit as fields become invigorated with life.

Another spring unfolds.

Changing Shades of Green

Pat and I walk my farm. We are an odd couple: he's trained as a scientist and an entomologist, I'm a farmer with a degree in sociology and rural studies. We compare what we see on the farm, but what's more important is what we don't see.

I've walked these fields thousands of times, he's entered hundreds of orchards. Oddly, those facts interfere with our perspectives, for we sometimes overlook the obvious. We both agree that walking may be the best management tool for farmers and researchers. Nothing replaces the personal and intimate sensibility of walking a farm, feeling the earth, seeing and smelling an orchard. But it's getting harder and harder to walk. Walking takes precious time, we can't cover a lot of ground, and first we have to break old habits and relearn the very act of walking.

I remember watching my children take their first steps. Walking was far more than a physiological task of muscle control and balance; it was driven by something inside, a motivation to explore. Adults often think of walking as merely a function of getting from one place to another, the start and finish is all that matters. But for children, a new dimension bursts open when they start walking, a new world of motion, of adventure, of discovery. They see a new world when they learn to walk.

Pat and I try to re-create our first steps into an orchard and see what's really in front of us, to capture the magical innocence of children and their endless curiosity about a new world. We wander through familiar workplaces with no questions in mind, attempting to walk without a destination.

"It's slow," I warn Pat.

"Almost painful," he adds.

As we leave the farmhouse porch and head toward the Sun Crest peaches, we agree to think out loud and share observations. Pat comments about my small five- and ten-acre blocks of vineyards, with dirt avenues dividing the fields. My equally small parcels of peach trees rise above the vines and break the horizon line. Other farms have been replanted in large forty- or eighty-acre sections, solid blocks of vines and trees. We both try to envision my farm from the sky, I imagine it looks like a patchwork quilt with a green appliqué.

"Think my small field size makes a difference?" I ask.

"It might," he says.

We allow ourselves to explore the topic. I can see him thinking of the possibilities: the advantages of mixed habitat for beneficial insects, the rich diversity of species, the problems of monocropping and the spread of pathogens or pests. I interrupt his mental calculations. "Small fields mean if I screw up in one, I only mess up a little." We smile. It's so easy to get too technical about this farming game.

We approach the Sun Crest orchard, and I focus on the weakest tree. Daily I pass this spot and am reminded of its frail condition. "I can't figure out what's the matter with that tree. It just doesn't like me," I comment.

"What tree?" Pat says and grins.

Pat slowly pans the entire field. Then he crouches to peer down a row. I join him. "Ever notice the changing shades of green?" he says.

I think of Paul, a farmer and oil painter friend. He enjoys experimenting with green, capturing the subtle nuances of a fresh leaf or the thriving growth of mid-spring or the weak yellow green of a cover crop on bad soil. When a group of us visit Paul's house, the farmers tend to gather around certain paintings. Paul knows his paintings work when we gravitate toward a few, attracted by the colors, and begin talking about his greens. The true green of a field has depth, like the mysterious colors of a clear but deep lake. Each shade has meaning we all interpret differently. Paul says farmers are his best art critics, we know of more greens than anyone else.

Pat and I enter the field. Sounds envelop us, birds call and sing, insects buzz and flutter. Each step sounds distinct. Underfoot lies a rough collection of stalks and stems, sticks and twigs, leaves and wildflowers. Diversity dwells in my fields.

We both experiment with the mechanics of walking and looking. I crouch low, feeling like an imitation Native American in my desperate effort to be one with nature. I try listening to my footsteps and establish a deliberate, methodical cadence that forces me to go slower. It's uncomfortable. I compare it to riding in a car with someone who drives with excruciating caution.

I hear myself breathing and discover a type of efficiency in movement. With a slow, patient stride, I can check the vigor of the cover crop, the dryness of the soil, the health of the leaves. I begin to notice the slumping peach shoots where a worm has struck, the different shades of green where mites establish their home. Instead of making three or four different checks of a field for specific pests or problems, I find I can get an impression of the whole orchard in one visit. This means decisions will be easier to make.

I turn to ask my companion how he's doing. I discover he's on the other side of the field. He looks dazed, without direction, almost expressionless, and I realize I must appear exactly the same.

I try to move even more slowly, turning my head from left to right, right to left, consciously panning the orchard. After a while my method seems to work, I begin to see hints of color I had overlooked. The younger limbs, perhaps only a few years old, push vibrant green shoots, the hue is light, and the surface appears shiny. Growth on the old thick branches seems darker and duller. Then I realize that the two sets of leaves are not the same age. The green on the established branches is maturer, with longer, more developed shoots, while not only do the young limbs have newer shoots but the nodes are closer together. The vibrant green may be a result of denser growth.

I'm not sure this makes a difference, but I do know that, on the same tree, peaches from old branches will ripen days earlier than those on younger limbs. Dad claims that old-growth peaches taste sweeter, but I've always thought he had an affinity for the old wood.

Tiny peaches cling to the slender limbs, and I catch myself envisioning them a few months from now at harvesttime. Two or three old branches do not look right, and I sense they may die before harvest. My conclusion is based only on a hunch that comes from having worked with these trees for decades. The trees provide subtle clues in a grand mystery that can alternately frustrate and torment or amaze and initiate.

I hear steps behind me. Pat is smiling. "We're getting the hang of it," he says, breaking the spell.

We continue to walk in silence. Then he turns.

"I'm sorry but I just can't help it." He pulls out a small hand lens dangling around his neck. "I've been trained as an entomologist for too long. I have to revert to my old ways." I give my approval, thankful he doesn't ask what I was just thinking. My thoughts have wandered too. I am calculating how many boxes of fruit I can pull from this orchard and what the different pricing schemes and potential profit margins will be this year.

He drops to the ground and examines some drying cover crop leaves. "They're full of mites," he announces.

A knot instantly forms in my stomach. Immediately I think of the damage mites can cause and what I could spray to control them. Old habits are hard to break.

"But I've never seen this species in a peach tree."

I relax, embarrassed by my reaction. I look through his lens, don't recognize the little spiderlike creatures, and am happy they would rather stay in the clover. We both walk out of the orchard with the knowledge that the peach crop will probably be fine. Should we become too confident, nature will put a stop to our foolishness. In the meantime, it's wonderful to feel satisfied without knowing or even caring exactly why.

Five Worms

"Five worms."

I ask Pat to repeat.

"Five worms, I found five worms in your peaches." Pat has just finished one of his weekly data-gathering searches at my farm.

"What kind of worms?"

His voice is calm. "OFM. Oriental fruit moth."

That's not what I mean. I want to know the size of the worms, their color, and are they eating leaves or peaches? I ask, "Are the worms ugly?"

He pauses and I try to collect my thoughts. Then he says, "I'm not as familiar with OFM," and tries to comfort the shaken farmer by adding, "The peach twig borer populations are low, real low."

My eyes grow wide and I stare blankly out toward my fields. I mumble "Five worms" to myself.

I drive out to the field and Pat follows in his truck. The green peaches are growing fat, the size of Christmas decorations. The leaves flutter in a breeze like thousands of baby bird wings. Nervous anxiety builds and I start to search for worms, but I stop. I have no idea where to look.

Pat sits in his truck, procrastinating with a data log before joining me in the field. I plunge into a dozen questions. "What do OFM larvae look like at this time of year? They aren't after my green peaches yet, are they? Do other farmers have an outbreak?" I end with my most important one: "Pat, how many more worms are there?"

Pat shrugs. "I'm not sure. Like I said, OFM's not my thing. But I did do some reading." He launches into a ten-minute lecture on oriental fruit moth, and I learn more in those few minutes than in all my years on the farm. When five worms munch on your trees, your learning curve accelerates.

Initially I want to quantify the problem, break it down into dollars and cents.

Before, I used to apply a pesticide in winter that took care of all these worm problems. It wasn't expensive, maybe $20 per acre, for which I'd also get a low-stress spring and summer. But my natural-farming attempt is quickly becoming expensive for the nerves.

I ask, "Where did you find the five worms? Does each tree have five worms? Each branch?"

"Oh, no," Pat answers. "I looked at dozens of trees."

I relax a little. Five worms divided by two dozen trees means only a few worms per acre. But this could be the beginning of a new hatch, with only the first wave having emerged.

Pat explains how he found the worms. He inspects each branch for tiny half-inch or smaller worms or any visible signs of their feeding. It requires hours to inspect a dozen trees. "You've never found an OFM?" he asks.

"To tell you the truth, I've never looked," I blurt. "And I doubt if any farmer has ever committed an entire day to searching hundreds of branches for worms. No wonder you found some, looking so damned hard." It occurs to me that I may always have had five worms in my spring orchard and never knew it because no one spent hours obsessed with finding them. I ask again, "So how many worms do you think are out here?"

Pat shrugs again.

I'm not used to that kind of answer. Pesticide salesmen never shrug their shoulders. In fact they would love my situation: five worms, peach crop threatened, worried farmer, instant sales. Farmer paranoia and good sales commissions go hand in hand.

"What do five worms mean?" I mumble out loud. Pat smiles and says that sounds like a Zen master's question. I glare at him and he wanders over to another row of peaches.

The five worms challenge my attempt to farm these peaches differently. Their discovery threatens my organic methods, all the work I've tried this year. I sense a coming crisis of faith, knowing I could spray and kill all the worms in the field but then possibly repeat another ordinary harvest of homeless peaches. I have been hoping my alternative farming practices would become a marketing tool, leverage to get attention for these wonderful-tasting fruits.

But how can I live with nature? By learning to live with five worms and my stress? I realize that for the rest of the season, with the early morning rising sun or at nightfall with the heat lingering in the air, I'll stand on my farmhouse porch thinking about five worms.

I join Pat and we scan a few branches of leaves and green peaches. "Thanks for letting me know about the five worms," I say. He nods. "By the way, what did you do with them?" I grin. "I'd like to see their squashed bodies."

Pat turns to me with wide eyes and a blank look.

Learning to Fail

The farm is never far away from my family. Our produce comes from the work of family. On the Masumoto farm our fruits and garden vegetables have been family food for generations.

My eight-year-old daughter, Nikiko, has witnessed both the successes and the failures of our farm. She has touched and tasted ripening fruits and has watched the power of weather unleashed on the fields. She knows her father is vulnerable to things out of his control. The farm is part of her picture drawing. She watches spring thunderstorms march into our valley and ravage tender green shoots with a downpour of hail. As the first ice balls crash down from the heavens, she sees me stand outside under the darkened sky and cry out, "Stop!" Later she draws a picture of the storm with a farmer wearing a big hat to protect himself.

We plant an annual vegetable garden, and this year Nikiko helps plant some of the seeds and seedlings. But after growing initially, they begin to die.

Nikiko's garden is failing. A virus attacks the fragile squash, causing the leaves to yellow and the delicate growth to wither. Her eggplants glisten from a sticky juice secreted by a herd of aphids with a company of tending ants. A phantom creature even munches on the hardy marigolds, taking huge circular bites out of the dangling leaves.

Daily I monitor the slow death, assessing the new damage, wondering if I should do something drastic. I consider using a garden spray, but when I read the label from the typical hardware store garden dust or pest spray, I realize it would be deadlier than anything I use on the farm. It will kill the aphids along with everything else, not the lesson I would want the garden to convey to my child. I face the same dilemma as I try to find a home for my Sun Crest peaches. If something doesn't work right I have to fight the tendency to find a quick solution.

"It's OK, Dad," Niki explains. "We have other squash plants." Then she quickly gives the napping dog a hug and skips over to the sunning cats for their afternoon tea together.

Nikiko helps me realize the difference between disappointment and losing. Her garden, like farming, teaches me that at times failure is OK.

I've lost raisin crops, peach harvests, whole trees and vines. I've lost money, time, and my labor. I've lost my temper, my patience, and, at times, hope. Most of the time, it's due to things beyond my control, like the weather, market prices, or insects or disease. Even in situations where I believe I am in charge—cover-crop seeding, management of workers, the timing of harvest—I now know I can never really have complete control.

Ironically, the moment I step off my farm I enter a world where it seems that everything, life and nature, is regulated and managed. Homes are built to insulate families from the outside weather. People work in climate-controlled environments designed to reduce the impact of the weather. The government develops bureaucracies and statutes to safeguard against failure and protect us from risk. In America, a lack of control implies failure.

As a kid I was taught that sports is a great training field for life, where you learn about the difference between winning and losing. But you also learn to make excuses to avoid looking like a failure. It's far easier to blame someone or something—a teammate who couldn't catch a fly ball, a lousy referee—than it is to learn to live with losses.

On the farm, the foul lines aren't marked and nature doesn't play by a rule book. There are no winners and losers and the game is never finished. There's always next year and the next harvest, more dark clouds on the horizon or aphids in your child's garden.

I also learned something about failure from my father. One year it began to rain on our raisin crop. A year's worth of work lay on the ground,
exposed and vulnerable to the elements. The rain would soon begin to rot
the harvest. I remember running outside to tell the clouds to go away. I
came back inside and watched my father grow angry too. Restless, we
walked back and forth to the window to check the march of dark clouds
and listened to the *tap-tap-tap* of rain on the roof.

"What can we do?" I blurted out in frustration.

"What *can* you do?" he answered. "Make it stop raining?"

We lost most of the crop that year. We failed. But the grapes grew the
next year and it didn't rain.

When I farm or garden, I learn to fail without winners or losers.

The Furin

A small *fūrin* hangs on our farmhouse porch. Its miniature bell delicately
jingles with the slightest breeze. A long strip of paper captures the air cur-
rents and translates the movement into sound. I can peer out over the fields,
watching the advancing spring season with its green blankets of foliage,
and hear the wind.

Nikiko likes the fragile sounds. The metal chime rings like a whisper,
the voice tiny like a child's. Occasional spring winds in the valley blow
strong enough to snap the outstretched vine canes. Most of the time soft
breezes brush our cheeks with such subtleties that we ignore their presence. A *fūrin* reminds grown-ups what children already sense. Niki says
she hears the wind singing.

I spend the spring battling nature, trying to farm differently, hoping
somehow I am contributing to the quest to save my peach. The more I
struggle, the more the burden seems to weigh. Each new approach gen-
erates more questions; the complexity of working with nature slips into a
growing pattern of chaos.

I remember a Japanese saying about the power of bamboo. Its strength
is not found in a rigid structure that blocks the wind; instead, the stalks
bend with the wind. Their power resides in their very flexibility. I'm working on becoming like bamboo. I've abandoned my attempts to control
and compete with nature, but letting go has been a challenge.

I'm trying to listen to my farm. Before, I had no reason to hear the sounds of nature. The sole strategy of conventional farming seems to be dominance. Now, with each passing week, I venture into fields full of life and change, clinging to a belief in my work and a hope that it's working.

As I recall the past spring from my porch, the ringing of the *fūrin* helps me understand as it flutters in a subtle breeze. For the first time in my life, I see the wind.

Sue Hubbell

From

A COUNTRY YEAR
Living the Questions

Sue Hubbell bases her writing career in farming—not crops but insects. She owns
a honeybee farm in the Ozark Mountains of southeast Missouri and lives part
of the year in Washington, D.C. Her book *A Country Year: Living the Questions*
recounts her life on the bee farm and brought her to national prominence. In
these two selections from *A Country Year,* Hubbell reflects on her involvement
in nature. Cutting trees in her woodlot and intervening in the lives and deaths
of mice, chickens, and snakes involves stepping into life's processes. There she mod-
ifies the natural world, as does every other creature. With attention to the complexity of life's web and a conscious affirmation of responsibility, such active participation in nature becomes a central part of being at home on the earth.

This week I have started cutting my firewood. It should be cut months
ahead of time to let it dry and cure, so that it will burn hot in the winter.
It is June now, and almost too late to be cutting firewood, but during the
spring I was working with the bees from sunup until sundown and didn't
have time. By midday it is stifling back in the woods, so I go out at sun-
rise and cut wood for a few hours, load it into the pickup and bring it
back to stack below the barn.

I like being out there early. The spiders have spun webs to catch night-
flying insects, and as the rising sun slants through the trees, the dewdrops
that line the webs are turned into exquisite, delicate jewels. The woodlot
smells of shade, leaf mold and damp soil. Wild turkey have left fresh bare
spots where they scratched away the leaves looking for beetles and grubs.

My dogs like being there too, and today snuffled excitedly in a hollow at the base of a tree. The beagle shrieked into it, his baying muffled. The squirrel who may have denned in the tree last night temporarily escaped their notice and sat on a low limb eying the two dogs suspiciously, tail twitching. A sunbeam lit up a tall thistle topped with a luxuriant purple blossom from which one butterfly and one honeybee sipped nectar. Red-eyed vireos sang high in the treetops where I could not see them.

For me their song ended when I started the chain saw. It makes a terrible racket, but I am fond of it. It is one of the first tools I learned to master on my own, and it is also important to me. My woodstove, a simple black cast-iron-and-sheet-metal affair, is the only source of heat for my cabin in the winter, and if I do not have firewood to burn in it, the dogs, cat, the houseplants, the water in my pipes and I will all freeze. It is wonderfully simple and direct: cut wood or die.

When Paul was here he cut the firewood and I, like all Ozark wives, carried the cut wood to the pickup. When he left, he left his chain saw, but it was a heavy, vibrating, ill-tempered thing. I weigh a hundred and five pounds, and although I could lift it, once I had it running it shook my hands so much that it became impossibly dangerous to use. One year I hired a man to cut my wood, but I was not pleased with the job he did, and so the next year, although I could not afford it, I bought the finest, lightest, best-made chain saw money could buy. It is a brand that many woodcutters use, and has an antivibration device built into even its smaller models.

The best chain saws are formidable and dangerous tools. My brother nearly cut off his arm with one. A neighbor who earns his living in timber just managed to kill the engine on his when he was cutting overhead and a branch snapped the saw back toward him. The chain did not stop running until it had cut through the beak of his cap. He was very solemn when I told him that I had bought my own chain saw, and he gave me a good piece of advice. "The time to worry about a chain saw," he said, "is when you stop being afraid of it."

I am cautious. I spend a lot of time sizing up a tree before I fell it. Once it is down, I clear away the surrounding brush before I start cutting it into lengths. That way I will not trip and lose my balance with the saw running. A dull chain and a poorly running saw are dangerous, so I've learned to keep mine in good shape and I sharpen the chain each time I use it.

This morning I finished sawing up a tree from the place where I had been cutting for the past week. In the process I lost, in the fallen leaves somewhere, my scrench—part screwdriver, part wrench—that I use to make adjustments on the saw. I shouldn't have been carrying it in my pocket, but the chain on the saw's bar had been loose; I had tightened it and had not walked back to the pickup to put it away. Scolding myself for being so careless, I began looking for another tree to cut, but stopped to watch a fawn that I had frightened from his night's sleeping place. He was young and his coat was still spotted, but he ran so quickly and silently that the two dogs, still sniffing after the squirrel, never saw him.

I like to cut the dead trees from my woodlot, leaving the ones still alive to flourish, and I noticed a big one that had recently died. This one was bigger than I feel comfortable about felling. I've been cutting my own firewood for six years now, but I am still awed by the size and weight of a tree as it crashes to the ground, and I have to nerve myself to cut the really big ones.

I wanted this tree to fall on a stretch of open ground that was free of other trees and brush, so I cut a wedge-shaped notch on that side of it. The theory is that the tree, thus weakened, will fall slowly in the direction of the notch when the serious cut, slightly above the notch on the other side, is made. The trouble is that trees, particularly dead ones that may have rot on the inside, do not know the theory and may fall in an unexpected direction. That is the way accidents happen. I was aware of this, and scared, besides, to be cutting down such a big tree; as a result, perhaps I cut too timid a wedge. I started sawing through on the other side, keeping an eye on the tree top to detect the characteristic tremble that signals a fall. I did not have time to jam the plastic wedge in my back pocket into the cut to hold it open because the tree began to fall in my direction, exactly opposite where I had intended. I killed the engine on the saw and jumped out of the way.

There was no danger, however. Directly in back of where I had been standing were a number of other trees, which was why I had wanted to have the sawed one fall in the opposite direction; as my big tree started to topple, its upper branches snagged in another one, and it fell no further. I had sawed completely through the tree, but now the butt end had trapped my saw against the stump. I had cut what is descriptively called a "widow maker." If I had been cutting with someone else, we could have used a second saw to cut out mine and perhaps brought down the tree, but this is dangerous and I don't like to do it. I could not even free my saw by taking it apart, for I had lost my scrench, so I drove back to the barn and gathered up the tools I needed; a socket wrench, chains and a portable winch known as come-along. A come-along is a cheery, sensible tool for a woman. It has a big hook at one end and another hook connected to a steel cable at the other. The cable is wound around a ratchet gear operated by a long handle to give leverage. It divides a heavy job up into small manageable bits that require no more than female strength, and I have used it many times to pull my pickup free from mud and snow.

The day was warming up and I was sweating by the time I got back to the woods, but I was determined to repair the botch I had made of the morning's woodcutting. Using the socket wrench, I removed the bar and chain from the saw's body and set it aside. The weight of the saw gone, I worked free the bar and chain pinched under the butt of the tree. Then I sat down on the ground, drank ice water from my thermos and figured out how I was going to pull down the tree.

Looking at the widow maker, I decided that if I could wind one of the chains around the butt of it, and another chain around a nearby standing tree, then connect the two with the come-along, I might be able to winch the tree to the ground. I attached the chains and come-along appropriately and began. Slowly, with each pump of the handle against the ratchet gear, the tree sank to the ground.

The sun was high in the sky, the heat oppressive and my shirt and jeans were soaked with sweat, so I decided to leave the job of cutting up the tree until tomorrow. I gathered my tools together, and in the process found the scrench, almost hidden in the leaf mold. Then I threw all the tools into the back of the pickup, and sat on the tailgate to finish off the rest of the ice water and listen to the red-eyed vireo singing.

It is satisfying, of course, to build up a supply of winter warmth, free except for the labor. But there is also something heady about becoming a part of the forest process. It sounds straightforward enough to say that when I cut firewood I cull and thin my woods, but that puts me in the business of deciding which trees should be encouraged and which should be taken.

I like my great tall black walnut, so I have cut the trees around it to give it the space and light it needs to grow generously. Dogwoods don't care.

They frost the woods with white blossoms in the spring, and grow extravagantly in close company. If I clear a patch, within a year or two pine seedlings move in, grow up exuberantly, compete and thin themselves to tolerable spacing. If I don't cut a diseased tree, its neighbors may sicken and die. If I cut away one half of a forked white oak, the remaining trunk will grow straight and sturdy. Sap gone, a standing dead tree like the one I cut today will make good firewood, and so invites cutting. But if I leave it, it will make a home for woodpeckers, and later for flying squirrels and screech owls. Where I leave a brush pile of top branches, rabbits make a home. If I leave a fallen tree, others will benefit: ants, spiders, beetles and wood roaches will use it for shelter and food, and lovely delicate fungi will grow out of it before it mixes with leaf mold to become a part of a new layer of soil.

One person with a chain saw makes a difference in the woods, and by making a difference becomes part of the woodland cycle, a part of the abstraction that is the forest community.

Snakes again. Black rat snakes this time. I can't tell one five-foot black rat snake from another, so I don't know if the one that has been showing up in the chicken coop each and every Friday all summer long is the same individual or not, but I rather think he is. My theory is that a week is the time it takes him to digest his meal of mice and an occasional egg. This is theory only, for none of my books tell me when mealtime is for five-foot black rat snakes; it is something I must ask my herpetologist friend the next time I see him.

Black rat snakes are some of the largest common snakes found around here. I estimate the one in the chicken coop to be five feet, but they can grow six feet or more. They are shiny black as adults, but patterned strikingly with brownish and blackish markings when they are young. The vaguest hint of blotchings can sometimes be seen on adults, and this gives them their scientific name, *Elaphe obsoleta obsoleta*. *Elaphe* allies them with their kind, the other rat and corn snakes, and *obsoleta* is a term used in biology to mean indistinct. Their common name hints at their diet.

I have named this one Friday.

Far be it from me to wish a mouse ill, but the mice were rather out of hand in the chicken coop this spring, eating so much of the chopped corn put out for the chickens that I was keeping more mice than chickens. The trouble was that I was fresh out of cats, my pair of barn cats having died within months of each other last winter after fifteen and seventeen years of full and inscrutable lives. Late in the spring, I adopted a kitten, but he had some growing to do before he became a mouser; in the meantime, the mice, unchecked, multiplied rapidly until they became a bold nuisance to me and the chickens.

So I was pleased when I saw the first black rat snake in the spring. There were mice in the barn, mice in the chicken coop, and soon there were black rat snakes of all sizes everywhere. One of the reasons I think Friday must be the same snake is that he has grown self-assured in his sense of possession of the chicken coop, where he soon had the mouse population reduced to tolerable levels. His species can be fierce and will bite if attacked, but Friday seems to understand that I do not intend to hurt him and he ignores me. The day that I found him coiled up in a nest, the three eggs he had swallowed clearly apparent in his midsection, he looked at me calmly; he was too lumpy to slither away quickly. Last Friday, when I went out to gather the eggs, he was in the coop again. The day was a hot one, and the two-inch-wide circle of water at the base of the chicken-watering fountain had enticed him to try a bit of a bath. He looked me square in the eye as I stood laughing at him. No supposed serpentine dignity could keep him from being anything but ridiculous as he tried to loop and jam his entire five-foot length into the small circle of available water.

Black rat snakes also feed on birds, and in deference to their tastes I brood the dozen pullets I buy each spring in the cabin. I keep them under an electric light in a refrigerator carton near the wood stove. Their downy softness is a delight for a week or so, but they grow gawky rapidly, and stupidly peck one another if they do not have enough space. Their sawdust litter needs constant replenishing; they are untidy with their feed and water, and I soon grow weary of them as roommates. One spring I put them out too soon and the next morning found a dead pullet, too big for a black rat snake to swallow, but small enough for it to kill. They kill animals that size by constriction, and the snake's spiral grip was clearly printed on the pullet's strangely elongated corpse. Now I keep the pullets in the cabin until they are too big to be a snake's prey.

Another time I was able to save a pair of baby phoebes from a black rat snake. The parent birds had built their nest just under the eaves of the honey house, and I had been watching them off and on all spring through the window. The two eggs had hatched, and there were two fledglings in the nest when I was working in the honey house one day and heard a terrible ruckus outside. The parent birds were in a nearby persimmon tree crying out in distress. A black rat snake, like the good climber his breed is, had slithered up the side of the honey house and was looped around the nest calmly swallowing the two baby birds. I ran outside, grabbed the snake by the tail and shook him hard. The baby birds dropped from his mouth, wet but undigested. I threw the snake as far as I could, scooped up the babies and put them back in the nest. The parent birds remained in a state of ineffectual confusion all day, alternately repelled by and drawn to their offspring. At nightfall they finally returned, and the pair of young phoebes lived to fly from the nest on their own.

And there we are, with my meddling, back to the human responsible for putting a flock of chickens in prime mouse habitat, setting the process in motion in the first place. I like to think of it as a circle. If I take one step out of the center, I find myself a part of that circle—a circle made of chickens, chopped corn, mice, snakes, phoebes, me, and back to the chickens again, a tidy diagram that only hints at the complexity of the whole. For each of us is a part of other figures, too, the resulting interconnecting whole faceted, weblike, subtle, flexible, fragile. As a human being I am a great meddler; I fiddle, alter, modify. This is neither good nor bad, merely human, in the same way that the snake who eats mice and phoebes is merely serpentish. But being human I have the kind of mind which can recognize that when I fiddle and twitch any part of the circle there are reverberations throughout the whole.

LIVING BETWEEN
CITY AND COUNTRY

Rick Bass

ON WILLOW CREEK

Rick Bass was raised in Texas and now lives with his family in Yaak Valley in northwestern Montana. He is a prolific nature writer whose books include *Wild to the Heart*. In his essays, as well as in more direct political efforts, he has fought hard for the preservation of wilderness and endangered species. Bass's writing is often characterized by an easy, conversational style and an evocation of human camaraderie tinged with good humor—qualities that emerge out of his family's storytelling tradition. In this selection, he discusses his family's ties to the hill country of Texas. He grew up in between city and country, playing in remnant wilderness areas near housing developments. His father drove to Houston for work, but he and other men in the family also would drive to deer country to hunt. Bass emphasizes the deep tie between nature and language, between the sense of family and the experience of the land. Nature is an active force working on those who feel an allegiance to it.

I don't know how to start, but perhaps that's no matter. I am only thirty-five years old, and the land is over a billion; how can I be expected to know what to say beyond "Please" and "Thank you" and "Ma'am"? The language of the hill country of Texas, or of any sacred place, is not the language of pen on paper, or even of the human voice. It is the language of water cutting down through the country's humped chest of granite, cutting down to the heart and soul of the earth, down to a thing that lies far below and beyond our memory.

Being frail and human, however, memory is all we have to work with. I have to believe that somewhere out there is a point where my language—memory—will intersect with the hill country's language: the scent of cedar, the feel of morning mist, the blood of deer, glint of moon, shimmering heat, crackle of ice, mountain lions, scorpions, centipedes, rattlesnakes, and cactus. The cool dark oaks and gold-leaved hickories along the creeks; the language of the hill country seems always to return to water. Along the creeks is where most of the wildlife is found. It is along a creek that the men in my family built a hunting cabin sixty years ago. We have lived in Texas for a hundred and twenty years, and the men in my family have always hunted deer—hunting them in Tennessee before that, and Mississippi, and perhaps all the way back to the dawn of man, to the first hunter—perhaps that link across the generations is completely unbroken, one of the few unfragmented systems remaining in this century—*The Basses hunt deer*—a small thing, but still whole and intact.

It is only for the last sixty years, however, that we've hunted deer—once a year, in November—on this thousand acres deep in the hill country.

Sixty years. The land changes so much more slowly than we do. We race across it, gathering it all in—the scents, the sounds, the feel of that thousand acres. Granddaddy's gone, now; Uncle Horace, John Dallas, Howard, gone too: already I've lived long enough to see these men in my family cross that intersection where they finally learn and embrace the real language of the earth—the language of granite, and history—leaving us, the survivors, behind, still speaking of them in terms of memory.

We have not yet quite caught up with the billion-year-old land we love and which harbors us, but as we get older, we're beginning to learn a word or two, and beginning to see (especially as we have children) how our own lives start to cut knifelike down through all that granite, the stone hump of the hill country, until we are like rivers and creeks ourselves, and we reach the end and the bottom, and *then* we understand . . .

Water. The cities and towns to the south and east of the hill country— Austin, San Antonio, Houston, La Grange, Uvalde, Goliad—I could chart them all, thousands of them, for they are all my home—these towns, these cities, and these people drink from the heart of the hill country. The water in their bodies is the water that has come from beneath the hills, from the mystical two-hundred-mile-long underground river called the Edwards Aquifer. The water is gathered in the hill country by the forces of nature, percolates down through the hills and mountains and flows south, underground, toward the ocean.

That water which we don't drink or pump onto our crops or give to our livestock—that tiny part which eludes us—continues on to the Gulf

Coast, into the bays and estuaries, where delicate moisture contents, delicate salinities are maintained for the birds, shrimp, and other coastal inhabitants that at first glance seem to be far away from and unrelated to the inland mountains.

A scientist will tell you that it's all connected—that if you live in Texas you must protect the honor and integrity of that country's core, for you are tied to it, it is as much a part of you as family—but if you are a child and given to daydreaming and wondering, I believe that you'll understand this by instinct. You don't need proof that the water moving through those shady creeks up in the wild hills and mountains is the same that later moves through your body. You can instead stand outside—even in the city, even in such a place as Houston, and look north with the wind in your face (or with a salt breeze at your back, carrying your essence back to the hill country like an offering), and you can feel the tremble and shimmer of that magic underground river, the yearning and timelessness of it, just beneath your seven-year-old feet. You can *know* of the allegiance you owe it, can sense this in a way that not even the scientists know. It is more like the way when you are in your mother's arms, or your grandmother's, that you know it's all tied together, and that someday you are going to understand it all.

Of course that's the point of this story, that I was one of those children, and that I am here to say thank you to the country in which I was birthed, and to ask "please" that the last good part of it not be divided into halves and then quarters and then eighths, and on, then, further divided into the invisibility of neglect or dishonor . . .

The men would go north in the fall—my father and his brother Jimmy, driving up to the hill country from Houston, while Granddaddy—only barely a granddaddy then, which now seems unimaginable—came down from Fort Worth.

They would meet up in the high hills and low mountains, in the center of the state. I'd stand there on the back porch in Houston with my mother and watch them drive off—it would often be raining, and I'd step out into the rain to feel it on my face—and I'd know that they were going to a place of wildness, a place where they came from. I'd know it was an act of honor, of ritual, of integrity. I was that boy, and knew these things, but did not seriously believe that I would ever be old enough to go in the fall myself.

Instead, I sought out those woods I could reach. We lived out near the west edge of Houston, near what is now the Beltway, a few hundred yards from the slow curls of Buffalo Bayou. While the men in my family went up into the hill country (and at all other times of the year), I would spend my time in the tiny de facto wilderness between outlying subdivisions. Back in those still-undeveloped woods was a stagnating swamp, an old oxbow cut off from the rest of the bayou; you had to almost get lost to find it. I called it "Hidden Lake," and I would wade out into the swamp and seine for minnows, crawdads, mud puppies, and polliwogs with a soup strainer. In those woods, not a mile from the Houston city limits, I saw turtles, bats, skunks, snakes, raccoons, deer, flying squirrels, rabbits, and armadillos. There were bamboo thickets too, and of course the bayou itself, with giant alligator gars floating in patches of sunlit chocolate water, and Spanish moss hanging back in the old forest, and wild violets growing along the bayou's banks. A lot of wildness can exist in a small place, if it is the right kind of country: a good country.

That country was of course too rich to last. The thick oaks fell to the saws, as did the dense giant hickories and the sun-towering, wind-murmuring pines. It's all concrete now; even the banks of the bayou have been channeled with cement. I remember my shock of finding the first survey stakes, out in the grasslands (where once there had been buffalo) leading into those big woods along the bayou's rich edge. I remember asking my mother if the survey stakes meant someone was going to build a house out there—a cabin, perhaps. When told that a road was coming, I pulled the stakes up, but the road came anyway, and then the office buildings, and the highway, and the subdivisions.

The men would come back from the woods after a week. They would have bounty with them—a deer strapped to the hood of the car, heavy with antlers (in those days people in the city did not have trucks), or a wild turkey. A pocket of blackjack acorns; a piece of granite. An old rusting wolf trap found while out walking; an arrowhead. A piece of iron ore, red as rubies. A quartz boulder for my mother's garden. And always, they brought back stories: more stories, it seemed, than you could ever tell.

Sometimes my father or uncle would have something new about him— something that I had not seen when he'd left. A cut in the webbing of his hand from where he'd been cleaning the deer. Or a light in his eyes, a kind of *easiness*. A smell of woodsmoke. Beard stubble, sometimes. These were men who had moved to the city and taken city jobs, who drove to work every morning wearing a suit, but they came back from the hill country with the beginnings of beards. There was always something different about them. The woods had marked them.

Because my parents could see that I had an instinctive draw to the animal world—to be more frank, because they could see that I was aflame with the wild—they did their best to keep me nourished, there in the city. My mother took me to the zoo every week, where I'd spend hours looking at the animals with a joy and an excitement, looking at exhibits which would now crush me with sadness. We went to the Museum of Natural History every Saturday. I heard lectures on jumping spiders and wolf spiders. I breathed window fog against the aquarium panes as I watched the giant soft-shelled turtles paddle slowly through their underwater eerie green light. I bought a little rock sample of magnetite from the gift shop. The little placard that came with the magnetite said it had come from Llano County, Texas. That was one of the two counties my father and uncle and grandfather hunted (the thousand acres straddled Llano and Gillespie counties). This only fueled the fire of my love for a country I had not even seen—a country I could feel in my heart, however, and could feel in my hands, all the way to the tips of my fingers: a country whose energy, whose shimmering life-force, resonated all the way out into the plains, down into the flatlands.

All that sweet water, just beneath our feet. But only so much of it: not inexhaustible. We couldn't, or weren't supposed to, take more than was given to us. That was one of the rules of the system. My father, and the other men who hunted it, understood about this system, and other such systems; for them, the land—like our family itself—was a continuum. Each year, each step hiked across those steep slickrock hills cut down deeper into the rocks, deeper into memory, gave them more stories, more knowledge, and at the same time, took them ever closer to the mystery that lay at the base of it.

I'd grip that rough glittering magnetite like a talisman, would put my fingers to it and try to feel how it was different from other rocks—would try to feel the pull, the affinity it had for things made of iron. I'd hold it up to my arms and try to feel if it stirred my blood, and I believed that I *could* feel it . . .

I'd fall asleep listening to the murmur of the baseball game on the radio with the rock stuck magically to the iron frame of my bed. In the morning I would sometimes take the rock and place it up against my father's compass. I'd watch as the needle always followed the magnetite, and I felt my heart, and everything else inside me, swing with that compass needle, too.

When we run out of country, we will run out of stories.

When we run out of stories, we will run out of sanity.

We will not be able to depend on each other for anything—not for friendship or mercy, and certainly not for love or understanding.

Of course we shouldn't protect a wild core such as the Texas hill country because it is a system still intact with the logic and sanity that these days too often eludes our lives in the cities. We should instead protect the hill country simply for its own sake, to show that we are still capable of understanding (and practicing) the concept of honor: loving a thing the way it is, and trying, for once, not to change it.

I like to think that in the sixty years we've been hunting and camping on that rough, hidden thousand acres—through which Willow Creek cuts, flows, forks, and twists, with murmuring little waterfalls over one- and two-foot ledges, the water sparkling—that we have not changed the humped land one bit.

I know that it has changed us. My grandfather hunted that country, as have his sons, and now we, my brothers and cousins, hunt it with them, and in the spring, we now bring our young children into the country to show them the part, the huge part, that is not hunting (and yet which for us is all inseparable from the hunting): the fields of bluebonnets and crimson paintbrushes, the baby raccoons, the quail, the zone-tail hawks and buzzards circling Hudson Mountain, the pink capitol domes of granite rising all through the land as if once here lived a civilization even more ancient than our parents, grandparents, and great-grandparents.

A continuous thing is so rare these days, when fragmentation seems more than ever to be the rule. I remember the first time I walked with my daughter on the thousand acres, on the land our family calls the "deer pasture." The loose disintegrating granite chat crunched under her tiny tennis shoes and she gripped my finger tight to keep from falling, and the sound of that gravel underfoot (the pink mountains being worn away, along with our bodies) was a sound I'd heard all my life at the deer pasture, but this time, this first time with my daughter gripping my finger and looking down at the loose pink gravel that was making that sound, it affected me so strongly that I felt faint, felt so light that I thought I might take flight . . .

A country, a landscape, can be sacred in an infinite number of ways. The quartz boulders in my mother's garden: my father brought her one each year, and I thought, and still think, it was one of the most romantic things I'd seen, that even while he was in the midst of wildness that one week each year, he was still thinking of her.

Other families had store-bought Doug fir or blue spruce trees for Christmas; we had the spindly strange mountain juniper ("cedar") from the deer pasture. Even though we lived to the south, we were still connected to that wild core, and these rituals and traditions were important to us, so fiercely felt and believed in that one might even call them a form of worship. We were raised Protestants, but in our hearts' and bodies' innocence were cutting a very fine line, tightroping along the mystical edge of pantheism. When Granddaddy was dying, just this side of his ninetieth year, and we went to see him in the hospital room in Fort Worth, I took a handful of arrowhead fragments from the deer pasture and put them under his bed. It seemed inconceivable to me that he not die as he had lived, always in some kind of contact with that wildness, and the specificity of that thousand acres.

When Mom was sick—small, young, and beautiful, the strongest and best patient the doctors had ever had, they all said—and she was sick a long time, living for years solely on the fire and passion within, long after the marrow had left her bones and the doctors could not bring it back, and when she still never had anything other than a smile for each day—my father and brothers and I would take turns bringing her flowers from the deer pasture.

One of us would walk in through the door with that vase from the wild. There would be store-bought flowers, too, but those splashes of reds, yellows, and blues, from lands she'd walked, lands she knew, are what lit up her face the most. The specificity of our lives together, and of our love: those colors said it as well as the land can say anything—which is to say, perfectly. Indian paintbrushes. Bluebonnets. Liatris. Shooting stars. I'm certain those flowers helped her as much as did our platelets, the very blood and iron of ourselves, which we also shared with her. She really loved wildflowers, and she really loved the hill and brush country of Texas, and she really *loved us.*

My mother loved to drink iced tea. Sometimes she and my father and brothers and I would go up to the deer pasture in the dead sullen heat of summer, in the shimmering brightness. We'd ride around in the jeep wearing straw hats. We'd get out and walk down the creek, to the rock slide: a stream-polished half-dome of pink granite with a sheet of water trickling over it, a twenty-foot slide into the plunge pool below, with cool clear water six feet deep, and a mud turtle (his face striped yellow, as if with war paint) and two big Midland soft-shelled turtles living in that pond. An osprey nest, huge branches and sticks, rested up in the dead cottonwood at the pool's edge.

My brothers and I would slide down that half-dome and into the pool again and again. A hundred degrees, in the summer, and we'd go up and down that algae-slick rock like otters. We'd chase the turtles, would hold our breath and swim after them, paddling underwater in that lucid water, while our parents sat up in the rocks above and watched. What a gift it is, to see one's children happy, and engaged in the world, loving it.

We'd walk farther down the creek, then: a family. Fuller. My mother would finish her tea; would rattle the ice cubes in her plastic cup. She'd crunch the ice cubes, in that heat. She always drank her tea with a sprig of mint in it. At some point on one of our walks she must have tossed her ice cubes and mint sprig out, because now there are two little mint fields along the creek: one by the camp house, and one down at the water gap. I like to sit in the rocks above those little mint patches for hours, and look, and listen, and smell, and think. I feel the sun dappling on my arms, and watch the small birds flying around in the old oak and cedar along the creek. Goshawks courting, in April, and wild turkeys gobbling. I like to sit there above the mint fields and feel my soul cutting down through that bedrock. It's happening fast. I too am becoming the earth.

Seen from below as it drifts high in the hot blue sky, a zonetail hawk looks just like the vultures it floats with, save for its yellow legs. (Vultures' legs are gray.) The zonetail's prey will glance up, study the vultures for a moment, and then resume nibbling grass. Then the zonetail will drop from that flock of vultures like a bowling ball.

Afterwards, if there is anything left of the prey, perhaps the vultures can share in the kill.

Golden-cheeked warblers come up into this country from Mexico, endangered, exotic blazes of color who have chosen to grace the hill country with their nests in the spring. They place their hopes for the future, for survival, deep in the cool shade of the old-growth cedars, in only the oldest cedars whose bark peels off in tatters and wisps like feathers, the feathery old bark which the warblers must have to build their nests. But as the old-growth cedar is cut to make way for more and more rangeland, the brown cowbird, a drab bully that follows the heavy ways of cattle, lays its eggs in the warblers' delicate nests and then flees, leaving the warbler mother with these extra eggs to take care of. The cowbird nestlings are larger, and they outclamor the warbler babies for food, and push the beautiful gold-cheeked warbler babies out of the nest.

Why must the ways of man, and the things associated with man, be so clumsy? Can't we relearn grace (and all the other things that follow from that: mercy, love, friendship, understanding) by studying the honor and integrity of a system, one of the last systems, that's still intact? Why must we bring our cowbirds with us, everywhere we go? Must we break everything that is special to us, or sacred—unknown, and holy—into halves, and then fourths, and then eighths?

What happens to us when all the sacred, all the *whole* is gone—when there is no more whole? There will be only fragments of stories, fragments of culture, fragments of integrity. Even a child standing on the porch in Houston with the rain in his face can look north and know that it is all tied together, that we are the warblers, we are the zonetails, we are the underground river: that it is all holy, and that some of it should not be allowed to disappear, as has so much, and so many of us, already.

Sycamores grow by running water; cottonwoods grow by still water. If we know the simple mysteries, then think of all the complex mysteries that lie just beneath us, buried in the bedrock: the bedrock we have been entrusted with protecting. How could we dare do anything other than protect and honor this last core, the land from which we came, the land that has marked us, and whose essence, whose mystery, contains our own essence and mystery? How can we *conceive* of severing that last connection? Surely all internal fire, all passion, would vanish.

Stories. On my Uncle Jimmy's left calf, there is a scar from where the wild pigs caught him one night. He and my father were coming back to camp after dark when they got between a sow and boar and their piglets. The piglets squealed in fright, which ignited the rage of the sow and boar. My father went up one tree and Uncle Jimmy up another, but the boar caught Jimmy with his tusk, cut the muscle clean to the bone.

Back in camp, Granddaddy and John Dallas and Howard and old Mr. Brooks (there for dominoes, that night) heard all the yelling, as did their dogs. The men came running with hounds and lanterns, globes of light swinging crazily through the woods. They stumbled into the middle of the pigs, too. My father and Uncle Jimmy were up in the tops of small trees like raccoons. There were pigs everywhere, pigs and dogs fighting, men dropping their lanterns and climbing trees . . . That one sow and boar could have held an entire *town* at bay. They ran the dogs off and kept the men treed there in the darkness for over an hour, Uncle Jimmy's pants leg wet with blood, and fireflies blinking down on the creek below, and the boar's angry grunts, the sow's furious snufflings below, and the frightened murmurs and squeals of the little pigs. The logic of that system was inescapable: *don't get between a sow and boar and their young.*

The land, and our stories, have marked us.

My father and I are geologists. Uncle Jimmy and his two youngest sons manufacture steel pipe and sell it for use in drilling down through bedrock in search of oil, gas, and water. Our hunting cabin is made of stone. We have a penchant for building stone walls. Our very lives are a metaphor for embracing the earth: for gripping boulders and lifting them to our chest and stacking them and building a life in and around and among the country's heart. I've sat in those same boulders on the east side and watched a mother bobcat and her two kittens come down to the creek to drink. There used to be an occasional jaguar in this part of the world, traveling up from Mexico, but that was almost a hundred years ago. Granddaddy would be ninety this October. He and the old guy we leased from, Howard, were born in the same year, 1903, which was the number we used for the lock combination on the last gate leading into the property. It's one of the last places in the world that still makes sense to me. It is the place of my family, but it is more: it is a place that still abides by its own rules. The creeks have not yet been channeled with concrete. There is still a wildness beating beneath the rocks, and in the atoms of every thing.

Each year, we grow closer to the land. Each year, it marks us deeper. The lightning strike that burned the top of what is now called the Burned-Off Hill: we saw firsthand how for twenty years the wildlife preferred that area, but finally the protein content has been lowered again, and it is time for another fire.

The dead rattlesnake my cousin Rick and I found out on the highway two years ago: we put it in the back of the truck along with the wood for that night's campfire: put it down there in the middle of all that wood. That night Russell and Randy unloaded the wood, gathering great big armloads of it. Rick and I shined the flashlights in Russell's face then, and he realized he'd gathered up a great big armload of rattlesnake. We yelled at him to drop that snake, but he couldn't, it was all tangled up everywhere, all around his arms.

The land and its stories, and our stories: the time Randy and I were picking up one of what would be the new cabin's four cornerstones, to load into the truck. August. Randy dropped his end of the sandstone slab (about the size of a coffin) but didn't get his hand free in time. It might have been my fault. The quarter-ton of rock smashed off the end of his left pinky. No more tea sipping for Cousin Randy. He sat down, stunned in the heat, and stared at the crushed pulpy end of that little finger. I thought strangely how some small part of it was already mashed in between the atoms of the rock, and how his blood was already dripping back into the iron-rich soil. Randy tried to shake off the pain, tried to stand and resume work, but the second he did his eyes rolled heavenward and he turned ghost-white in that awful heat and fell to the ground, and began rolling down the steep hill, to the bottom of the gulch. All the little birds and other animals back in the cool shade of the oaks and cedars were resting, waiting for night to cool things off. What an odd creature man is, they had to be thinking. But we couldn't wait for night, or its coolness. We were aflame with a love for that wild land, and our long, rock-sure history on it: our loving place on it.

Granddaddy knew the old Texan's trick of luring an armadillo in close by tossing pebbles in the dry leaves. The armadillo, with its radar-dish ears, believes the sound is that of jumping insects, and will follow the sound of your tossed pebbles right up to your feet before it understands the near-sighted image of your boot or tennis shoe and leaps straight up, sneezes, then flees in wild alarm.

There is a startling assemblage of what I think of as "tender" life up there, seemingly a paradox for such a harsh, rocky, hot country. Cattails along the creeks, tucked in between those folds of granite, those narrow canyons with names like Fat Man's Misery and boulder-strewn cataclysms such as Hell's Half Acre. Newts, polliwogs, bullfrogs, leopard frogs, mud turtles, pipits and wagtails, luna moths and viceroys, ferns and mosses . . .

The old rock, the beautiful outcrops, are the power of the hill country, but the secret, the mystery, is the water; that's what brings the rock to life.

It's so hard to write about such nearly indefinable abstractions as yearn-ing or mystery, or to convince someone who's not yet convinced about the necessity and holiness of wildness. It's hard in this day and age to con-vince people of just how tiny and short-lived we are, and how that makes the wild more, not less, important. All of the hill country's creatures had helped me in this regard. It was along Willow Creek where as a child of nine or ten I had gone down with a flashlight to get a bucket of water. It was December, Christmas Eve, and bitterly cold. In the creek's eddies there was half an inch of ice over the shallow pools. I had never before seen ice in the wild.

I shined my flashlight onto that ice. The creek made its trickling mur-mur, cutting down the center of the stream between the ice banks on ei-ther side, cutting through the ice like a knife, but in the eddies the ice was thick enough to hold the weight of a fallen branch or a small rock, a piece of iron ore.

There were fish swimming under that ice! Little green perch. The creek was only a few yards wide, but it had fish in it, living just beneath the ice! Why weren't they dead? How could they live beneath the surface of ice, as if in another system, another universe? Wasn't it too cold for them?

The blaze of my flashlight stunned them into a hanging kind of paralysis; they hung as suspended as mobiles, unblinking.

I tapped on the ice and they stirred a little, but still I could not get their full attention. They were listening to something else—to the gurgle of the creek, to the tilt of the planet, or the pull of the moon. I tapped on the ice again. Up at the cabin, someone called my name. I was getting cold, and had to go back. Perhaps I left the first bit of my civility—my first grateful relinquishing of it—there under that strange ice, for the little green fish to carry downstream and return to its proper place, to the muck and moss beneath an old submerged log. I ran up to the cabin with the bucket of cold water, as fresh and alive as we can ever hope to be, having been graced with the sight and idea of something new, something wild, something just beyond my reach.

I remember one winter night, camped down at the deer pasture, when a rimy ice fog had moved in, blanketing the hill country. I was just a teenager. I had stepped outside for a moment for the fresh cold air; everyone else was still in the cabin, playing dominoes. (Granddaddy smoked like a chimney.) I couldn't see a thing in all that cold fog. There was just the sound of the creek running past camp; as it always has, as I hope it always will.

Then I heard the sound of a goose honking—approaching from the north. There is no sound more beautiful, especially at night, and I stood there and listened. Another goose joined in—that wild, magnificent honking—and then another.

It seemed, standing there in the dark, with the cabin's light behind me (the *snap! snap! snap!* sound of Granddaddy the domino king playing his ivories against the linoleum table), that I could barely stand the hugeness, the unlimited future of life. I could feel my youth, could feel my heart beating, and it seemed those geese were coming straight for me, as if they too could feel that barely controlled wildness, and were attracted to it.

When they were directly above me, they began to fly in circles, more geese joining them. They came lower and lower, until I could hear the underlying readiness of those resonant honks; I could hear their grunts, their intake of air before each honk.

My father came out to see what was going on.

"They must be lost," he said. "This fog must be all over the hill country. Our light may be the only one they can see for miles," he said. "They're probably looking for a place to land, to rest for the night, but can't find their way down through the fog."

The geese were still honking and flying in circles, not a hundred feet over our heads. I'm sure they could hear the gurgle of the creek below. I stared up into the fog, expecting to see the first brave goose come slipping down through that fog, wings set in a glide of faith for the water it knew was just below. *They were so close to it.*

But they did not come. They circled our camp all night, keeping us awake; trying, it seemed, to *pray* that fog away with their honking, their sweet music; and in the morning, both the fog and the geese were gone, and it seemed that some part of me was gone with them, some tame or civilized part, and they had left behind a boy, a young man, who was now thoroughly wild, and who thoroughly loved wild things. And I often still have the dream I had that night, that I was up with the geese, up in the cold night, peering down at the fuzzy glow of the cabin lights in the fog, that dim beacon of hope and mystery, safety and longing.

The geese flew away with the last of my civility that night, but I realize now it was a theft that had begun much earlier in life. That's one of the greatest blessings of the hill country, and all wildness: it is a salve, a twentieth-century poultice to take away the crippling fever of too much civility, too much numbness.

The first longing years of my life that were spent exploring those small and doomed hemmed-in woods around Houston sometimes seem like days of the imagination, compared against my later days in the hill country. It seemed, when I went to Hidden Lake, or to the zoo, or the arboretum, or the museum, that I was only treading water.

I fell asleep each night with my aquariums bubbling, the post-game baseball show murmuring on the radio. That magic rock from Llano County, the magnetite, stuck to the side of my bed like a remora, or a guardian, seeing me through the night, and perhaps filling me with a strange energy, a strange allegiance for a place I had not yet seen.

Finally the day came when I was old enough for my first hunting trip up to the deer pasture. My father took me up there for "the second hunt," in late December. I would not go on the first hunt, the November hunt, until after I was out of college, and a hunter. The "second hunt" was a euphemism for just camping, for hiking around, and for occasionally carrying a rifle.

My father and I drove through the night in his old green-and-white 1956 Ford—through country I'd never seen, beneath stars I'd never seen. My father poured black coffee from an old thermos to stay awake. The trip took a long time, in those days—over six hours, with gravel clattering beneath the car for the last couple of hours.

I put my hand against the car window. It was colder, up in the hills. The stars were brighter. When I couldn't stay awake any longer—overwhelmed by the senses—I climbed into the back seat and wrapped up in an old Hudson's Bay blanket and lay down and slept. The land's rough murmur and jostling beneath me was a lullaby.

When I awoke, we had stopped for gas in Llano. We were the only car at the service station. We were surrounded by a pool of light. I could see the dark woods at the edge of the gravel parking lot, could smell the cedar. My father was talking to the gas-station attendant. Before I was all the way awake, I grabbed a flashlight and got out and hurried out toward the woods. I went into the cedars, got down on my hands and knees, and with the flashlight began searching for the magnetite that I was sure was all over the place. I picked up small red rocks and held them against the metal flashlight to see if they'd stick.

When my father and the attendant came and got me out of the woods and asked where I had been going and what I'd been doing, I told them, "Looking for magnetite." How hard it must be, to be an adult.

We drove on: an improbable series of twists and turns, down washed-out canyons and up ridges, following thin caliche roads that shone ghostly white in the moonlight. I did not know then that I would come to learn every bend in those roads, every dip and rise, by heart. We clattered across a high-centered narrow cattle guard, and then another, and were on the property that we'd been leasing for thirty years—the thousand acres, our heart.

It was so cold. We were on our land. We did not own it, but it was ours because we loved it, belonged to it, and because we were engaged in its system. It dictated our movements as surely as it did those of any winter-range deer herd, any migrating warbler. It was ours because we loved it.

We descended toward the creek, and our cabin. The country came into view, brilliant in the headlights. Nighthawks flittered and flipped in the road before us, danced eerie acrobatic flights that looked as if they were trying to smother the dust in the road with their soft wings. Their eyes were glittering red in the headlights. It was as if we had stumbled into a witches' coven, but I wasn't frightened. They weren't bad witches; they were just wild.

Giant jackrabbits, with ears as tall again as they were, raced back and forth before us—leaped six feet into the air and reversed direction mid-leap, hit the ground running: a sea of jackrabbits before us, flowing, the high side of their seven-year cycle. A coyote darted into our headlights' beams, grabbed a jackrabbit, and raced away. One jackrabbit sailed over the hood of our car, coming so close to the windshield that I could see his wide, manic eyes, looking so human. A buck deer loped across the road, just ahead. It was an explosion of life, all around us. Moths swarmed our headlights.

We had arrived at the wild place.

John Hanson Mitchell

CEREMONIAL TIME

John Hanson Mitchell lives in Littleton, Massachusetts. His pursuit of a sense of place first became widely known through his book *Ceremonial Time: Fifteen Thousand Years on One Square Mile,* which has been followed by other books of natural history. In the following essay, the first chapter of *Ceremonial Time,* Mitchell emphasizes the importance of a sense of time for a sense of place. To know the land—"the undiscovered country of the nearby"—is to know its geological and human history. The book is a double story: of his own life on the land, and of the last fifteen thousand years of Scratch Flat, from the Proto-Indians through the colonists and up to encroaching urbanism. By learning from Native Americans still living in the area, Mitchell develops the beginnings of a shamanistic sense of "ceremonial time" in which the distant past reveals itself. Conventional distinctions between past and present, as well as between nature and culture, are blurred. The result is an expanded and integrated view of place.

There is a plum grove just above the house in which I live, a tangled, unproductive group of some twelve trees that were planted sometime in the late 1920s by an old curmudgeon who lived in the house in the decades following the turn of the century. Every morning between April and November, weather permitting, I take a pot of coffee up to that grove to watch the sun come up over the lower fields and to think about things. More and more now I find myself thinking there about time, how it drifts in from the future, how it brushes past us briefly in the present, and then drifts off again to become the past, and how none of these stages, neither past, nor present, nor future, are really knowable. Presented with this dilemma, I have come in recent years to accept the primitive concept of ceremonial time, in which past, present, and future can all be perceived in a single moment, generally during some dance or sacred ritual. Ceremonial time was perceived easily by the people who lived on the land around the plum grove for most of human history. The Pawtucket Indians would summon it up regularly during certain periods of the year, and I have found that it is a convenient method of understanding the changes that have taken place on this particular patch of earth over the last fifteen thousand years.

I should say at the outset, since I am writing about time and place, that history hangs heavily in this area. Fifteen thousand years ago the last of three glacial advances smoothed the rough edges of a small patch of land about ten miles north of the Concord River. After the glacier retreated, it left behind on that particular section of land a deep bed of sand and gravel which, in subsequent centuries, was overlaid with a rich layer of topsoil. Even before the last ice of the glacier had melted from the barren, rolling hills, small bands of fur-clad hunters, known technically as Paleo-Indians, moved into the region in search of game. In due time, that is, after some five thousand years, the descendants of these Paleo people settled into semi-permanent villages, some of which were located not far from the square-mile tract of land in question. A thousand years ago these Indians, who by now had organized themselves into a tribe known as the Pawtuckets, found that by clearing off some of the existing vegetation in the area and replacing it with other plants, the production of food could be substantially increased. This revolutionary development gave birth to an agricultural economy which has survived on that little section of earth ever since.

Five or six centuries after the Pawtucket agricultural experiments began, a group of new settlers moved into the region and improved on the technique. These newcomers had white skin and brought with them from Europe new crops, exotic animals, and an attitude toward the land that, in the space of a few decades, altered the entire environment. Whereas in 1630 the area had been characterized by deep woods broken only by a few primitive garden clearings, by 1790 the land consisted, for the most part, of open, rolling fields of English hay, rough grazing meadows, orchards, and large kitchen gardens.

The white settlers who moved into the area also constructed a new kind of shelter. In contrast to the rounded wickiups of the Pawtuckets, these were squared-off, framed structures designed to keep the natural world at bay. By 1850, there were about seven of these buildings in the little patch of land that the glacier scraped off. One of these, a small farmhouse, was constructed on an east-facing slope by a farmer named Peter Farwell. About one hundred fifty years later, I moved into that house and as a result have come to know and love the square-mile tract of land that surrounds it.

My understanding of this land is circumscribed by time as we measure it here in the West. I seem almost always to be stuck in this little slice of history we call the present, but there are days, there are periods, when some obscure combination of forces seems to release an awareness of ceremonial time so I can see the history of this little stretch of land in sharpened detail. Invariably on these days I get up from my chair in the plum grove and begin to walk, and invariably I seem to cover a certain territory on these walks, not unlike a dog or a bird. It is bordered on the south by a highway, known locally as the Great Road, which runs from Concord, Massachusetts, north-northwest to the small villages of southern New Hampshire. The Great Road was originally an Indian trail which meandered through what is now known as the Nashoba Valley. In its recent history, the road carried a number of important personages and was involved in a small, obscure way, in national events. For sixty or seventy years, the brightest and the best in the American establishment traveled on this highway between Groton School and Harvard University in Cambridge. And one April morning in the late eighteenth century, a group of militant farmers marched down the Great Road to a bridge over the Concord River to start a revolution. But all that is another story.

To the east and north, the territory in question is bordered by a stream known as Beaver Brook which the glacier gouged out during its retreat. It is a pleasant little body of water, offering clear, and in places, deep waters for swimming and good courses for skating in winter. In any other part of the world, Beaver Brook might be termed a river; it is slow-flowing and deep in some sections, and in places it widens to fifty yards or more. As do most of the rivers in the region south of the Merrimack River, the brook flows northward. Its wide grassy marshes provide excellent habitat for ducks, geese, otters, muskrat, as well as a few rarer species of plants and animals. The brook curves westward at the northern end of its course and empties into a shallow lake which the early white settlers called Forge Pond. The waters of this lake are relatively clean and swimmable, and fishermen still seem to find something worth casting for there in spite of the fact that in recent years it has been surrounded with the habitations of modern-day Americans. The houses are of a type that were built originally as summer cottages and then later winterized for permanent dwellings. On a point of land, so far undeveloped, on the southeast shore of the lake, the Pawtucket Indians and their progenitors would hold festivals and, if my sources are accurate, the normal flow of time as we now measure it, would stop, run backward, or collapse altogether so that the primal shamans of who knows how many generations, the spirits of dead bears and wolves, would come alive again and dance there in the half-lit regions between the firelight and the forest wall.

The western edge of the tract of land is bordered by a deep pine forest and a brooding larch swamp. Whippoorwills nest in the pine forest, and although I rarely see them, I can often hear barred owls, great horned owls, and screech owls calling from the darkened interior. On the east side of that pine forest and about an eighth of a mile behind my house, there is a grove of very old hemlock trees. Some of the trees in the grove are hollowed and broken, some may have been standing in the years when local rabble-rousers in the community were mobilizing against the British; and the general sense of the place is gloomy and dark, as if some unspeakable acts took place there, some brutal rite whose aura has been carried forward into the twentieth century. As you will see, this may or may not be the case, but I will come to that in due time.

Just south of the pine woods there is a wide field that is usually planted in corn by Matty Matthews, a hardworking dairy farmer who is determined to continue farming in spite of the fact that economies of this region appear to be working against him. Just south of Matthews's cornfield, you will come again to the Great Road. There are five farms in this square-mile tract, four of which are located on the main highway. Next to the Matthews place there is a 120-acre spread known as Sherman's Acres which, in recent years, has sprouted a lucrative crop of suburban tract houses. East of Sherman's there is a farm run by a Greek immigrant named Jimmy-George Starkos, which is by far the most pleasant and the best-tended of the five farms in the square-mile tract. Jimmy-George's farm is made up of beet and bean fields which rise up to a wooded ridge to the east. Beyond the ridge there is another farm which, for more than eighty years, housed local paupers and transients. The house is still there, but a few years ago the farmer sold off his hayfields to developers and now there are several large, flat buildings on the land, owned for the most part by computer companies. The place was once known as Beaver Brook Farm;

now it is called—without a touch of conscious irony—Beaver Brook Industrial Park.

Walk north of the industrial park along the banks of Beaver Brook and you will come full circle. There is a stretch of oak and pine woods owned by a local sportsmen's club (again, no irony in the name) and just to the north you will come to a group of fields which are more or less central to this story. For one thing, this particular farm lies at the center of the square-mile tract that I am describing, and for another, a lot of history has been played out in that two hundred acres of old fields and woods. The property is owned by a man named Charlie Lignos who owns a dairy farm in the next town and who, for some obscure reason, is allowing perfectly good agricultural land to grow up to woods. The farm consists of some five fields, each separated by stone walls and hedgerows. The fields rise up from Beaver Brook in a series of terraces and are interspersed with untended apple orchards and patches of dense woods. The soil is good in the area and in all likelihood, given the location, the land has been farmed for more than five hundred years, first by the Pawtuckets, then by Christianized Indians, and then finally by white Europeans.

A man named Jeremiah Caswell was the first European to work this land; in the mid-eighteenth century he cleared most of the tract, planted orchards, and unlike his Indian predecessors, brought in livestock—oxen, dairy cows, pigs, goats, and later horses and sheep. In 1973 there were three barns and three houses associated with the original Caswell holdings; by 1979 there were only two structures left. Vandals had burned two barns and an abandoned house, and the town had torn down the third barn because, officials said, it was an attractive nuisance, an indication, in my opinion, of the economic direction that the community is taking. The main house, the old Caswell estate, has been restored and is now surrounded by extensive flower gardens. The four acres of land surrounding the other Caswell house are being farmed once more in an odd sort of way, but the house itself, although sturdy enough, is in continual need of repair; I know this for a fact, since I am the one who lives there.

During the brighter years in this town, that is, during the height of the nineteenth-century agricultural period, the square-mile section of land which I have described was called Scratch Flat. One local legend suggests that Scratch Flat was so named because in the 1860s a number of families living there suffered from a "certain cutaneous itch" for seven years. More likely the tract got its name from the fact that the flat land surrounding a low hill in the area was so thoroughly cultivated. Whereas the rest of the community was known for its apple and pear orchards, Scratch Flat was always known for its good soil and its truck farms. My friend Margaret Lacey, a ninety-five-year-old woman who had ice blue eyes and a long memory, told me that on summer nights during the 1890s the air in Scratch Flat was heavy with the smell of celery, and even up to the 1950s the area was known for its farms. Billy Sherman used to be called the Cauliflower King by the buyers in the Haymarket in Boston, and Jimmy-George Starkos sent three sons to college on the money earned from a roadside stand which was open only four months of the year.

All of them, Starkos, Sherman, Caswell, and the Pawtuckets, can thank the glacier for their success in life. The deep bed of sand and gravel, the easy slopes, the drainage patterns, and the deep layer of organic topsoil made it easy to farm in this area. It is no accident that the industrial development that swept through New England during the nineteenth century skipped over Scratch Flat and the valley in which the town is located. On the other hand, the same factors that make the land good for farming also make it good for housing and modern industrial development; and, in spite of the good soil, in spite of the fact that arable land is something of a rare commodity in New England, more and more now, computer companies and new houses are appearing on the farmlands of the town.

All this is really only one side of the history of Scratch Flat, however. It should be borne in mind that the greater number of living things that inhabit this little section of the planet are nonhuman and most of them have lived in the region in an unbroken continuum for thousands of years. There are at present approximately one hundred fifty people on Scratch Flat, most of them living along the Great Road, in Billy Sherman's housing development, and on Beaver Brook Road which cuts through the eastern section of the tract. There is also at least one family of gray foxes, one family of great horned owls, one or possibly two barred owl families, innumerable families of red foxes, skunks, raccoons, squirrels, groundhogs, rabbits, mice, voles, and bats, as well as at least one otter and several families of mink, muskrat, and short-tailed weasel. Least bitterns, sora rails, wood ducks, and other species of water birds nest in the Beaver Brook marshes, and any number of common and, in cases, uncommon species of birds nest in the woods and old fields. I have seen eagles flying over

Charlie Lignos's fields; I once saw an eastern coyote track here; I have seen deer; and I have heard, seen, and even caught any number of species of reptiles and amphibians, one of which, the blue-spotted salamander, proved to be rare and endangered.

In spite of the abundance of wildlife, however, the human community in the area, with a few exceptions, is not aware of the animal community, so that when I tell some neighbor that there are great horned owls living in the white pines beyond Matthews's farm, they tend to doubt my word. They are interested, of course, but not so interested that they would get up from their comfortable chairs and walk out through the snowy woods to witness that chaos of hooting and yowling that takes place during the great horned owl nesting season at the end of February. Wilderness and wildlife, history, life itself, for that matter, is something that takes place somewhere else, it seems. You must travel to witness it, you must get in your car in summer and go off to look at things which some "expert," such as the National Park Service, tells you is important, or beautiful, or historic. In spite of their admitted grandeur, I find such well-documented places somewhat boring. What I prefer, and the thing that is my subject here, is that undiscovered country of the nearby, the secret world that lurks beyond the night windows and at the fringes of cultivated backyards.

I have gotten into the habit recently of walking through Scratch Flat at night; it offers an exotic alternative to a walk during the day. Time collapses more easily then; the world entirely alters itself and the true and almost frighteningly inhuman landscape that characterized the area for most of its history reasserts itself. On summer nights in the lower fields near Beaver Brook, I can hear the intense energy of the Carboniferous period in the calls of katydids, cone-headed grasshoppers, and snowy tree crickets. I can hear the Jurassic in the caterwauling of the great horned owls; and in winter, in the dark line of hills beyond the icy marsh, in the spare spruce-dotted bogs, I can sense something of the lifeless, barren landscape of the glacial Pleistocene. For all our frenetic work and our apparent ability to alter the biosphere, we human beings are insignificant little creatures in the perspective of geologic time.

Nevertheless, even at night, our present has a way of insinuating itself into these vast time scales. One of the things that I can hear at night, along with the timeless calls of the Carboniferous and the Jurassic, is a strange roaring hiss that sounds something like a distant rushing stream. That sound is created by Route 495, which runs on the other side of the ridge that separates Scratch Flat from the town in which the tract of land is located. In 1965 a number of local officials, most of whom owned farmland in the area, arranged to have the highway constructed through the western edge of the town, no more than half a mile from the town common. For a few years after the highway came through, nothing much changed. Traffic decreased slightly on the Great Road, a few farmhouses were torn down or moved, a good pear orchard which was split in two by the highway went out of business; but other than that, Route 495 did not seem to have much of an effect on the economy of the place. Then quite abruptly things began to change. Ted Demogenes sold off the former town poor farm and the industrial development that once skipped over the place began to work its way in. If Scratch Flat would not come to the future during the nineteenth century, if it refused to give in to current economic trends, then the future, in its inexorable way, would come to Scratch Flat.

In our time, if you ask people in the town where Scratch Flat is, no one will know. In effect, the place died sometime in the early twentieth century when transportation and communication lines improved and the quarters of the town—the West End, Hog End, and Scratch Flat—became more or less unified. And if you were to drive along the Great Road, apart from the marshes of the Beaver Brook, and perhaps the beauty of the rolling farmlands of Jimmy-George Starkos and Billy Sherman, you would not say that this place is any different from any other place in this section of New England. But that is only the superficial appearance of things. Scratch Flat is at once a real and imaginary country; it is nowhere, and it is everywhere, unique on the one hand and totally indistinguishable on the other.

I first came to Scratch Flat not because it was a region of rolling farmlands and pleasing vistas, but because there happened to be an old house for sale there and my wife and I were looking for a place to live in the general area. It seemed a pleasant enough place to settle. The dwelling was a small farmhouse built sometime in the early 1800s; the four acres of land that came with the house sloped gently up from the house to a dark stand of pines; and, although in a semiwild state, it was clear that the two or three acres of open land had been cultivated in the not too distant past. Just behind the house there was a square of short grass that served for a lawn, on a rise on the southwest side of the property there was a fallen barn, and beside the ruin, there was the tangled and overgrown remnant of a plum grove. Open meadows, a few old apple trees made up the rest of the open lands, and in this forgotten, overgrown landscape there lived leopard frogs, snakes, toads, rabbits, meadowlarks, woodchucks, yellow garden spiders, crickets, grasshoppers, butterflies, and all the other plants, mammals, birds, insects, reptiles, and amphibians that are commonly associated with an old-field ecosystem. The woods behind the meadow were made up of white pine on the southwest corner of the property and a mixture of deciduous trees on the northwest side. To the east, across the road, there were more woodlands, and north and northeast of the property the land was surrounded by terraced hayfields, old barns, and cows belonging to Charlie Lignos. Given its proximity to Boston and its western suburbs, the place was a demi-paradise if you were of a mind to enjoy that sort of thing, which I was.

Shortly after I moved to Scratch Flat I began to wander—first east to the Beaver Brook and the hayfields and orchards, then west and north through the woods to the lake and the cultivated fields of the farms over the hill behind the house. From the very beginning, I felt there was something about the lands surrounding the property, some vague and almost indefinable quality of time, or space, or history, that lingered in the area. Clearly Scratch Flat had been intensely cultivated, had been lived upon and walked over, cleared and plowed, planted and then planted again. Everywhere you looked you could see the evidence of previous habitation, in the cellar holes of ruined farmhouses, in the isolated stone-lined wells, in the carefully constructed stone walls running through the pine woods and the swamps, and in the fallen and dying barns, the numerous bottle dumps, and the rutted memory of old carriage roads. Something was alive amidst these ruins that could not be seen, there was a definite presence in the area.

At first, during my early walks, I thought this presence might be some kind of an animal, a bobcat perhaps or a coyote, or even possibly a mountain lion. Such things had been reported from time to time in the area and there was, it seemed to me, enough territory in the northwest section of the tract to hide, if not support, one of these larger predators. But the more I walked over the land, the more convinced I became that whatever was lurking at the dark edges of the woods at Scratch Flat was not an animal. It seemed to be human, and yet at the same time, definitely nonhuman. By the end of the first year, I began to believe that something had happened on Scratch Flat at some point in its history, some act, or event, or continuum of events that had managed to transcend time. At the end of the second year, after I had gotten to know a number of the old families in the area, I decided to actively search out the thing or the event, grab it by the tail, so to speak, and drag it out into the light of the present.

This was, I realize now, just one more journey, one more voyage of exploration for me. Ever since I was able to leave the confines of my own backyard, I have been fascinated by the idea of trespassing, exploring either legally or illegally the backyards of the larger estates in the town in which I grew up. As I grew older, I extended these explorations to nearby woodlands, and then later still, when I was about ten or twelve, to a long neck of woods that ran along the Palisades on the Hudson River, woods that were dotted, in those days, with the ruins of estates, overgrown gardens and escaped daffodils and periwinkles. Later still I extended these explorations even farther, developed for a while a definite wanderlust, so that sometimes I would travel simply for the sake of the trip, simply to know what this or that place was like. There is nothing unusual about all this, I suppose; it is just one more aspect of the American restlessness, all a part of the lack of a sense of place that seems to be a defining characteristic of the culture.

When I began to explore Scratch Flat, I had a sense that I was setting out on another one of these earlier journeys. I began to learn more about the history of the place, and the more I learned, the farther back in time I found I had to travel, until finally I reached into prehistory and bumped up against the great white wall of the glacier. There was no sense in going any farther. Before the glacier there were no people in the area and therefore there could be no history, no human perception of the place. And it was at this point that I realized that I was embarked on the greatest trespass of all. I was not exploring a square-mile tract of land thirty-five miles west of Boston; I was exploring time.

About a year after I began my research, after it had come to me that Indians had lived the better part of the history of this place, I met a man named Fred Williams who is part Pawtucket and part Micmac Indian. Williams's "real" name, he says, is Nompenekit, or Man Born Twice. The name was given to him by his grandfather and later in his life, when he became active in Indian affairs, Williams resumed the name. He is a man of about fifty or sixty with the deeply lined face of an old man, bright black eyes, and the trim body of a young man. His hair is a rich gray, the color of the cloudy winter sky, and he wears it long, sometimes in braids, sometimes held in place with a decorative headband. He has a classical American Indian face, hooked nose, reddish-brown skin, and full, chiseled lips, and, like many of the Indian people that I have come to know in recent years, he smokes a lot of cigarettes. When I first met him, he seemed diffident, almost painfully shy and polite, yet always willing to share his views. Later, after I came to know him better, I realized that this apparent diffidence was actually a state of calm fortitude which seemed to spring from a deep confidence in his worldview. He was very firm in his beliefs, very steady, as if he were operating according to certain basic truths which were unknowable to me, a white man.

Nompenekit was a fairly well known figure among the few remaining New England Indians and was known also in the white community. He would occasionally appear at lectures and similar events to give the Native American side of the history, although his views were decidedly radical, and not always appreciated even by Indians. I met Nompenekit in connection with an educational program I happened to be involved with once in the Lowell school system, and after I started my exploration of Scratch Flat, I called him to ask if he had any information on the native peoples that might have lived in the area. He directed me, as you will see, to an excellent and unique source; but more importantly, he was the one that taught me to think in Indian time.

Indian time, Nompenekit explained, does not move according to Western tradition. Morning is when the first light shows. Noon is when the sun is at its highest point. Spring comes—or used to come—when the herring appear in the rivers; fall comes, Nompenekit said, not in October or September, but in August when the migratory birds start to collect together at the woodland edges. Indian time stretches itself out on occasion, on occasion contracts or reverses its apparent flow. It is not exacting, not measured by dials or digits on a lighted screen, and at the base of this system is the concept of ceremonial time. It is then, said Nompenekit, that you can actually see events that took place in the past. You can see people and animals who have been dead for a thousand years; you can walk in their place, see and touch the plants of their world. And more importantly, when ceremonial time collapses, the spirit world can be seen, the gods, ghosts, and monsters of the Indians manifest themselves.

Nompenekit's Indian time more or less came naturally to me. I am not one who is particularly obsessed with the measurement of hours or days. But ceremonial time, the more interesting aspect of this way of thinking, did not come so easily, and steeped as I am in Western tradition, it is likely that I will never be able to thoroughly free myself from the belief that time flows linearly from past to present to future. But after I learned about ceremonial time, I began to try to use it as a tool to explore the past. As I said, there are moments on Scratch Flat when the past seems to me to be closer to the surface, when events that I know took place there seem to be somehow more real; this is a phenomenon that has happened to me most of my life, and after I met Nompenekit, I began to think that this state of mind was close to the idea of ceremonial time, and began to consciously exploit it. I found that when the moment was right, by concentrating on some external object, an arrowhead that was found on Scratch Flat, for example, or the running walls or foundations of the area, I was able to perceive something more than a simple mental picture of what some past event was like. I not only could see the event or the place in my mind's eye, but would also hear it, smell the woodfires; and sometimes, for just a flash, a microsecond if you care to measure things, I would actually be there, or so it seemed. This is nothing like the experience with the madeleine in *Remembrance of Things Past;* what I would sense is the reality of an event that I could never have witnessed. Nor is it anything mystical; I don't claim to have experienced these things in some previous existence. It was simply a heightened awareness or perception of the way things must have been. And yet, I learned from Nompenekit, that is all that is necessary. "If you see those things in your mind," he told me once, "you must believe that is what happened. That is the only thing you can know."

There are many versions of history according to Nompenekit; there is the Indian version, there is the written version of the white man, and there may be another version, something somewhere between the two. He never denied official history, he simply would say that that is the way the white man believes things happened, but they might have happened in another way.

More than anything else, I have found that this liberal attitude toward reality is the key to understanding the past in Scratch Flat. One aspect of the history of the area, the formal history of the politics, of the crops that were grown and of the people that served on the various town boards, is fairly well documented for the two hundred sixty years of the town's existence. That history does not record, however, the struggle, the sorrows, the ecstasies, the joys, and the anger of the people that actually lived and worked on Scratch Flat. Furthermore, the recorded history of the general region tells only of approximately three hundred to four hundred years; the rest of human history, the fifteen-thousand-year stretch between the arrival of the Paleo-Indians and the recent past, is unwritten. But I have learned from Nompenekit and his friends that this past is not entirely unknowable; it exists in the legends and the folk tales of the local Indian tribes and, to some extent, in the racial memory of the descendants of the people who lived in the region for most of its history.

It occurred to me, after I came to know Nompenekit, that if I were to thoroughly understand Scratch Flat, genuinely dig out the story of the things that happened here, I could not rely solely on the maps, town records, and other official documents; I would have to get all the sources. And so I began asking everyone I could think of who might know something about the place or its past—archeologists, historians, old farmers, local eccentrics, Indian shamans, developers, newer residents, and local farmhands. I began to take on all comers, so to speak, all views of the past, present and future, and all the official and unofficial histories. And from these various sources, all of which I set down here without prejudice, I think I have uncovered the mystery; I think I have discovered what it is that I sensed in the woods and fields on my first walk over this insignificant little patch of the planet.

Robert Finch

INTO THE MAZE

Robert Finch lives in Cape Cod, a place particularly rich in the history of American nature writing. He is the author of several collections of essays, including *The Primal Place*. Finch's writings reflect the land he lives in. Rather than presenting striking imagery of magnificent mountains or tales of adventures in a vast wilderness, he introduces us to an intimate place long tied to human culture. He also offers small but crucial pieces of wisdom that come from a life finely tuned to one's homeland. In his writings, small town society and New England history are incised by the surging alewives that course upriver, and the lives of birds and toads are incorporated into his family life. It is a land, however, that is slowly being altered by the spread of urban life. In this selection, Finch discusses the changes that are occurring in his place, the need for becoming a true resident, and his craving for entrance into nature, which comes not from willful entry but from listening to the land.

I

One of the occupational hazards of living in a place like Cape Cod is not always knowing where you are. The sea fog that rolls in regularly over the mud flats and salt marshes is not entirely to blame for such chronic disorientation. Nor are the winter northeasterlies whose heavy surf and storm surges break through barrier beaches, destroy parking lots, silt up harbors, and claim waterfront property all that dislocate us.

Change is the coin of this sandy realm, and as long as we are not too close to it, such change delights us. The seasons flow in their rhythmic variety, a little out of sync with the mainland due to the ocean's moderating influence—which pleases our sense of separateness. With them come in the streaming tides of shorebirds, migrating alewives and striped bass, pack ice in Cape Cod Bay, spring peepers in the bogs, gypsy moths in the oaks, and tourists in the motels and restaurants.

Years flow and bring still broader changes, sometimes surprising, not always welcome. Bald heaths grow up to pine barrens, meadows fill in with juniper, abandoned bogs return to cedar swamps or maple swamps, oaks replace the pines, and a charming water view from the deck or terrace disappears under a rising horizon of leaves.

With these changes some new bird species appear, others grow scarcer. Fish populations fluctuate, ponds slowly silt in. New areas of tidal flats are claimed by spreading salt-marsh grasses, and each year a few more feet of the ocean cliffs topple into the surf, taking a beach cottage or two with them. Major alterations in the shape of the coastline can and do take place within a man's lifetime, adding a feeling of shared mortality in our relationship with this thin spar of glacial leavings. Yet through all this variety of natural change we also sense a continuity, not always to our liking, perhaps, but with a fittingness and perceptible identity of its own, an interplay of great and connected forces.

To this natural change, however, we have added our own, in a way that we share with most other parts of the country. In the beginning we may have desired only to "fit in" to this natural scene, to enjoy what it has to offer; and yet in doing so on such a mass scale and on our own terms, we have inevitably introduced forces that have had increasing repercussions of their own.

We move here in winter onto some quiet street and find the following summer that traffic makes it unsafe to cross the road for our mail. A piece of woods where we used to walk our dogs is turned, almost overnight, into roads and building lots. An open stretch of coastal bluffs that once formed a background to our clamming on the mud flats is now clotted with condominiums. Along the Mid-Cape Highway the deer we noticed for years are one day no longer there; in their stead are houses and tennis courts. Back roads and open fields, where fox stalked and woodcock courted, all at once sprout shopping malls, golf courses, new schools, and sewage-treatment plants. And so on.

Countryside is suddenly suburban, suburban areas become densely developed, and in places our highways and urbanized areas begin to take on an aspect that makes us look hard at the exit and street signs in order to reassure ourselves we are not in Boston or New Bedford, yet. Having increased our individual mobility in both the physical and social sense—the speed and ease with which we can travel from place to place as well as the power to choose our hometowns—we find ourselves less and less sure of where it is we have finally arrived.

Sometimes, watching a chickadee or a junco at the window feeder at the end of a winter's day, ruffled and tossed by a wet wind and alone at the coming of darkness, I am tempted to pity its lack of human comforts and security. But the bird at least was born to the condition in which it lives. It is part of an unbroken past of this land and knows where to find itself, despite all human and natural change, during the night and in the morning. Can I say as much for myself?

What is Cape Cod today? Rural? Semirural? Suburban? Seasonally urban? Bits and parts of each, perhaps. For this particular moment, at least, the term *subrural* seems as accurate as any: a patchwork of conflicting claims and uses hanging on to the remnants of a distinct rural culture that now exists almost completely in the past. And once we have named it, what then? What are we to make of it? How are we to know where we are? How are we to get here, once we have arrived?

2

The first step must be to see clearly what is there. This is often more difficult than it might appear, for nature has no guile, which is one of the things that makes it so hard for us to see. The bare, uncompromising face of the land is too much for us to behold, and so we clothe it in myth, sentiment, and imposed expectations.

In West Brewster, for instance, where I live, the scene outside my window looks more like western Connecticut or Minnesota than like what most people think of as a typical Cape Cod landscape. No sandy shores or low dunes, no salt marshes or wide ocean waters stretch out before me. Rather, the house I built here a few years ago sits well inland, tucked into the wooded, hilly terrain of a low, broken line of glacial hills known as the Sandwich Moraine. The moraine begins west at the Cape Cod Canal, rises quickly to a height of just over three hundred feet, runs east along the edge of Cape Cod Bay for some forty miles in a descending and increasingly interrupted ridge of loose till and rocks, and eventually peters out into the Atlantic at Orleans, where the arm of the Cape bends north toward Provincetown.

My house is situated near the eastern end of this moraine, on one of the lower crests about eighty feet above mean sea level. It faces south, on the north side of a roughly circular ridge of hills. These hills enclose a steep-sided bowl, or kettle hole, about a quarter of a mile in diameter, known locally as Berry's Hole.

The house is also circular in shape—octagonal, to be exact—with wide overhangs that combine with the higher hills around it to effectively block out most of the sky from inside, even in winter. When it was built, the top of the hill was leveled off and lowered a few feet, so that the yard, which stretches south from the house to the edge of the kettle hole, appears to leap off into nothing, into some great abyss, rather than falling off, as it does, into the rather modest hollow below.

The soil in these hills is sandy by mainland standards, but compared with beach sand it is heavy with clay and studded not only with small stones but also with many large glacial boulders twenty feet or more in length, called glacial erratics. Likewise, there is little of the low seaside vegetation generally associated with a shoreline environment—beach plum, bayberry, pitch pine. Instead, the surrounding slopes are covered with nearly pure stands of oak, that inland tree. For as far as I can see, unbroken stands of black and white oak lift their gray, lichen-spotted trunks and branches crookedly skyward.

Since the soil is relatively poor in nutrients, the oaks tend to be dwarfed in stature and prone to insect infestations. Nevertheless, they combine with the land to create an illusion of size. Stunted and twisted by poor soil, overcutting, and salt-laden winds, these trees possess the crooked look of age. They do not dominate the low hills but fit in proportion to them, so that together they give the impression of a far greater scale than either really has. It is easy to look out at them and see full-sized forests lining the flanks of mountain ranges that stretch for miles across some formidable gorge. The Cape has its own scale, and, to one not used to it, its landscape is full of such tricks of proportion and perspective.

No shorebirds, terns, herons, or crabs inhabit the immediate area. Rather, my wild neighbors are woodland fauna—deer, crows, owls, grouse, and a fox who lives in a burrow halfway down the hollow. Wood thrushes and phoebes nest about the house in summer, whippoorwills sing at night, and red-tailed hawks wheel slowly overhead, sending down sibilant screams from a high October sky. In the spring the slopes of Berry's Hole are covered with star flowers, lady's-slipper orchids, and trailing arbutus, or mayflower, while out of its deep, wet throat comes the tumultuous, insistent, nighttime chorus of wood frogs and spring peepers.

In short, although my home, as the herring gull flies, is less than half a mile inland from the salt marshes and shallow waters of Cape Cod Bay, it often takes an effort of will to remind myself that I live, not deep in the heart of the continent, but on an exposed and vulnerable headland thirty miles out into the open Atlantic, on the thin shores of a narrow land.

3

One May morning, several months after moving into the house, I looked up from the table where I had been typing and saw the stiff, gray, intersecting patterns of the oak trunks and branches outside the window. I saw them, as though for the first time, for what they really were: a maze, a vast, living maze stretching out beyond my lines of sight. And all at once I knew, with a clear and compelling conviction, that what I wanted, what I was seeking here, was entrance, or rather re-entrance, into that maze.

The trees are not an impenetrable thicket. They are, in fact, more like the original Cape Cod forest encountered by the Puritans during the *Mayflower*'s initial landfall at Provincetown in November of 1620 and described by Gov. William Bradford as "open and fit to go riding in." I can easily get up from my chair, open the door, cross the yard, and walk down the wooded slope to the bottom of the kettle hole. I have done so many times, before and since, but whenever I do my every noise and movement reveals me as an outsider, an intruder. I jangle my credentials as I go, crashing through the dry leaves, cursing as my jacket or pants leg catches on a barbed strand of catbrier.

What I want is to go silently and smoothly into the maze, without a rustle, as the light fox bounds with inborn agility across the rounded stone walls; as the soft rabbit threads itself surely and painlessly through the brier and viburnum jungles; as the lean, long-legged deer stops to look at me, sideways, with wet black eyes, then steps cleanly and quickly over brush and branch, disappearing up the slope without a word, as though into a fog; as the sharp-shinned hawk flits batlike through the web of branches; as the flicker leaps up and glides out through the layered oak boughs; as the green-and-gold garter snake, warming itself on a stone in the spring sun, suddenly bolts at my presence and, like a sand eel, vanishes in a glistening wriggle down into a crease in the earth and is gone.

These creatures tease me with their unconscious competence, a sureness that implies not so much prowess as belonging, of knowing where and who they are, of being local inhabitants in a way I am not.

Sometimes, frustrated by the unyielding rigidity of these woods in the face of my overtures, I go out with my chainsaw and cut down a few more of the trees around the house, pretending that I am getting firewood. For a few minutes the air is full of a geared thunder that obliterates all perception or participation, until the rashness of my deed catches up with me and I stop, finding myself in a space suddenly cleared and empty, surrounded by a quailed silence, having solved nothing and gotten nowhere.

There is no Gordian knot to cut here. Every part of the maze is a knot tied to every other part. To cut down the trees and scatter the animals, to make broad paths and wide clearings, is not to solve or enter the mystery, but to obliterate it and erect empty designs in its place. Such acts may give me passage and room to move about, but not entrance, and entrance is what I crave.

There is no quick, easy way into this or any other place, no sign pointing out the beginning of the path—no path to point out, for that matter. And yet, as I look out from this house into the round yard bordered by a sea of trees, and beyond them to the unseen shape of the peninsula itself, uncurling like a tendril growing into the sea, I seem to sense that this spot is as good as any from which to begin.

I take the sheet of paper, half-filled with sentences, out of the typewriter and hold it up before my eyes. Turning the sheet sideways, I look over its edge out the window to the trees beyond. When I do, the vertical lines of black ink begin to blur into the dark, rising bars of the trunks. It is a self-conscious gesture, but perhaps that is what it takes—a deliberate change of perspective, a loosening of focus, and a bending of your lines of sight to what it is you would see.

Or perhaps the secret is even simpler, as simple as the insistent, hidden song of the ovenbird, deep in the layered woods around me, that now begins to rise up out of the kettle hole in a ringing and ever more confident crescendo: *teach-er, Teach-er, TEACH-ER, **TEACH-ER!***

URBAN LIVING

Peter Sauer

WATER UNDER
AMERICAN GROUND
West 78th Street

Peter Sauer lives in New York City, where he cultivates a sense of place in the great American megalopolis. He edited *Finding Home: Writing on Nature and Culture from Orion Magazine,* and he is a contributing editor of the splendid journal of nature writing *Orion: People and Nature.* The following essay from *Orion* explores the nature of place and the place of nature in New York City. Sauer discovers an urban Galápagos of animals rarely noticed by city dwellers, explores the "peaceable kingdom" of the American Museum of Natural History, and reflects on the design of Central Park. In his natural history of this part of the city, he investigates the possibility that a brook has been buried. Throughout the essay, Sauer articulates a complex and integrated view of nature that includes urban life and museum displays, culture and wildness, past and present.

For three evenings in June the sun sets directly between the buildings that form the canyon walls of West 78th Street and projects long shadows of people crossing the street all the way up the gently sloped blacktop pavement, from Broadway, across Amsterdam and Columbus Avenue, east to the American Museum of Natural History. During the last two minutes before the sun drops beneath the Palisades above the far shore of the Hudson River, its light beams in horizontally, close to the ground, flickering as it passes between the moving taxis, cars, and trucks north- and southbound on Broadway, steady in the intervals when traffic signals stop them. I timed my dog walks to coincide with this event, hurried out when the air was clear, zigzagged back and forth across the street and up the block, stopping when the traffic stopped, to see how far the shadow of the family's little dog would stretch and if mine would be cast as far as the museum's west wall, which in this light glows like the headwall of a ceremonial Anasazi canyon.

Like summer's first light blinking through the aperture of moving traffic, there was a now-you-see-it-now-you-don't quality to every aspect of the natural history I learned while living on West 78th Street. Wildness itself seemed modulated, as if rewired through an urban black box to add layers of human artifice to every manifestation of its force, and the neighborhood flora and fauna could be classified by these distortions: The museum biota—mounted specimens, skeletons, glass models, and plaster casts—represented natural history heavily laced with nineteenth-century, pre-anthropological empire building. The splendidly abundant Central Park biota—especially of migratory birds—in its trampled but nevertheless fantastical pastoral landscape, represented nature annually amplified by art and enthusiasm. The gutsy, entrepreneurial, street biota, less noticed and less fashionable, ignored by science—except for that of commercial exterminators and municipal rat and pigeon controllers—seemed mine alone to study and celebrate as the wildest, most contemporary music of all.

House sparrows nested in looted parking meters; kestrels in a hole in a high decorative minaret of brick. The spiders were organizing exterior building walls into mutually exclusive, stratified life zones: from the first to the third, the fourth to the seventh, and the eighth floor and above. One summer, in a London plane tree that a winter storm had shoved precariously over the middle of the street, robins constructed a nest festooned with ribbons of glistening video- and black and yellow police-line tape that dangled over the hot pavement like the tentacles of a tree-dwelling Caribbean jellyfish and fluttered in the slipstream of every passing delivery truck, as if grasping for escaping prey. While I watched, this resilient gypsy biota was constructing its own urban Galápagos.

The first street birds to sing in the spring were house finches, descendants of caged birds imported from western mountain slopes and released in Long Island City by a pet wholesaler after Congress passed a law prohibiting trade in native species. Separated from their natural habitat, and the biological pool from which their ancestors had sprung, the West 78th Street finches belonged to a yet unrecognized species, an inchoate evolutionary work-in-progress, developing, on this block anyway, a predisposition for nesting in and under exterior window air conditioning units. As several species of Old World insects also colonized these appliances, I imagined a twenty-first century Darwin would discover that the window finches had become cockroach carnivores.

Compared to life on the street, the museum's version of nature and humanity was peaceable kingdom. Natural biota and primitive people coexisted as faunal partners in ecosystems disconnected from the present and unhinged from their pasts. Bits and pieces of captured moments were displayed like snapshots in a sprawling album. The dusty mahogany-skinned, larger-than-life Northwest boatpeople have been pushing their heroic ocean-going war canoe eastward through the museum's 77th Street lobby for at least as long as since I was a child. A diorama, in the Teddy Roosevelt Wing as I recall, displays a group of now-endangered East Asian pygmy rhinos, labeled (since the 1930s) with a credit to the cooperative colonial bureaucrats who granted the museum's permission to collect them. Every corner of the world is presented as it might have appeared in the summer of its discovery. The full-sized whale suspended over the Hall of Fishes poises at the silent edge of a gentle dive into the last instant of a pristine, unpolluted sea.

In contrast, east of the museum—the same direction the canoeists are heading—through the entrance called Naturalists Gate, Central Park teems with living biota in a landscape constructed to make nature a cultural event. Here, the spring bird migrations arrive as bright waves of prehistoric bits of gossamer protoplasm dropping nightly from vernal skies to feed, and rest, and fill up this wood with song, and to be greeted by a spontaneous, running, voice-over, interpretive commentary, involuntarily delivered by hundreds of euphoric birders. One late-May morning in the Ramble section of Central Park, an authoritative voice spoke from the underbrush: "Did you get a good look at it?" it asked—of whom I was not sure—and without waiting for a reply, explained: "The yellow warbler is the only *yellow* warbler with yellow feather shafts." The migration is thoroughly covered by experienced observers; no detail, no rare individual goes unremarked. For several years, the cop on the Central Park beat was a birder, who scootered through the chilly morning wood with a walkie-talkie and binoculars around his neck, stopping in strategic places to peer into the brush, as though assigned to radio his sightings into a registry at headquarters. Once, a squad of hardy, country-booted, camera- and scope-toting birders directed me to a rare Brewster's warbler. It was just beyond the far northeast edge of the Ramble, they informed me, "along the West Drive, in the cherry branch that hangs over the sixth guardrail post north of a Sabrett's hot dog vendor."

It was.

Central Park, Olmsted's masterpiece of earth-moving legerdemain, allows one to be immersed in nature, yet never at a far remove from a deli. Passing through the park's distinctive gray stone perimeter wall at Naturalists Gate, for example, one is immediately at treetop level, crossing the high, arched Buttress Bridge, from which the entry road descends into an oak and wisteria Victorian lakeshore forest. The city is out of sight; its sounds, muffled by foliage, give way to water lapping. A second footbridge crosses a lagoon to a rise on the north shore; the Ramble, where, on a good day, the warblers are as rainforest-dense as are the birds in any zoo on earth.

For almost a decade, the three biota, of street, museum, and park, appeared utterly disparate and unrelated. I had no clue how to imagine a coherent ecosystem for them, until I began looking for the West 78th Street Brook and its headwaters.

In the city, natural forces are elusive. Except when Con Ed certifies that lightning striking a substation in far-away northern Westchester has triggered a blackout, disasters are blamed on political, economic, social, or cultural forces. For example, less regularly than the annual migration, but every few years, the boiler room of our building filled with water and we were without hot water and heat for two or three chilly April days. Though these floods coincided with unusually wet springs following snowy winters, I read them as service interruptions; standard West Side conspiracies— the greedy landlord, super, and fuel oil company gouging each other to gouge me. The surprising possibility that the floods were a natural phenomenon was introduced to me by Bob Napoli, the building's most independent superintendent, and the only super I ever trusted to be in cahoots with no one.

During the twenty years I resided in the thick-walled, prewar apartment building, on the south side of the block between Broadway and Amsterdam Avenue, its operations, including the machinations of the boiler bellowing in all seasons from beneath the lobby floor, were in the charge of a succession of superintendents who, with union blessings, came and left like itinerant workers birddogging their ways across the five boroughs toward retirement seasons in Florida. With a sense of place as peripatetic as their lives, all but one defined the building's location solely by its interchangeable couplings to the city's sewers, conduits and mains, which were also the absolute boundaries of their union certification and job responsibilities. Bob Napoli was the exception. Wherever he went, his leery constitution demanded a geographic context. He loved talking about places where the lay of the land was visible; Bear Mountain Park; his wife's family's place in Puerto Rico, or the ex-urban homestead his grown son had settled, no doubt following paternal instincts. A year after Bob Napoli arrived on 78th Street, he showed me the three-and-a-half-foot-deep bunkerlike trench in the floor of the portion of the boiler room that lay beneath the sidewalk. "This was constructed," he declared, as we stood inside it, "to catch the flood of a brook that used to flow here and allow it to drain away without disabling the furnace. It worked," he added, voicing admiration for the builder, "until the city's storm drains clogged."

Tantalized by a possible geological dimension that might add continuity to the neighborhood's disorderly natural history, I set about to find additional evidence to support the Brook Hypothesis, to build a theory so circumstantially elegant that April water erupting from the basement floor would be as compelling evidence for the existence of the brook as observations of starlight being bent by the sun's gravity were of relativity.

The lower course of the brook was easy to imagine. Seventy-eighth Street lies in a shallow valley between the low hills of 77th and 79th Streets. The same tilt toward the river that elongates solstice shadows in June carries January's modern glacial ooze of meltwater, slush, and street detritus down from Columbus Avenue to Broadway. There it pools over backed-up storm drains, turns sluggishly northward to 79th Street and Broadway, and turns again, to cascade down a steep slope toward the 79th Street Boat Basin at the edge of the Hudson in Riverside Park. Without the two sharp corners, this was, I decided, the brook's approximate course.

Tracing the brook upstream, east of Columbus Avenue, to its headwaters, presented more difficulty. From the American Museum of Natural History, across Central Park West and into Central Park, the original land surface has been transformed by at least three major city-building constructions. The museum sits in the middle of an enigmatic plain that, at first glance, resembles the low bed of a former pond. The depression is an illusion, however, created by an excavated truck ramp on the building's west side and by a slight ridge that rises to its east, which, though it appears to be a natural divide, is almost certainly made of fill left over after the tunnel that carries the "A" train was cut beneath Central Park West. East of Central Park West, opposite the museum, the land surface drops abruptly on the inside of Central Park's perimeter wall to about twenty feet below street level. If the top of the watershed had been a pond where the museum now stands, the surface of land offered no evidence of it nor of the original direction of the drainage.

Before the Upper West Side of Manhattan became a city neighborhood it was old farmland, which fallowed, awaiting development, had become a squatters' shantytown. The eviction of the squatters and the construction of the streets happened at about the same time that Frederick Law Olmsted built Central Park and the first museum building was erected on its adjacent parcel of park land.

In a photograph displayed at the museum, taken at a time when squatters' huts still stand in the neighborhood and work on the park is well underway, the first museum building sits alone in a dry and dusty landscape. To its west a grid of city streets has been raised as causeways, high enough above the old farmland's surface that digging basements for the buildings that will fill the empty blocks requires no more than a few feet of excavation. No water is visible along 78th Street, though the photograph does show a shadow of a valley there, in which, it appears, the elevation of a stream in flood stage would be above that of the present boiler room floor.

East of the tiny museum in the photograph, Central Park stretches as a barren horizonless moonscape, across which hundreds of men and wagons are redistributing cubic acres of earth into a new terrain—hills, valleys, and a lake, being imagined and reified by human tectonics. The crater that will be Central Park Lake is under construction, and the land surrounding it is being regraded to drain into it. I had my clue.

By the time he began designing Central Park, the city had already tapped upstate mountains for drinking water, and Olmsted was free to use Manhattan water as pigment for his landscape. The key to understanding the natural history of the neighborhood I was experiencing was not where the local water had flowed, but how it had been valued and used. Replaced by mountain water, local water, with which squatters presumably washed their feet, had become commercially superfluous, collectable nature, to be used as decoration, or homeless nature, to be ignored and piped away.

After that revelation, proving the brook existed or tracing its course seemed less important to me, and though I was no longer searching for it at the time, the closest I believe I ever got to its headwaters came a few years later in a springtime mire at the edge of what used to be the bed of Butterfly Pond, beneath Buttress Bridge, just inside the Naturalists Gate. As I see it, Olmsted constructed Butterfly Pond to serve two purposes. As park plumbing, it captured water, which had previously run west under the museum, and redirected it eastward into Central Park Lake. As design and drama, the pond's wings were spread wide below both sides of the bridge so that light reflected from them would capture visitors' eyes and delay their discoveries of the lake ahead until they had descended deep enough into the landscape to be fully surrounded by its illusion.

Butterfly Pond was one of several Olmsted water bodies drained or filled early this century when shallow standing water became associated with miasma and disease. The pond's southern wing subsequently metamorphosed into an asphalt playground (mostly childless, except when our children visited it). But each spring, the dormant northern wing flickers to life with muddy seeps, from which I collected samples for my elementary science classes to ogle at the wriggling squirming organisms they contained and to be amazed at the strange forms life could take.

For my part, I was collecting a sample of time—water from the holy Holocene; from before the museum, Frederick Law Olmsted, and the "A" train turned the local watershed around; before city water came from the Catskills; before the war canoe was lifted from the Pacific and sent east over the great divide.

Alan Thein Durning

From

THIS PLACE ON EARTH
Home and the Practice of Permanence

Alan Thein Durning grew up in Seattle. He became a distinguished environmental researcher for the Worldwatch Institute in Washington, D.C., and published an award-winning book on the consumer society, *How Much Is Enough?* Not long after the book was published, he and his family decided to move to Seattle to cultivate a deep sense of place. In his hometown he has been active in the Northwest Environment Watch, focusing on bioregional research. His book *This Place on Earth: Home and the Practice of Permanence* describes various innovations in sustainable living throughout the Pacific Northwest and offers an account of his own family's attempt to make Seattle a bioregional community. The following selection consists of three excerpts from *This Place on Earth.* The first, from the opening of the book, relates his motivations for returning home, while placing Seattle in the broader context of the Northwest. The last two excerpts come from the end of the book. His family, living in a troubled neighborhood, seeks to develop community through setting up a basketball hoop, taking neighborhood walks with a baby stroller, and petitioning government for better urban design. Throughout the book, Durning gives us a realistic but hopeful vision of a bioregional city, one that consists of a true human community linked intimately with the broader natural community.

August

I am back in Seattle. I am exhausted, lonely, and off-balance—the damp air smells disconcertingly like childhood. At the moment, being here feels like defeat. It reminds me of the times when my brother and sister swam out to the log and I turned tail and crawled onto the beach.

I am haunted by the fear that by coming here I have turned tail on the cause that has occupied my last decade. I tell myself I am changing tactics, but I do not always trust this idea. At a minimum, I cannot fully explain my reasons for being here, nor why I am so determined to stay.

I came here, I suppose, to find out what it means to live responsibly in desperate times. Perhaps I came here in hopes of finding out what *permanence* would look and feel like—and to practice it while we still have the chance. Perhaps I came to confront head-on the pain and paradox of living in an economy that seems to thrive on the death of nature. Maybe I came here in the hope that *place* might be the escape hatch for a fractured society hurtling toward the environmental brink.

All I can say with confidence is that I came here because, a year ago, a grinning barefoot peasant in the Philippines pitied me—the one thing I could not stand—and her pity became like a seed in my shoe. It sprouted, grew into my dreams, and tormented me. It sent me scurrying to the only place that ever felt like home. And it put down a taproot that has now bound me here, in this moss-cloaked neighborhood where everything is smaller than my memories.

Coming home did not come naturally because allegiance to locale is alien to my family. I am from a line that reveres wanderers. My father, second son of a self-taught Irish merchant and a Polish Jew, fled the bigotry of the South at age sixteen and never looked back. My mother is a tenth-generation descendant of Puritans who sailed to Massachusetts from England after the *Mayflower's* voyage. Beginning with the third generation in the New World, the family began moving to a new town with each generation. By the sixth generation, they had crossed the Mississippi. The seventh generation reached the Pacific; the eighth crossed to Asia. The ninth and tenth also kept moving. For two centuries or more, my ancestors died in different states than the ones in which they were born. I grew up hearing the stories of these people—pioneer farmers, merchants, missionaries, military officers, and geographers.

Even the friends my family has attracted have been international vagabonds: my grandmother's guest books, kept since she was first married, record all the places where her many visitors ever lived. Seven ink-filled volumes stand on her shelf, reading like catalogs of exotic ports. I grew up paging through them, dreaming of the places I would one day inscribe in Grandma's book. Recently, I found an entry in uneven script: "Alan Durning, age 11, world traveler."

The three of us in my litter have collected stamps in our passports the way we used to collect bottle caps. Until recently, it has been uncommon for any two of us to be in the same time zone at once. I have been especially successful at mobility. The longest I have ever lived in the same room is three years; in the same house, six. Most of my life, I have surpassed the national average of moving every fifth year; I have rarely put up more than two consecutive calendars at the same address. Shortly after college, I set up base camp in Washington, D.C., where I joined the staff of a research center charged with monitoring the world's social and ecological health. A few years of seventy-hour weeks later I had been promoted and began hopscotching the globe myself, studying everything from poverty to atmospheric chemistry. It was urgent stuff: documenting injustice, testifying before Congress, jet-setting on behalf of future generations.

Then came the seed. I was in the Philippines interviewing members of remote hill tribes about their land and livelihood. On a sweltering day in the forested terrain of the Banwa'on people, a gap-toothed chief showed me the trees, streams, and farm plots that his tribe had tended for centuries. It was territory, he insisted, they would defend with their lives. As the sun finally slid lower in the sky, he introduced me to a frail old woman who was revered by the others as a traditional priestess. We sat under a sacred tree near her farm and looked out over the Ma'asam River. She asked through an interpreter, "What is your homeland like?"

She looked at me with an expectant smile, but I was speechless. My eyes dropped. Should I tell her about my neighborhood on the edge of Washington, D.C., the one where I then lived with my wife, Amy, and our son, Gary? The one where we could not let Gary play outside our apartment because of the traffic?

She repeated the question, thinking I had not heard. "Tell me about your place." Again, I could not answer. Should I tell her about the neighborhood we had previously fled, the one where the dead bodies of young men kept turning up in the alleys? The one where police helicopters were always shining their spotlights through our windows? The one that had since erupted in riots and suffered the psychotic nonchalance of a serial killer? I said nothing.

The truth was I lacked any connection to my base in Washington, D.C., and for some reason, for the first time, it shamed me. I had breakfasted with senators and shaken hands with presidents, but I was tongue-tied before this barefoot old woman. "In America," I finally admitted, "we have careers, not places." Looking up, I recognized pity in her eyes.

Picture North America from space. Look at the upper left and start an imaginary line on the rugged coast of southern Alaska. Climb the ridges that encircle Prince William Sound. Cross the snowy teeth of the Chugach Mountains and descend through kettle-pond country to the feet of the towering Alaska Range. Rise again to the bitter heights and, turning southeast along the crest, clip the corner of the Yukon Territory. Enter British Columbia and veer east through its folding north.

Turn your line south when you reach the Continental Divide in the Rocky Mountains. Follow that divide down the thousand-mile spine of British Columbia, across Montana, along the buttressed ridges of the Idaho border, and into Wyoming as far as Jackson Hole.

There, leave the divide and turn westward toward the coast. Following the swells and benches that limit the Columbia Basin, dip southward into Utah and Nevada, then northward again around the high desert of central Oregon. When you approach the Cascade Mountains, veer southwest through the tangled topography of northern California to the crest of the Coast Range. Just north of San Francisco Bay, descend to the shores of the Pacific.

The line you have drawn is an unfamiliar one. You won't find it on maps by Rand McNally. But it shows a geographical unit more real, in an ecological sense, than any of the lines governments draw. You have drawn a biological region—a bioregion. Specifically, you have outlined the watersheds of rivers flowing into the Pacific Ocean through North America's temperate rain forest zone.

Rain forests, the largest outside of the tropics, stretch along the coast from San Francisco Bay to Prince William Sound in a fifteen-hundred-mile belt. Running through this landscape of mammoth evergreens are salmon-filled rivers that rise inland—sometimes hundreds of miles inland—among corrugated ranges and desert plateaus.

The unity of this diverse bioregion is in the movement of its water; every ounce of moisture that the ocean throws into the sky and the sky hurls down on the land inside this region's borders tumbles toward the rain forest coast. If it does not evaporate or get trapped in underground aquifers along the way, the water will reach that dripping shoreline through one of several hundred swift, cold rivers. Most likely, it will travel through the Columbia—the biggest Pacific-bound flow in the Americas—or the Fraser—home to the Earth's greatest populations of migrating salmon.

But water that falls outside the boundaries will never touch the rain forest. It will run off in other directions—into the Yukon River and Bering Sea, into the Mackenzie and Saskatchewan Rivers and the Arctic Ocean, into the Missouri and Mississippi Rivers and the Gulf of Mexico, into the salt pans and dry washes of the landlocked Great Basin, or into the Sacramento River and San Francisco Bay. It will define other natural places, other units of ecology, but it will not glide through the mossy rot of temperate rain forests.

This place, defined by water running to woodlands, has no perfect name. You could call it the Rain Forest Province, the North Pacific Slope, or—as some do—Cascadia. But it is simpler to press into service a name from common parlance, a name that already denotes the place's economic and demographic center of gravity. It is best to call this place—the part of northwestern North America that is connected to the Pacific through rain forests—the Pacific Northwest.

After all, the human settlement patterns in the Pacific Northwest already give many of its people a cultural sense of kinship that roughly coincides with this natural unity. The place has a densely populated core and a vast, buffering hinterland. Its heart extends along a corridor from Vancouver and Victoria, British Columbia, through Seattle and Tacoma, Washington, to Portland and Eugene, Oregon. If you travel away from this urbanized strip in almost any direction, population diminishes in an unbroken gradient until you have crossed into other bioregions with other human hubs.

For reasons both cultural and ecological, therefore, the Pacific Northwest is one of the Earth's natural places. It exists apart from any government's recognition of it as a single place. It exists in a more fundamental way. It is manifest on the face of the land. It is there. It can be discovered.

Natural units of place such as this have always mattered more to people than has humanity in general or the planet in its entirety. Indeed, history is unequivocal: people will sacrifice for villages, homelands, or nations, even giving their lives. But humans seem unwilling to sacrifice for their planet, despite the fact that it is now suffering proportionately greater losses from social decay and environmental destruction than do most countries at war.

Specialists have known for decades that burgeoning numbers of people and their surging consumption of material resources were making the scale of human impacts on the Earth unsupportable. Homo sapiens has produced far more protoplasm—more mass of living tissue—than any other species in the four-billion-year evolutionary record. Earth's 5.8 billion people and their domesticated animals eat 3 percent of all the plant matter that grows on land each year—the staple of terrestrial food chains. Add the habitats burned, paved, plowed, grazed, cut down, or otherwise turned to human ends and the figure rises to 39 percent. Humans appropriate two-fifths of all plant matter that grows on land each year, a state of affairs that cannot last. This extreme disruption of ecosystems will end. The question is whether people will end it voluntarily and creatively, or whether nature will end it for them, savagely and catastrophically.

Humanity's failure to act in defense of the Earth is conventionally explained as a problem of knowledge: not enough people yet understand the dangers or know what to do about them. An alternative explanation is that this failure reflects a fundamental problem of motivation. People know enough, but they do not care enough. They do not care enough because they do not identify themselves with the world as a whole. The Earth is such a big place that it might as well be no place at all.

If places motivate but the planet does not, a curious paradox emerges. The wrenching global problems that the world's leading thinkers so earnestly warn about—crises such as deforestation, hunger, population growth, climate change, the proliferation of hazardous materials, and the loss of cultural and biological diversity—may submit to solutions only obliquely. The only cures possible may be local and motivated by a sentiment—the love of home—that global thinkers have often regarded as divisive or provincial. Thus, it may be possible to diagnose global problems globally, but impossible to solve them globally. There may not be any ways to save the world that are not, first and foremost, ways for people to save their own places.

April

As the last nut goes into place, a balding white man I've seen next door to Tyrone's house comes over. He introduces himself as Andy. "I've been meaning to have you folks over to pop a bottle of something for months. I see your kid out on his bike all the time. His name's Gary, right?" I climb down the ladder and stand with him looking up at the hoop, talking about this and that.

Andy helps me pull the ladder off the trellis, which sets off a stampede from down the block. Gary and the others charge toward us, veering off course only to scoop up basketballs, kickballs, and dog-chewed tennis balls from the front stoops and shrub-skirted hideaways of neighboring houses. When the herd is about thirty feet out, the balls start to fly. And the music of basketball begins, to continue uninterrupted for weeks on end: the dark clap of balls striking fiberglass, the vibrating ring of the steel rim.

The noise brings Amy outside with Kathryn and Peter. We stand around, holding the little ones and watching the play. Other adults stop to watch, too, replacing each other slowly on the sidewalk. The hoop makes it easy to be neighborly. You just watch the kids play. You don't have to think of what to say. There is Hanna, our next-door neighbor; Gerri, who lives beyond her, and Gina, whose driveway circles behind our place.

Over the days ahead we meet more neighbors: George, who has just moved in between us and the yellow house; Ray, who is Daron and Devon's father; Junior, who is—we think—Marcus's father; and Hillary, who lives up a block but has a kid the same age as Kathryn. Other folks stop too, folks who walk this way to the bus or the minimart. Amy and I find we are spending more time out front, visiting there when our parents drop by, rather than going inside right away. When we were looking for housing, we had wanted a front porch big enough to sit on. We did not find one, but the basketball court performed some of the same function.

The hoop starts to pay off in tangible ways, too. My work ethic has always made me regard sidewalk chatter as idle and unproductive; in fact, it is highly productive. It is like putting money in the bank. When we need curry powder, we know from courtside conversations that George is a bit of a cook, and, sure enough, he has a little stash. When we need garden tools to beat down the weeds behind the house, we know that Hanna has a good collection. And when Hanna needs somebody to walk her dog, she knows it will make Gary's day. Daron's dad, Ray, invites Gary to play on a basketball team he is going to coach in the winter. Eleven-year-old Sara proves so good with Peter and Kathryn that Amy invites her to come over after school to help out. Petty con artists sometimes knock on our door, saying they live just across the way and need ten bucks to take a sick relative to the hospital by cab. Before we knew our neighbors, we did not know what to believe. Now we can't be fooled.

After the hoop has been up for a couple of months, Tyrone comes over to stand with me as Gary practices three-pointers and Peter crawls on the pavement. "It's a blessing!"

"Yes, it is!" I agree. He compliments Gary on his shooting. I ask how his wife is doing. We discuss the weather. He and I have talked a fair bit since the hoop went up. I am no longer uncomfortable.

After a quiet spell, he lowers his voice. I can tell he's going to give me an update on the yellow house. "You know, they've been doin' better, 'specially the kids. The whole family is doin' better. It's a blessing!"

"Yes, it is!" I still have no idea how he knows what he knows, nor whether to believe him. But it is nice to hear that he thinks matters are improving on our troubled block. I think they are too.

May

Amy is out front by the hoop when Julie stops by, her stroller loaded with her two kids. She lives in the next block in a walk-up duplex. She and Amy get to talking about traffic. "It just goes too fast, doesn't it? I'm afraid to let the kids play outside. I'm afraid to cross the street." Amy agrees. While I have been attempting to weave community with a basketball hoop, Amy has been doing it with a baby stroller. She has been walking places: she has become the best customer of a new produce stand that opened three blocks away, and she visits a nearby children's consignment store almost every week.

"A friend of mine passed a petition around among her neighbors to request a traffic island from the city," says Julie. The city measured traffic speed and found it was over the speed limit. It built a planting circle in the middle of the intersection. Cars slowed down. People felt safer.

"Maybe we could get one on our street, too," says Amy. "Let's do a petition."

Amy has begun pointing out to me the traffic circles and diverters that are going in all over the city's neighborhoods. We watch them sprout from the blacktop like alder in a clear-cut. First come the spray-painted shapes on the pavement, then the Engineering Department's orange cones, then holes in the ground, then fresh concrete, and then soil and shrubs. The pace at each calms down.

When we are walking in our neighborhood nowadays, Amy points to the intersections where she wants bumps, bends, bubbles, and circles. She points to the sidewalks that are too narrow and the corners where the curb is impassable with a stroller. She points to empty lots that could become playgrounds or corner stores. A new landscape is taking shape in her head: what our community could be.

The petition, cooked up beside the basketball court, goes up and down the street quickly, and Julie mails it downtown. We are waiting for a response.

The Pacific Northwest. No part of the industrial world has as large a share of its ecosystems intact. And no other place on the continent matches its depth and breadth of sustainability initiatives, efforts undertaken by businesses, citizens, communities, and governments. A single biological region stretching from Prince William Sound to the Redwood Coast of California and from the Pacific Ocean to the crest of the Rockies, an economic region encompassing fourteen million people and $300 billion of annual production, the Pacific Northwest can be the test case for sustainability.

Drawing on its tradition of turning outlandish dreams into practical realities, the Northwest may be the place that demonstrates how to trade the old worldview for the new, and in the process exchange sprawl and malls for compact, vibrant cities; clear-cuts and monoculture for enduring farms, forests, and fisheries; throwaways, overpackaging, and rapid obsolescence for durability, reuse, and repair; volume for value; and consumerism for community.

The Northwest could model a way of life comprising less stuff and more time, fewer toys and more fun. Above all, it could become a place whose civility, whose culture—whose humanity—are as stunning as its scenery.

The politics of place is a politics of hope. It is sustained by a faith—somewhat mystical perhaps—in *place* itself. Whether they are descendants of Asian hunters who crossed the Bering land bridge during the Ice Age or mongrels with New England Puritan–Irish–Polish–Jewish blood, all people who put down roots are shaped by their home ground. Over time it seeps into them, and they become natives. In the Northwest this means they look up at twilight and draw strength from the mountains. They seek renewal at the rivers and the shores. They taste communion in the pink flesh of the salmon. The rains cease to annoy.

Here is the hope: that this generation becomes the next wave of natives, first in this place on Earth and then in others. That newfound permanence allows the quiet murmur of localities to become audible again. And that not long thereafter, perhaps very soon, the places of this Earth will be healed and whole again.

From Port Arthur in British Columbia, maverick timber boss A. J. Auden of the Abitibi Power and Paper Company had it right fifty years ago when he said, "We have spent these past two hundred and fifty years . . . in restless movement, recklessly skimming off the cream of superabundant resources, but we have not used the land in the true sense of the word, nor have we done ourselves much permanent good. It's high time that we . . . settled down, not for a hundred years, but for a thousand, forever."

Richard Rodriguez

NOTHING LASTS
A HUNDRED YEARS

Richard Rodriguez has written two literary autobiographies, including *Days of Obligation: An Argument with My Mexican Father*. He grew up in California, spending much of his youth in Sacramento, then a small but growing city. He now lives in San Francisco. Rodriguez's autobiographical literature is unique and powerful. Different periods of time overlap each other, and his style is marked by a directness and simplicity that contains honesty, insight, and keen perception. His upbringing blended different cultures, not only Mexican and American, but also Irish and Asian Indian. Family and cultures are always braided with experiences of the natural world. In this selection he evokes the mixture of cultures and nature in California and Mexico. The earth is not placed center stage in this essay, unlike in traditional nature writing, but its presence is ongoing and fundamental.

A waiter bowed. The dining room was flooded with sunlight. I saw my mother sitting alone at a table near the window.

Where's Papa?

I turned to see my father enter the dining room. His hand moved to adjust his tie. Some pleasure tempted his lips.

He had gotten up early. He had taken a walk. He had gone to the Capuchin church on the Via Veneto. I remembered the church—the monk murmuring at the drop of a coin—and, several flights down, I remembered the harvest of skulls.

For years I had dreamed of this trip with my parents. We were many years from Sacramento. We were in Rome at the Eden Hotel. This was to have been my majority—the grand tour—proof of my sophistication, my easy way with the world. This was to have been the culmination of our lives together, a kind of antiheaven. My father should have been impressed.

But nothing I could show my father, no Michelangelo, no Bernini, no cathedral or fountain or square, would so rekindle an enthusiasm in my father's eyes as that paltry catacomb he had found on his own. He had seen the final things. He was confirmed in his estimate of nature. He was satisfied.

I was born in the year 1632, in the city of York, of a good family, though not of that country, my father being a foreigner of Bremen. . . . I was called Robinson Kreutznaer; but by the usual corruption of words in England we are now called, nay, we call ourselves, and write our name 'Crusoe' . . .

Being the third son of the family, and not bred to any trade, my head began to be filled very early with rambling thoughts. . . . My father, a wise and grave man, gave me serious and excellent counsel against what he foresaw was my design.

When I was fourteen and my father was fifty, we toyed with the argument that had once torn Europe, South from North, Catholic from Protestant, as we polished the blue DeSoto.

"Life is harder than you think, boy."

"You're thinking of Mexico, Papa."

"You'll see."

We arrived late on a summer afternoon in an old black car. The streets were arcades of elm trees. The houses were white. The horizon was flat.

Sacramento, California, lies on a map around five hundred miles from the ruffled skirt of Mexico. Growing up in Sacramento, I found the distance between the two countries to be farther than any map could account for. But the distance was proximate also, like the masks of comedy and tragedy painted over the screen at the Alhambra Theater.

Both of my parents came from Mexican villages where the bells rang within an hour of the clocks of California. I was born in San Francisco, the third of four children.

When my older brother developed asthma, the doctors advised a drier climate. We moved one hundred miles inland to Sacramento.

Sacramento was a ladies' town—"the Camellia Capital of the World." Old ladies in summer dresses ruled the sidewalks. Nature was rendered in

Sacramento, as in a recipe, through screens—screens on the windows; screens on all the doors. My mother would close the windows and pull down the shades on the west side of the house "to keep out the heat" through the long afternoons.

My father hated Sacramento. He liked an open window. When my father moved away from the ocean, he lost the hearing in one ear.

Soon my mother's camellias grew as fat and as waxy as the others on that street. She twisted the pink blossoms from their stems to float them in shallow bowls.

Because of my mother there is movement, there is change in my life. Within ten years of our arrival in Sacramento, we would leap from one sociological chart onto another, and from house to house to house—each house larger than the one before—all of them on the east side of town. By the time I went to high school, we lived on "Eye" Street, in a two-story house. We had two cars and a combination Silvertone stereo-television. My bedroom was up in the trees.

I am not unconscious. I cherish our fabulous mythology. My father makes false teeth. My father received three years of a Mexican grammar-school education. My mother has an American high-school diploma. My mother types eighty words per minute. My mother works in the governor's office, where the walls are green. Edmund G. "Pat" Brown is governor. Famous people walk by my mother's desk. Chief Justice Earl Warren says hi to my mother.

After mass on Sundays, my mother comes home, steps out of her high-heel shoes, opens the hatch of the mahogany stereo, threads three Mexican records onto the spindle. By the time the needle sinks into the artery of memory, my mother has already unwrapped the roast and is clattering her pans and dinking her bowls in the kitchen.

It was always a man's voice. Mexico pleaded with my mother. He wanted her back. Mexico swore he could not live without her. Mexico cried like a woman. Mexico raged like a bull. He would cut her throat. He would die if she didn't come back.

My mother hummed a little as she stirred her yellow cake.

My father paid no attention to the music on the phonograph. He was turning to stone. He was going deaf.

I am trying to think of something my father enjoyed.

Sweets.

Any kind of sweets. Candies. Nuts. Especially the gore oozing from the baker's wreath. Carlyle writes in *The French Revolution* about the predilection of the human race for sweets; that so much of life is unhappiness and tragedy. Is it any wonder that we crave sweets? Just so did my father, who made false teeth, love sweets. Just so does my father, to this day, disregard warnings on labels. Cancer. Cholesterol. As though death were the thing most to be feared in life.

My mother remembered death as a girl. When a girl of my mother's village died, they dressed the dead girl in a communion dress and laid her on a high bed. My mother was made to look; whether my mother was made to kiss that cold girl I do not know, but probably she did kiss her, for my mother remembered the scene as a smell of milk.

My mother would never look again. To this day, whenever we go to a funeral, my mother kneels at the back of the church.

But Mexico drew near. Strangers, getting out of dusty cars, hitching up their pants, smoothing their skirts, turned out to be relatives, kissing me on the front porch. Coming out of nowhere—full-blown lives—staying a month (I couldn't remember our lives before they came), then disappearing when back-to-school ads began to appear in the evening paper.

Only my Aunt Luna, my mother's older sister, lives in Sacramento. Aunt Luna is married to my uncle from India, his name an incantation: Raja Raman. We call him Raj. My uncle and aunt came to the Valley before us. Raj is a dentist and he finds work where he can, driving out on weekends to those airless quonset-hut villages where farmworkers live. His patients are men like himself—dark men from far countries—men from India, from Mexico, from the Philippines.

One Sunday in summer my father and I went with my Uncle Raj and my Aunt Luna to Lodi, about thirty miles south of Sacramento. There was a brown lake in the center of Lodi where blond teenagers skied. We stopped to eat lunch in the shade of a tree and then we drove on, past dust-covered vineyards.

We stopped at an old house. I remember the look on my Aunt Luna's face. My father and my uncle got out of the car. There was some question about whether or not I should go with them. Aunt Luna fretted. "Don't be afraid of anything you'll see," she said. "It's just an old house where some men live." Aunt Luna stayed in the car.

Inside, the house is dark. The front-room windows are painted over.

There are cots along the walls. On several cots men recline. They are dressed. Are they sick? They watch as we pass. We hear only the sound of our steps on the boards of the floor.

A crack of light shines from behind a door at the rear of the house. My uncle pushes open the door. A man wearing an apron is stirring a pot.

Romesh!

Romesh quickly covers the pot. He kisses my uncle on the mouth. He shakes hands with my father. Then, turning to me, he salutes: "General."

Romesh was Raj's older brother. Every Christmas, when Romesh came to my uncle's house, he called me the general. My brother was the colonel. Romesh came with his sister—"the doctor." One time he stood on his head. Every Christmas, Romesh and his sister gave me presents that either had no sex or should have gone to a girl. Once, a green cup; another year, a string of pearls. I was never sure if there was menace in Romesh.

Uncle Raj offered my father a job managing a "boardinghouse"—like the one in Lodi—where derelicts slept.

In private my mother said no, Leo, no.

My father ended up working in the back room of my uncle's office on J Street, making false teeth for several dentists. My father and Uncle Raj became closest friends.

My classmates at Sacred Heart School, two blocks from our house, belong to families with names that come from Italy and Portugal and Germany. We carry aluminum lunch boxes decorated with scenes from the lives of Hopalong Cassidy and Roy Rogers. We are an American classroom. And yet we are a dominion of Ireland, the Emerald Isle, the darling land. "Our lovely Ireland," the nuns always call her.

During the hot Sacramento summers, I passed afternoons in the long reading gallery of nineteenth-century English fiction. I took an impression of London and of the English landscape. Ireland held no comparable place in my literary imagination. But from its influence on my life I should have imagined Ireland to be much larger than its picayune place on the map. As a Catholic schoolboy I learned to put on the brogue in order to tell Catholic jokes, of grave diggers and drunkards and priests. Ireland sprang from the tongue. Ireland set the towering stalks of the litanies of the Church to clanging by its inflection. Ireland was droll. Ireland was omniscient, Ireland seeping through the screen of the confessional box.

And did your mother come from Ireland? Around March 17, a Catholic holiday, my Mexican mother—that free-floating patriot—my mother begins to bristle a bit. "If it's so wonderful, why did they all leave?" But it is her joke sometimes, too, that we are Irish. My mother's surname is Moran, her father a black Irishman? Her father was tall with eyes as green as leaves. There were Irish in nineteenth-century Mexico, my mother says. But there is no family tree to blow one way or the other. The other way would lead to Spain. For Moran is a common enough name in Spain, as throughout Latin America. Could it have been taken, not from Ireland but to Ireland, by Spaniards—Spanish sailors shipwrecked by Elizabeth's navy?

When my younger sister asked me to help her with an essay for school (the topic was Ireland), I dictated a mouthful of clover about Dublin's Jewish mayor and Ed Sullivan, Dennis Day, Mayor Daley, Carmel Quinn. "Ireland, mother of us all. . . ."

The essay won for my sister an award from the local Hibernian society. I taunted my sister the night she had to dress up for the awards banquet. My mother, though, returned from the banquet full of humor. They had all trooped into the hall behind the Irish colors—my sister, my mother, my father, an assortment of ladies, and some white-haired priests.

When Father O'Neil came back from his first trip home to Ireland, I was in third grade. There was a general assembly at school so we could see his slides, rectangles of an impossible green bisected by a plane's wing. The relations lined up in front of white houses, waving to us or just standing there. There was something so sad about Father then, behind the cone of light from the projector, in Sacramento, at Sacred Heart School, so far from the faces of home and those faces so sad.

Ireland was where old priests returned to live with their widowed sisters and (one never said it) to die. So it was a big white cake and off you go. Ireland was our heart's home. I imagined the place from St. Patrick's Day cards—a cottage, a bell on the breeze, the breeze at my back, through quilted meadows and over the winding road.

Sacramento, my Sacramento, then, must seem to Father O'Neil as flat and as far away as Africa in the Maryknoll missionary movies. Life was the journey far from home, or so I decided as I watched Father O'Neil popping squares of memory upside down into a projector.

My mother remembered a train ride across the Mexican desert. Her brother, her only, her darling Juan, had come to California to find work. When he earned money enough he sent for his widowed mother and his five sisters. My mother was eight years old when she left Mexico. Poking her head out of the carriage window, she got cinders in her hair, which made her sisters laugh.

On that same train were nuns disguised in cotton dresses. They wore hats and gloves. The nuns were fleeing religious persecution in Mexico. An Irish pastor had promised them a convent in California. My mother sang for them.

In my own version of my life, I was not yet the hero—perhaps California was the hero, perhaps my mother. I used to lie awake in the dark and imagine myself on a train far, far away, hurtling toward the present age of my parents. Forty-six. Forty-six. I used to imagine my future as the story of the Welsh coal miner's son who leaves home to take the high road to London. But, as it was, I didn't come from Ireland or India. I was born at the destination.

In the 1950s, billboards appeared on the horizon that beckoned restless Americans toward California. Sacramento of the 1950s was the end of the Middle Ages and Sacramento growing was the beginning of London.

In those days, people were leaving their villages and their mothers' maiden names to live among strangers in tract houses and God spoke to each ambition through the GI Bill. Highways swelled into freeways. If you asked, people in Sacramento said they were from Arkansas or from Portugal. Somewhere else.

It was my father who told me that an explorer with my surname, Juan Rodriguez Cabrillo, had been the first European to see California, rising and falling on the sea. The Irish nun at school confirmed the sighting. California was the farthest outpost of the Spanish colonial empire, Sister said. "Mexico City was the capital of the New World."

Mexico was the old country. In the basement of my Aunt Luna's house, I'd seen the fifty-gallon drums destined for Mexico, drums filled with blankets, flannel shirts, wrinkled dresses, faded curtains. When things got old enough they went to Mexico, where the earth shook and buildings fell down and old people waited patiently amid the rubble for their new old clothes.

I was repelled by Mexico's association with the old. On the map in Sister Mary Regis's classroom, Mexico was designated OLD MEXICO. In my imagination, Mexico was a bewhiskered hag huddled upon an expanse of rumpled canvas that bore her legend: Old Mexico.

Mexico City had universities and printing presses, cathedrals, palanquins, periwigs, long before there were British colonies in New England, Sister said. Long before there were cathedrals in Mexico, or periwigs or palanquins, there had been Indians in California. They had long hair. They wore no clothes. They ate acorns. They moved camp often. The fifth-grade textbook couldn't remember much else about them. (They looked like me.)

Alongside the duck pond at Sutter's Fort was a replica of an Indian teepee, but the wrong kind—a Plains Indian teepee—a tripod covered with painted leather.

Tall silvery grasses were bound into sheaflike water boats. California Indians paddled up and down the watery marshes of the Central Valley, which at that time looked very much like a duck-hunting print, said Sister, holding one up: a wedge of ducks driven into a rosy dawn.

In the nineteenth century, an unnamed Spanish explorer had come over the foothills from San Francisco Bay. The unnamed explorer nevertheless brought names; he flung names like blue-rocks; he consigned names to every creek and river. He named the valley Sacramento to honor the sacramental transformation of bread and wine into the body and blood of Christ. The river, which Californians would later call the Sacramento, the explorer named Jesús María. There were saints' names and Mary's name all up and down California.

In the 1950s, it seemed odd to me that non-Catholics went along with all this. They mispronounced the Spanish words, it's true. In Spanish, Sacramento gets a pinwheel in the middle—a twirling "r." Valley pronunciation flattened the word—trampled the "sack"—but then the Valley was flat. And Sacramento was a Protestant town.

My school was named to honor the Sacred Heart, which symbolized the ardor of Christ for His people—a heart with an open valve, spewing flame. Public schools in town were named to honor nineteenth-century American men, adventurers and civilizers, men crucial to the Protestant novel: Kit Carson, John Frémont, C. K. McClatchy, James Marshall. The most common naming name was that of John Sutter, Sacramento's founding father. Sutter's name attached to two hospitals in town; a boulevard; a men's club across from the state capitol; a public park; a tennis club.

Sutter's Fort was our historical landmark. Sutter's Fort was across the street from the new Stop'n'Shop, a ten-minute bicycle ride from my house. Sutter's Fort held no mystery for me. The grass was mowed once a week.

The fort was surrounded on weekdays by yellow school buses. Not that Sacramento's memory of John Sutter was an unmixed pride. Sutter was a founding father notable for his failure. His story spelled a lesson in the Protestant annals.

Johann Sutter arrived in the 1830s, when California was Mexican territory. He had come from a low, delftish sky, from Bavaria, from Calvin, from Zwingli. When Sutter arrived in Monterey, he proposed to Mexican officials that he would build a fort in the great valley over the coastal hills. The fort would be a European settlement—New Helvetia he called it—a wall against the Indians. Mexico granted permission. Sutter paid no money to become a duke of wind and grass, the last European in a nineteenth-century opera.

As a young man, as a silent man, courting my mother, my father spent what little money he had on opera tickets, purchasing the extravagant gesture. When my father was seven years old, his mother died giving birth to a baby named Jesús. My father remembered lightning. How it rained that night! His father bundled up the blood-soaked sheets and the shift she wore, and with his son (my father carried the lantern), he went out into the storm to bury them. A few months later the baby died.

My father remembered the funeral of his father—the coffin floating on the shoulders of the men of the village, as if on a river, down the hill to the cemetery. As the casket was lowered into the pit, my father stepped forward to look down and he saw the bones of a hand reaching upward. My father never afterward passed up an opportunity to look into an open casket.

Infrequently, after dinner, my father told ghost stories.

"It doesn't happen here," my mother would say to her children, leaning into the story like an unwanted shaft of sunlight. "It happened in Mexico. Those things happen in old countries. During the Revolution, people used to bury their gold. When they died, they needed to come back to tell their children to dig up the money, so they could rest in peace. It doesn't happen here."

At the Saturday matinee at the Alhambra Theater we sat in the dark, beneath proximate grimaces of comedy and tragedy, laughing at death— we laughed at that pathetic tourist, the Creature from the Black Lagoon. For we were the sons and daughters of Arkies and Okies and the Isles of the Azores. Parents, grandparents—someone near enough to touch, someone close enough to whisper—had left tragedy behind. Our parents had crossed the American River, had come to Sacramento where death had no dominion. To anyone who looked back from the distance of California, the words of the dead were like mouths opening and closing in a silent film.

Sacramento's ceremonial entrance was the Tower Bridge, where a sign proclaimed the town's population as 139,000. From the bridge you could see the state capitol—a wedding cake topped by a golden dome. Then, for six blocks, Sacramento posted BAIL BONDS; WEEKLY RATES; JESUS SAVES. Skid Row was what remained of the nineteenth-century river town, the Sacramento one sees in the early lithographs—a view from the river in the 1850s: young trees curling upward like calligraphic plumes; wooden sidewalks; optimistic storefronts; saloons; hotels; the Eagle Theater.

In the 1950s, Sacramento had begun to turn away from the land. Men who "worked for the state" wore white short-sleeved shirts downtown. There were office buildings, hotels, senators. Sacramento seemed to me a long way from the Okie evangelists at the far end of the car radio. Except for Mexican farmworkers, I rarely saw men wearing cowboy hats downtown.

The urban progress of Sacramento in the 1950s—the pouring of cement and of asphalt—imitated, even as it attempted to check, the feared reclamation of California by nature. But in the 1950s there was plenty of nature left. On summer evenings, houses became intolerable. We lolled on blankets on the grass. We were that much closer to becoming Indians.

Summer days were long and warm and free and I could make of them what I liked. America rose, even as the grasses, even as the heat, even as planes rose. America opened like a sprinkler's fan, or like a book in summer. At Clunie Library the books which pleased me most were about boyhood and summer and America; synonyms.

I hate the summer of Sacramento. It is flat and it is dull. Though it is not yet noon, the dry heat of Sacramento promises to rise above the leaves to a hundred degrees. Just after noon, the California Zephyr cuts through town, pauses for five minutes, stopping traffic on K and L, and for those five minutes I inhabit the train's fabulous destination. But then the train sweeps aside like the curtain at the Memorial Auditorium, to reveal the familiar stage set for a rural comedy. A yellow train station.

Yet something about the Valley summer is elemental to me and I move easily through it—the cantaloupe-colored light, the puddles of shade on the street as I bicycle through. There is a scent of lawn.

When I think of Sacramento, I think of lawns—force-fed, prickling rectangles of green. Lawns are not natural to California. Even one season without water, without toil, is ruinous to a garden, everyone knows. The place that had been before—before California—would come back; a place the Indians would recognize. Lovely tall grasses of dandelion or mustard in spring would inevitably mean lapsarian weeds, tinder grass and puncture vines come summer.

On Saturdays I mow the front lawn. On my knees I trim the edges. Afterward I take off my shoes to water down the sidewalk. Around noontime, as I finish, the old ladies of Sacramento, who have powdered under their arms and tied on their summer straw hats, walk by and congratulate me for "keeping your house so pretty and clean. Whyn't you come over to my house now," the ladies say.

I smile because I know it matters to keep your lawn pretty and green. It mattered to me that my lawn was as nice as the other lawns on the block. Behind the American façade of our house, the problem was Ireland. The problem was India. The problem was Mexico.

Mexico orbited the memory of my family in bitter little globes of sorrow, rosary beads revolving through the crushing weight of my mother's fingers. Mexico. Mexico. My mother said Mexico had skyscrapers. "Do not judge Mexico by the poor people you see coming up to this country." Mexico had skyscrapers, pyramids, blonds.

Mexico is on the phone—long-distance.

Juanito murdered!

My mother shrieks, drops the phone in the dark. She cries for my father. For light.

A crow alights upon a humming wire, bobs up and down, needles the lice within his vest, surveys with clicking eyes the field, the cloud of mites, then dips into the milky air and flies away.

The earth quakes. The peso flies like chaff in the wind. The Mexican police chief purchases his mistress a mansion on the hill.

The doorbell rings.

I split the blinds to see three nuns standing on our front porch.

Mama. Mama.

Monsignor Lyons has sent three Mexican nuns over to meet my parents. The nuns have come to Sacramento to beg for Mexico at the eleven o'clock mass. We are the one family in the parish that speaks Spanish. As they file into our living room, the nuns smell pure, not sweet, pure, like candles or like laundry.

The nun with a black mustache sighs at the end of each story the other two tell: Orphan. Leper. Crutch. One-eye. Casket.

¡Qué lástima!

"Someday you will go there," my mother would say. "Someday you'll go down and with all your education you will be 'Don Ricardo.' All the pretty girls will be after you." We would turn magically rich in Mexico—such was the rate of exchange—our fortune would be multiplied by nine, like a dog's age. We would be rich, we would be happy in Mexico.

Of Mexico my father remembered the draconian, the male face—the mustache parted over the false premises of the city.

"What is there to miss?" My father leaned over the map of Mexico I had unfolded on my desk.

"Tell me about the village."

"It's not on the map." His finger moved back and forth across the desert, effacing.

"Tell me names, Papa, your family."

He was an orphan in Mexico. My father had no private Mexico, no feminine corner. From the age of eight my father worked for rich relatives, a poor relation on the sufferance of his uncle. He remembers a cousin, a teenage girl, who went to bed when the sun went down and wept all night. And there were aunts, young aunts with their hair packed into gleaming loaves; old aunts whose hair had shriveled into dry little buns. My father appears in none of the family photographs he has kept in a cigar box in the closet.

The family was prominent, conservative, Catholic in the Days of Wrath—years of anti-Catholic persecution in Mexico. My father saw a dead priest twirling from the branch of a tree. My father remembered a priest hiding in the attic of his uncle's house. My father heard crowds cheering as the haughty general approached. My father remembered people in the crowd asking one another which general was passing, which general had just passed.

The church was my father's home; both of his parents were in heaven; the horizon was my father's home. My father grew up near the sea and he dreamed of sailing away. One day he heard a sailor boast of Australia. My father decided to go there.

My father's hand rests upon the map, a solitary continent, veined, un-moored. His native village was near enough to the town of Colima so that at night, as a boy, he saw the new electric glow of Colima instead of the stars. Colima, the state capital, has grown very large (a star on the map); perhaps what had been my father's village is now only a suburb of Colima?

He shrugs.

My father made false teeth for Dr. Wang. Mrs. Wang was the recep-tionist. Mrs. Wang sat at a bare table in an empty room. An old Chinese man, Dr. Wang's father, climbed the stairs at intervals to berate his son and his son's wife in Chinese.

Because of my mother, we lived as Americans among the middle class. Because of my father, because of my uncle from India, we went to Chinese wedding receptions in vast basement restaurants downtown, near the Greyhound station. We sat with hundreds of people; we sat in back; we used forks. When the waiter unceremoniously plopped wobbly pink desserts in front of us, my mother pushed my plate away. "We'll finish at home."

My father and my uncle worked among outsiders. They knew a hand-some black doctor who sat alone in his office on Skid Row, reading the newspaper in his chair like a barber.

Sacramento was filling with thousands of new people each year—people fleeing the tanks of Hungary, people fleeing their fathers' debts or their fathers' ghosts or their fathers' eyes.

One of my aunts went back to Mexico to visit and she returned to tell my mother that the wooden step—the bottom step—of their old house near Guadalajara was still needing a nail. Thirty years later! They laughed.

My father said nothing. It was as close as he came to praising America.

We have just bought our secondhand but very beautiful blue DeSoto. "Nothing lasts a hundred years," my father says, regarding the blue De-Soto, as regarding all else. He says it all the time—his counsel. I will be sit-ting fat and comfortable in front of the TV, reading my *Time* magazine. My mother calls for me to take out the garbage. *Now!* My father looks over the edge of the newspaper and he says it: Nothing lasts a hundred years.

Holiday magazine published an essay about Sacramento by Joan Didion. The essay, an elegy for old Sacramento, was about ghostly ladies who perched on the veranda of the Senator Hotel and about their husbands, who owned the land and were selling the land. Joan Didion's Sacramento was nothing to do with me; families like mine meant the end of them. I so thoroughly missed the point of the essay as to be encouraged that a national magazine should notice my Sacramento.

Whenever Sacramento made it into the pages of *Time* magazine, I noticed the editors always affixed the explanatory *Calif.,* which I took as New York City's reminder. We were nothing. Still, that caliphate had already redeemed our lives. My mother, my father, they were different in California from what history had in store for them in Mexico. We breathed the air, we ate the cereal, we drank the soda, we swam in the pools.

My father was surprised by California and it interested him. It interested him that Sacramento was always repairing itself. A streetlight would burn out, a pothole would open in the asphalt, a tree limb would crack, and someone would come out from "the city" to fix it. The gringos were always ready to fix things, my father said.

In high school I worked as a delivery boy for Hobrecht Lighting Company. I delivered boxes of light fixtures to new homes on the north side of the river.

I remember standing outside a house near Auburn, waiting for the contractor to come with a key. I stood where the backyard would be. The March wind blew up from the fields and I regretted the loss of nature—the fields, the clear distance.

Yet California was elemental to me and I could no more regret California than I could regret myself. Not the dead California of Spaniards and forty-niners and Joan Didion's grandmother, but Kodachrome, CinemaScope, drive-in California—freeways and new cities, bright plastic pennants and spinning whirligigs announcing a subdivision of houses; hundreds of houses; houses where there used to be fields. A mall opened on Arden Way and we were first-nighters. I craved ALL-NEW and ALL-ELECTRIC, FREE MUGS, and KOOL INSIDE and DOUBLE GREEN STAMPS, NO MONEY DOWN, WHILE-U-WAIT, ALL YOU CAN EAT.

At a coffee shop—open 24 hours, 365 days a year—I approved the swipe of the waitress's rag which could erase history.

Through the years I was growing up there, Sacramento dreamed of its own redevelopment. Plans were proposed every few months to convert K Street downtown into a mall and to reclaim a section of Skid Row as "Old Town." The *Bee* published sketches of the carnival future—an expansive street scene of sidewalk cafés with banners and clouds and trees that were also clouds and elegant ladies with their purse arms extended, pausing on sidewalks that were made of glass.

A few years later, the future was built. Old Sacramento became a block of brick-front boutiques; some squat glass buildings were constructed on Capitol Avenue; and K Street, closed to traffic for several blocks, got a concrete fountain and some benches with winos asleep in the sun.

Never mind. Never mind that the future did not always meet America's dream of itself. I was born to America, to its Protestant faith in the future. I was going to be an architect and have a hand in building the city. There was only my father's smile that stood in my way.

It wasn't against me; his smile was loving. But the smile claimed knowledge. My father knew what most of the world knows by now—that tragedy wins; that talent is mockery. In the face of such knowledge, my father was mild and manly. If there is trouble, if there is a dead bird to pick up, or when the lady faints in church, you want my father around. When my mother wants water turned into wine, she nudges my father, for my father is holding up the world, such as it is.

My father remains Mexican in California. My father lives under the doctrine, under the very tree of Original Sin. Much in life is failure or compromise; like father, like son.

For several years in the 1950s, when one of my family makes a First Holy Communion, we all go to Sutter's Fort to have our pictures taken. John Sutter's wall against the Indians becomes a gauge for the living, a fixed mark for the progress of my mother's children. We stand in formal poses against the low white wall of the fort. One of my sisters wears a white dress and veil and a little coronet of seed pearls. Or, when it is a boy's turn, one of us wears a white shirt, white pants, and a red tie. We squint into the sun. My father is absent from all the photographs.

The Sacramento Valley was to have been John Sutter's Rhineland. He envisioned a town rising from his deed—a town he decided, after all, to name for himself—Sutterville. Sutter imagined himself inventing history. But in the Eastern cities of Boston and Philadelphia and New York, Americans were imagining symmetry. They were unrolling maps and fixing them

with weights set down upon the Pacific Ocean. Newcomers—Americans—
were arriving in Mexican territory.

Already there were cracks in the sidewalk where the roots of the elm
tree pushed up.

My father smiled.

Ask me what it was like to have grown up a Mexican kid in Sacramento
and I will think of my father's smile, its sweetness, its introspection, its
weight of sobriety. Mexico was most powerfully my father's smile, and not,
as you might otherwise imagine, not language, not pigment. My father's
smile seemed older than anything around me. Older than Sutter's Fort.

Priests were optimists. They were builders and golfers, drinkers of Scotch.
They bellowed their Latin. They drove fast in dark cars. They wore Hawai-
ian shirts to compensate for tragedy. Priests' boyhoods were spent in dark,
polished seminaries, as lovelorn, as masculine as my father's Mexico. Priests
wore skirts. Parishioners gave priests hand towels with crosses embroidered
on, or pen sets with crosses for clips, or handkerchiefs with little crosses
in the corners, or notepapers embossed with praying hands. Priests told
jokes to cover the embarrassment of such gifts; priests told jokes to cover
the embarrassment of collecting money; priests told jokes to cover the embarrassment of life, for priests had the power to forgive sins.

Nuns were pragmatists. They were embarrassed by nothing. The Sisters
of Mercy taught me confidence. When I came to their classrooms, unable,
unwilling to speak English, the nuns methodically elected me. They picked
on me. They would not let me be but I must speak louder, Richard, and
louder, Richard. I think of those women now, towers, linen-draped silos,
inclining this way and that, and only their faces showing; themselves country lasses, daughters of Ireland. They served as my link between Mexico
and America, between my father's dark Latin skepticism and the naïve
cherry tree of Protestant imagining.

The only exception to the rule of confidence at school came with religion class. At the start of each school day, after the "Morning Offering,"
after the Pledge of Allegiance to the Flag of the United States of America,
our young hearts were plunged in the cold bath of Ireland. For fifty minutes, life turned salt, a vale of tears. Our gallery, our history, our geography, was Ireland. The story of man was the story of sin, which could not
be overcome with any such thing as a Declaration of Independence. Earth

was clocks and bottles and heavy weights. Earth was wheels and rattles and sighs and death. We all must die. Heaven was bliss eternal. Heaven was a reign of grace bursting over the high city and over the mansions of that city. Earth was Ireland and heaven was Ireland. The dagger in Mary's heart was pain for her Son's passion. The bleeding heart of Jesus was sorrow for man's sin. Christ had instituted a church—a priesthood, sacraments, the mass—and men required all the constant intercession of the saints and the special help of Mother Mary to keep the high road. All alone, man would wander and err, like pagan Caesar or like Henry VIII.

At nine-thirty, the subject changed. The class turned to exercises of worldly ambition—to spelling, reading, writing—in preparation for adulthood in comic America. The nuns never reconciled the faces of comedy and tragedy and they never saw the need.

"Remember the Alamo," children in Sacramento learned to say. Remembering what?

Parades up Broadway on the Fourth of July enlisted equestrian clubs of blond businessmen dressed in tight pants, as Spanish dons, together with their señoritas, sidesaddle, on charming palominos. Men who had seen war in Asia and Europe, the woman who had lost her only true love—they waved to the crowd. The past was something that sparkled in the sun or the past was something preserved from the sun, like the adobe rooms at Sutter's Fort.

My father mutters about the intrigues of Masonic lodges in Mexico.

That's only Mexico, Papa.

Most boys my age in Sacramento are wearing coonskin caps when my father tells how America stole the Southwest from Mexico, how Americans died at the Alamo to make Texas a slave state.

The United States has a different version.

On Sunday nights, we gather around the TV to watch *The Ballad of Davy Crockett.* My father is interested at first. The Mexicans surrounding Walt Disney's Alamo are buffoons with white suspenders crossed over their bellies. My father returns to his newspaper.

At noontime exactly on a clear winter day, California will officially become the largest, by which we mean the most populous, state in the union. Governor Edmund G. "Pat" Brown wants fire sirens and factory whistles; he wants honking horns and church bells to detonate the hour of our numerical celebrity. The bureaucrat's triumphant tally will change California forever.

Sacred Heart Church in Sacramento has no bells, none that ring, nothing to hang in this clear blue sky. There is a brick tower, a campanile, a shaft of air. When the church was built, neighbors had complained first thing about bells. So no bells ever rang at Sacred Heart.

Five to twelve: The Irish nun stands at her blackboard. Tat. Tat. Tat. Slice. Tat. Tat. Tat. I strain to hear outside. Nothing, beyond the tide of traffic on H Street; the chain of the tether ball lifting in the wind, then dropping to lash its pole. Clank clink. Clank clink. At noontime exactly there is a scraping of chairs as we stand to pray the "Angelus" ("The angel of the Lord declared unto Mary . . . ").

One hundred miles away, the governor's son was also reciting the "Angelus." Edmund G. Brown, Jr.—Jerry Brown—was a seminarian in Los Altos, studying to become a priest. We saw his picture in the newspaper every year in the Christmas-tree photo from the governor's mansion—a young man with dark eyebrows, dressed in black.

Within twenty years Jerry Brown would assume his father's office. The ex-seminarian expounded upon limits, his creed having shriveled to "small is beautiful," a catchphrase of the sixties. Like John Sutter, Jr., Jerry Brown dismantled his father's huge optimism.

"Here tragedy begins," whispers Sister Mary Regis. "The wheel of fortune creaks downward toward a word buried for centuries in the bed of a stream. . . ."

The Irish nun, an unlikely Rhinemaiden, rehearses the Protestant parable for her fifth-grade class. John Sutter sent one of his men, James Marshall, up to the Sierra foothills to build a sawmill. It was January 1848. In the clear winter stream (here Sister hikes her skirt, shades her eyes with her hand; her eyes seem to scrutinize the linoleum), Marshall spied a glint. "It looked like a lady's brooch."

In the morning, or the next morning, or the next, Sutter dispatched several men to see if they could find more of the stuff. Sutter hoped to keep the discovery secret. But several merchants in the region made it their business to take the news over the hills to San Francisco. And so, within weeks, Sutter's kingdom—the kingdom intended for John Sutter by the providence of God—was lost in a rush of anarchy. Sutter was abandoned by his men, who would be kings themselves. His herd of cattle, his horses—

all were stolen. And his fort—that placid rectangle of dirt in an ocean of grass—his fort was overrun by men who heard the mystical word pronounced out loud.

GOLD.

There were stories. People vaulting from the dentist chair at the approach of my Uncle Raj. "No nigger dentist is going to stick his fingers in my mouth!" There was a price to be paid for living in Sacramento, the dark-green car, the green lawn, the big green house on 45th Street.

My Uncle Raj had three daughters. He wanted a son. I flirted with him. Every Christmas I would ask my Uncle Raj for expensive toys my parents couldn't afford. I wanted a miniature circus. I wanted a cavalry fort.

My uncle called me Coco.

Sutter's son inherited the shambles of his father's dream. John Sutter, Jr., was a tradesman and not a man of the land. John Sutter, Jr., recognized the advantages for trade in situating a new town alongside the river, two miles west of his father's fort. John Sutter, Jr., proposed giving the new river town the old Spanish name for the Valley—Sacramento. Thus Sacramento City flourished while Sutterville—which John Sutter had imagined as teeming, spired, as blessed as Geneva—Sutterville dried up and died.

In my bedroom I sketched visionary plans. A huge aquatic amusement park would parallel the river beneath an animated neon sign of a plunging diver. There would be a riverboat restaurant decked with Christmas lights and a dinner theater. (The movie *Show Boat* had recently been filmed near Sacramento.)

It was the father's failure Sacramento remembered, not the son's success. John Sutter abandoned his fort, retired to a farm. A short time later he left California for good. His bones are buried in Pennsylvania.

" . . . A victim of sudden good fortune," the Irish nun pronounced over him.

Such, too, was Sacramento's assessment of Sutter's life. The town may have owed its combustion to the Gold Rush, but when, within months, the vein of anarchy was exhausted, Sacramento would turn to regard the land itself as representing God's grace. Sacramento became a farm town, the largest in the Central Valley.

Toward the end of August, the air turned foul. Farmers were burning, people said—always this speculation on the cardinal winds—just as people said "peat dust" in March or "hay fever" in May or "alfalfa" in summer.

John Sutter served as a reminder to generations of farmers who lived by the seasons (Low Church lessons of slow growth, deferred reward). For his fall was steep, a lesson suitable to the moral education of generations of flatland teenagers—farm kids who came to Sacramento every August for the State Fair. We would see their pictures in the *Sacramento Bee,* kids from Manteca or Crow's Landing in their starched 4-H uniforms, holding sunflower ribbons over the heads of doomed beasts.

After work, my father and my Uncle Raj drove home together in Raj's new green car—the Mexican and the Indian. They sat in the car with the motor running.

"Go out and bring in your father," my mother would say.

I stole only bits of the story; the rest lay on a shelf too high for me. My Uncle Raj had gotten mixed up in some kind of politics. Once, Uncle Raj had taken my father to "a meeting" in San Francisco.

That was all I knew. That, and I once overheard my mother say on the phone, "We're afraid to have Leo apply for the job. There may be some record."

My father, as everyone knew, would have liked a job at the post office. But he never applied.

Alongside copies of *Life* and *Saturday Evening Post* on the mahogany table in Raj's waiting room were "international" pamphlets.

Was Raj a Communist?

Communists were atheists. Raj was a Catholic. He converted when he married my aunt. He went to mass every Sunday.

One afternoon a dental-supply salesman—his sample case and his hat were in his hand—came out into the waiting room with Raj. It was nearing six o'clock. I sat turning the pages of a magazine. My father was taking down the garbage. I could hear the trash barrel bumping down the stairwell. The man crossed to the table next to me, picked up the stack of pamphlets, and stooped to place them into the waste basket my father had just emptied. "Let's just get rid of these, Dr. Raman." His tone was not friendly but he smiled. "Why look for trouble, I always say," holding out his hand to Uncle Raj. Uncle Raj stared down into the waste basket.

Had my Uncle Raj conspired against paradise?

My uncle's eyes began to cloud at their perimeters. I heard them say he had a heart bother. I heard them say he was worried he might get deported.

My uncle had been in some kind of trouble with the Immigration Service. There had been "a trial."

My uncle put an Adlai Stevenson sticker on the back fender of his new green car.

But there were afternoons when my uncle's heart tightened like a fist at the prospect of losing California. In the back room of my uncle's office was a maroon sofa and, over the sofa, a painting of a blond lady being led by a leopard on a leash. Beneath the painting my uncle lay prostrate. At such times my father applied warm towels to the back of my uncle's skull.

Raj had come on ships all the way from Bombay when he was a boy. Now Raj hated the ocean. The swirling ocean was a function of the Immigration and Naturalization Service. The ocean would surely carry him back to India.

What was India, I pondered, but another Mexico. Indians in both places. "Cattle freely roam the streets of Bombay," according to the *World Book Encyclopedia.*

My mother remembered Mexico as a girl. She remembered the taste of Mexican ice cream, creamier than here. She remembered walking with her sisters round the plaza at night, the warm Guadalajara nights. She remembered a house—an address—tall shadows against a golden wall. In Mexico her mother made laces to sell, seeming to pluck the patterns out of the air with her fingers—laces fallen, like snowflakes, through time. My mother kept a cellophane bag full of lace in a drawer in the kitchen. She brought the bag out to show us, unfolding the laces tenderly as cobweb. Mexican women are real women, my mother said, caressing the antimacassar spread open upon the table. But the beauty of the lace troubled her. She admitted she never wanted to learn it.

Oh, but my mother's brother Juanito was tall as a tree, strong as a tree, with shade in his eyes. And people threw coins when my mother danced on a table in high-button shoes, tossing her head like a pony at the call of her nickname, Toyita. Toyita, she remembered the lyrics of a song. Ah, there are no love songs like the love songs of Mexico. This country is so dry, like toast, my mother said. Nothing like Mexico, my mother said, lapping the blue milk of the memory of Mexico.

My father is a man nearly as old as the century. As a boy he saw Hal-

ley's Comet and he gauged his life by the sighting. He said he would live
to see the comet's return and now he has surpassed Halley's Comet. My
father understands that life is as surprising as it is disappointing. He left
Mexico in his late twenties for Australia. He ended up in Sacramento in
a white coat, in a white room, surrounded by shelves of grinning false teeth.
Irony has no power over my father.

Our last house on "Eye" Street was across from an old cemetery. No
memory attached to it. The grass was watered and cut once a month by
the city. There were no scrolls or wrought-iron fences; no places to put
flowers. There were granite plaques level with the ground. Early dates. Solitary names. Men. Men who had come early to California and died young.

No grandsons or granddaughters came forward in the 1950s when Sacramento needed the land to build a school, a new Sutter Junior High School.
A plywood fence was hammered up around the cemetery and, within that
discretionary veil, bulldozers chugged and grunted, pulling up moist hairy
mounds of what had once been the light of day; trucks came to carry it
all away.

In early November, white tule fog rises from the valley floor. My father
is easy with this ancient weather reminiscent of the sea. My father is
whistling this morning as he scrambles two eggs. My mother turns away
from the window, pulling her blue bathrobe closer around her throat. I
am sitting at the kitchen table. I am sixteen years old. I am pouring milk
onto Sugar Frosted Flakes, watching milk rise in the bowl. My parents will
die. I will die. Everyone I know will someday be dead. The blue parakeet
my mother has taught to say "pretty boy" swings upon his little trapeze,
while my mother pours coffee.

I can no longer remember the cold. In my memory, it is always summer in Sacramento; the apricot tree in the backyard is heavy; the sky is
warm and white as a tent.

One summer, my uncle was beautiful. His skin was darker than Mexico. His skin wore shade. It was blue. It was black.

When I was seven years old, my girl cousins threw me into the lake at
Lodi and, with several islands to choose from, I swam toward the island
of my uncle. His eyes were black and so wide with surprise they reflected
the humor of the water. His nipples were blue and wet black fur dripped
down his front and floated in the water at his waist.

In the family album, Raj yet lifts me upside down by my legs. I am confident in my abandon as the trees whirl by. My aunt backs away from the camera, regret blurring from her eyes.

"Don't . . . Please. Put him down now, Raj."

Comedy and tragedy merged when I was sixteen. My uncle died.

He was extracting a tooth. He had just begun to tighten the clamp; the water swirled in the expectoral basin (within the patient's skull the awful grating, as of sepulchral stone), when my uncle began to sweat.

"I don't think I'm going to be able to finish. . . ."

The clamp banged down on the metal tray.

The receptionist's scream brought my father from the back lab, still drying his hands with a towel. My father placed the towel under my uncle's head. My father took my uncle's hand, where my uncle lay on the dark-green linoleum; my father easing my uncle down into the ocean.

"Keep me in your prayers," the nun would write years later to her fifth-grade student, remembering him as a boy on her deathbed. Before she died, Sister Mary Regis sent me a card, a confident, florid verse. Inside, she writes she will not be able to come to the lecture I am going to give in Sacramento, as she has a "chronic illness." (She is dying of cancer.)

"Keep me in your prayers, and I do you. Do you remember that you carried a notebook and asked millions of questions?"

The same question: Who is more right—the boy who wanted to be an architect, or his father, who knew that life is disappointment and reversal? (Is the old man's shrug truer than the boy's ambition simply because the shrug comes last?)

In Mexico my father had the freedom of the doves. He summoned the dawn. Each morning at five-thirty, my father would climb the forty steps of the church tower to pull the ropes that loosened the tongues of two fat bells. My father was the village orphan and it was his duty and his love and his mischief to wake the village, to watch it stir: the pious old ladies bending toward mass; the young men off to the fields; the eternal sea.

Starhawk

FANTASY OF A LIVING FUTURE

Starhawk lives in the San Francisco area, where she is active with the Reclaiming Collective, a group working to unify spirit and politics. She combines Buddhism and paganism, and is a practitioner in the Goddess tradition of myth and magic. She is also involved globally in environmental activism. Her book *Truth or Dare: Encounters with Power, Authority, and Mystery* details her spiritual politics, and in the following selection from that book, she envisions the possibility of a bioregional city. Fantasy has become an important avenue to explore our relationship with nature. This subgenre is based not on naivete but on the need to clarify our vision of a way of life that is grounded in place and community in order to see where we fall short and in what direction we need to move. In this brief ecotopia, Starhawk underscores the significance of diversity and the integration of culture and nature in the bioregional ideal.

The Hopis say that we all began together; that each race went on a journey to learn its own road to power, and changed; that now is the time for us to return, to put the pieces of the puzzle back together, to make the circle whole.* Through our differences, we complete each other. Together, we become a new whole. Mystery is vision. When I attempt to envision what the world renewed might look like, I imagine the following.

You are walking the dogs up on the hill they call La Matria, the Mother's Womb. Below is spread a sparkling panorama of the city, a living tapestry of rainbow colors on a warp of green. Toward the west, the Maiden's

* Buck Ghosthorse of the Institute for Culture and Creation. Spirituality taught me about the Hopi prophecies.

Breasts thrust their twin peaks up into a clear sky. All during Sunreturn Moon, fireworks lit the sky there, celebrating La Purisima, the festival of the conception of the Virgin. The streets were filled with processions, the Catholics and the Pagans dancing together without arguing about which Virgin they were celebrating, and everyone else in the city, it seemed, joining in just for the fun of it.

Now it is Fruit Blossom Moon, no fog, and the winter rains have turned the hillside green, dotted with the orange of a few early poppies. Three cows graze the hillside; the dogs are used to them and ignore them. You smile a greeting at the young girl who watches them; she is sprawled on her back in the sun, not working too hard. The cows are the project of the kids from your own child's school; the neighborhood market collective buys their milk and cream, and with the money and their own labor, they are constructing what you believe must be the world's most elaborate skateboard run.

Atop the hill stands a circle of stones. You pause for a moment, feeling the energy of the city, the hill, the sky all converge here, remembering the bonfires and the dancing and the rituals. On the Jewish New Year, they blow the shofar, the ancient ram's horn, here. On the Winter Solstice, you climb this hill at dawn to welcome the newborn sun.

To the east stretches the bay. The air is so clear today that you can see all the way to Coyote Mountain in the distant hills. Great flocks of pelicans and seabirds wheel and dive around the fleets of fishing boats, their bright-colored sails plumped out by the breeze. Among them sail the great ocean-going trade ships, their huge sails spread like wings. No need today to switch to the solar batteries; the wind is strong.

You call the dogs and head down the winding, processional way, reveling in the scent of the blossoms from the apple trees that line the walkway. You glance into the gardens of the houses on the hill; it would be a great day to double-dig your tomato bed and plant out the seedlings. The dogs run ahead as you follow the road down, past the park at the bottom of the hill. Sidewalk cafes line the park; you spend pleasant hours there watching the kids play on the slides and swings, taking your turn, as do most of the neighborhood adults, on playground watch.

Now the walkway narrows as you turn down your street. On your left are the front gardens of the old Victorian houses. On your right, a low greenhouse structure lines the roadbed where trolley cars and electric autos run on the one-way street. The greenhouse is the neighborhood waste treatment plant, where banked rows of water hyacinths are aquacultured to purify wastes and generate clean water and compost.*

You pass another small park, where a group of older people sit conversing under walnut and almond trees. Like everyone else on the street, they are a mix of races. Africa, Asia, the Americas, Europe, all contribute to their heritage, and you smile with pleasure, for to see a group of elders who embody the Four Quarters is considered extremely good fortune. "Blessed be the elders; blessed be the Four Quarters that complete the circle," you murmur as you pass.

There are several elders' houses on the block: equipped with elevators and intercoms, the older people can live independently in a suite of rooms with someone always on call; some take turns cooking and baking, some pool together and hire local teenagers to cook and clean. In your own house, each of you cooks once every two weeks. Once a week, you eat out at friends' or go to restaurants. On another night, you go to the neighborhood dining club, where, for a fixed membership fee, a collective provides a good organic meal. The dining club is a place to meet, talk, socialize, do informal business, and talk local politics.

The fruit trees that line the sidewalks are very old now, planted years ago as an attempt to provide free food for the hungry. Now, of course, no one goes hungry. The very thought is barbaric, amidst all this abundance. No one lacks shelter, or care when sick, or a chance to contribute the work that sustains abundance.

You open the door to your collective house. The dogs run in. Your computer sings to you: someone has left you a message. One of your housemates calls to you to tell you the news.

"The ship's in! The Chocolate Consortium called—they want everyone who can to come down there and help unload."

All thoughts of gardening disappear. You hop on your bicycle and speed down the path that winds past houses, shops, and parks to the docks.

The ship is in from Central America: one of the great winged traders, carrying your long-awaited shipment of cocoa beans and cane sugar. You

---

* Similar systems are described in Todd and Todd, *Bioshelters, Ocean Arks and City Farming,* pp. 98–105.

greet your co-workers from the Truffle Collective and say hello to your friends from the other collectives in the consortium: the Candymakers, the Bakers, the representative from the Ice Cream Consortium, the Chocolate Chip Cooperative. Together, you unload the heavy sacks, count the inventory, and examine their other wares: the finely crafted hammocks, the innovations in intelligent crystal technology in which Central America leads the way. The ship will return laden with fine Sonoma wines, precision tools from the East Bay foundries, artichokes from Santa Cruz, and, of course, a load of state-of-the-art skateboards from the City.

You have arranged this deal yourself and it has been a complicated one. Your work collective is part of an extensive tradeweb, involving the households of your members, your sister collectives in the Delta grain-growing region and the Wine Country, your lover, who works in an East Bay steel mill, where the worker cooperatives pride themselves on producing the finest alloys in the cleanest, safest plants in the country, your ex-lover, who is a computer genius, and your housemate's brother, who repairs and maintains ships. You can resort to currency if you need to: the City's money is good anywhere, but you prefer to trade when you can. Fortunately, with a few exceptions, everybody loves truffles. The Tofu and Tempeh Consortium won't touch sugar products, but many of the soybean growers have voracious sweet tooths, so it all works out.

The work is hard but you enjoy the physical labor as you all talk and joke together. It's a nice change from the candy kitchen and the computer terminal. The smells and the staccato sound of Spanish remind you of the winter you spent visiting the Cooperativa de Cacao, where the beans come from. You remember the lush fields of corn and vegetables, the sturdy children, the trees you helped plant to hold the slopes of the mountain, the doorways open to the mild nights and the people calling out as you took an evening stroll. The visit cemented the friendships that established your trade contacts.

Finally, the whole shipment is packed away on electrotrucks that will take it back to the factory. The captain invites you and your friends up to her cabin for a cold drink. After you ritually exchange compliments and computer software, you invite her and her compañeros to spend the evening with you. The moon will be full tonight; your ritual circle will meet up on the hill and guests will be welcome. You will dance to the moon and then head downtown, for it is Chinese New Year and the dragon will dance through the streets. There will be fireworks, parades, and celebrations.

You bicycle home. In the last hour of daylight, you have time to pull a few weeds and turn the compost. Your household, like most of the City's living groups, grows much of its own food, providing all its salad greens, most vegetables, many fruits, nuts, and herbs. Your housemate feeds the chickens and milks your goat. You can shower, soak your sore muscles in the hot tub, chat with your child, and relax before dressing for the celebration. It's been a long day—but a good one. Now for some good food, and you'll be ready to dance all night in the friendly streets aglow with moonlight.

CODA

Gary Snyder

THE REDISCOVERY
OF TURTLE ISLAND

For John Wesley Powell, watershed visionary,
and for Wallace Stegner

In "The Rediscovery of Turtle Island," Gary Snyder calls for a "panhumanism." By transcending the limits of traditional humanism, we can develop a deep sense of our kinship with all living beings and of the interpenetration of nature and culture. This integrated vision rejects not only the "user" mentality that treats the natural world as merely a resource, but also a "saver" view that seeks to preserve nature in the form of pristine wilderness free from human interference. The development of such a panhumanistic vision can be aided by learning from Native American cultures. The conception of this continent as Turtle Island can help us reinhabit the land in a bioregional way and become native to the land.

I

We human beings of the developed societies have once more been expelled from a garden—the formal garden of Euro-American humanism and its assumptions of human superiority, priority, uniqueness, and dominance. We have been thrown back into that other garden with all the other animals and fungi and insects, where we can no longer be sure we are so privileged. The walls between "nature" and "culture" begin to crumble as we enter a posthuman era. Darwinian insights force occidental people, often unwillingly, to acknowledge their literal kinship with critters.

Ecological science investigates the interconnections of organisms and their constant transactions with energy and matter. Human societies come into being along with the rest of nature. There is no name yet for a humanistic scholarship that embraces the nonhuman. I suggest (in a spirit of pagan play) we call it "panhumanism."

Environmental activists, ecological scientists, and panhumanists are still in the process of reevaluating how to think about, how to create policy with, nature. The professional resource managers of the Forest Service and the Bureau of Land Management have been driven (partly by people of conscience within their own ranks) into rethinking their old utilitarian view of the vast lands in their charge. This is a time of lively confluence, as scientists, self-taught ecosystem experts from the communities, land management agency experts, and a new breed of ecologically aware loggers and ranchers (a few, but growing) are beginning to get together.

In the more rarefied world of ecological and social theory, the confluence is rockier. Nature writing, environmental history, and ecological philosophy have become subjects of study in the humanities. There are, however, still a few otherwise humane historians and philosophers who unreflectingly assume that the natural world is primarily a building-supply yard for human projects. That is what the Occident has said and thought for a couple thousand years.

Right now there are two sets of ideas circling about each other. One group, which we could call the "Savers," places value on extensive preservation of wilderness areas and argues for the importance of the original condition of nature. This view has been tied to the idea that the mature condition of an ecosystem is a stable and diverse state technically called "climax." The other position holds that nature is constantly changing, that human agency has altered things to the point that there is no "natural condition" left, that there is no reason to value climax (or "fitness") over any other succession phase, and that human beings are not only part of nature but that they are also dominant over nature and should keep on using and changing it. They can be called the "Users." The Savers' view is attributed to the Sierra Club and other leading national organizations, to various "radical environmentalists," and to many environmental thinkers and writers. The Users' view, which has a few supporters in the biological sciences, has already become a favorite of the World Bank and those developers who are vexed by the problems associated with legislation that requires protection for creatures whose time and space are running out. It has been quickly seized on by the industry-sponsored pseudopopulist-flavored "Wise Use" movement.

Different as they are, both groups reflect the instrumentalist view of nature that has long been a mainstay of occidental thought. The Savers' idea of freezing some parts of nature into an icon of "pristine, uninhabited wilderness" is also to treat nature like a commodity, kept in a golden cage. Some preservationists have been insensitive to the plight of indigenous peoples whose home grounds were turned into protected wildlife preserves or parks, or to the plight of local workers and farmers who lose jobs as logging and grazing policies change.

The Users, in turn, are both pseudopopulist and multinational. On the local level they claim to speak for communities and workers (whose dilemma is real enough), but a little probing discloses industry funding. On the global scale their backers line up with huge forces of governments and corporations, with NAFTA and GATT, and raise the specter of further destruction of local communities. Their organizations are staffed by the sort of professionals whom Wendell Berry calls "hired itinerant vandals."

Postmodern theoreticians and critics have recently ventured into nature politics. Many of them have sided with the Users—they like to argue that nature is part of history, that human beings are part of nature, that there is little in the natural world that has not already been altered by human agency, that in any case our idea of "nature" is a projection of our social condition and that there is no sense in trying to preserve a theoretical wild. However, to say that the natural world is subject to continual change, that nature is shaped by history, or that our idea of reality is a self-serving illusion is not new. These positions still fail to come to grips with the question of how to deal with the pain and distress of real beings, plants and animals, as real as suffering humanity; and how to preserve natural variety. The need to protect worldwide biodiversity may be economically difficult and socially controversial, but there are strong scientific and practical arguments in support of it, and it is for many of us a profound ethical issue.

Hominids have obviously had some effect on the natural world, going back for half a million or more years. So we can totally drop the use of the word *pristine* in regard to nature as meaning "untouched by human agency." "Pristine" should now be understood as meaning "virtually" pristine. Almost any apparently untouched natural environment has in fact experienced some tiny degree of human impact. Historically there were huge preagricultural environments where the human impact, rather like deer or cougar activities, was normally almost invisible to any but a tracker's eye. The greatest single preagricultural human effect on wild nature, yet to be fully grasped, was the deliberate use of fire. In some cases human-caused fire seemed to mimic natural process, as with deliberate use of fire by native Californians. Alvar Núñez "Cabeza de Vaca," in his early-sixteenth-century walk across what is now Texas and the Southwest, found well-worn trails everywhere. But the fact still remains that there were great numbers of species, vast grasslands, fertile wetlands, and extensive forests in mosaics of all different stages in the preindustrial world. Barry Commoner has said that the greatest destruction of the world environment—by far—has taken place since 1950.

Furthermore, there is no "original condition" that once altered can never be redeemed. Original nature can be understood in terms of the myth of the "pool of Artemis"—the pool hidden in the forest that Artemis, goddess of wild things, visits to renew her virginity. The wild has—nay, *is*—a kind of hip, renewable virginity.

We are still laying the groundwork for a "culture of nature." The critique of the Judeo-Christian-Cartesian view of nature (by which complex of views all developed nations excuse themselves for their drastically destructive treatment of the landscape) is well under way. Some of us would hope to resume, reevaluate, re-create, and bring into line with complex science that old view that holds the whole phenomenal world to be our own being: multicentered, "alive" in its own manner, and effortlessly self-organizing in its own chaotic way. Elements of this view are found in a wide range of ancient vernacular philosophies, and it turns up in a variety of more sophisticated but still tentative forms in recent thought. It offers a third way, not caught up in the dualisms of body and mind, spirit and matter, or culture and nature. It is a noninstrumentalist view that extends intrinsic value to the nonhuman natural world.

Scouting parties are now following a skein of old tracks, aiming to cross and explore beyond the occidental (and postmodern) divide. I am going to lay out the case history of one of these probes. It's a potentially new story for the North American identity. It has already been in the making for more than thirty years. I call it "the rediscovery of Turtle Island."

2

In January 1969 I attended a gathering of Native American activists in southern California. Hundreds of people had come from all over the West.

After sundown we went out to a gravelly wash that came down from the desert mountains. Drums were set up, a fire started, and for most of the night we sang the pantribal songs called "forty-nines." The night conversations circled around the idea of a native-inspired cultural and ecological renaissance for all of North America. I first heard this continent called "Turtle Island" there by a man who said his work was to be a messenger. He had his dark brown long hair tied in a Navajo men's knot, and he wore dusty khakis. He said that Turtle Island was the term that the people were coming to, a new name to help us build the future of North America. I asked him whom or where it came from. He said, "There are many creation myths with Turtle, East Coast and West Coast. But also you can just hear it."

I had recently returned to the West Coast from a ten-year residence in Japan. It was instantly illuminating to hear this continent renamed "Turtle Island." The realignments that conversation suggested were rich and complex. I was reminded that the indigenous people here have a long history of subtle and effective ways of working with their home grounds. They have had an exuberant variety of cultures and economies and some distinctive social forms (such as communal households) that were found throughout the hemisphere. They sometimes fought with each other, but usually with a deep sense of mutual respect. Within each of their various forms of religious life lay a powerful spiritual teaching on the matter of human and natural relationships, and for some individuals a practice of self-realization that came with trying to see through nonhuman eyes. The landscape was intimately known, and the very idea of community and kinship embraced and included the huge populations of wild beings. Much of the truth of Native American history and culture has been obscured by the self-serving histories that were written on behalf of the conquerors, the present dominant society.

This gathering took place one year before the first Earth Day. As I reentered American life during the spring of 1969, I saw the use of the term "Turtle Island" spread through the fugitive Native American newsletters and other communications. I became aware that there was a notable groundswell of white people, too, who were seeing their life in the Western Hemisphere in a new way. Many whites figured that the best they could do on behalf of Turtle Island was to work for the environment, reinhabit the urban or rural margins, learn the landscape, and give support to Native Americans when asked. By 1970 I had moved with my family to the Sierra Nevada and was developing a forest homestead north of the South Yuba River. Many others entered the mountains and hills of the Pacific slope with virtually identical intentions, from the San Diego backcountry north into British Columbia. They had begun the reinhabitory move.

Through the early seventies I worked with my local forest community, but made regular trips to the cities, and was out on long swings around the country reading poems or leading workshops—many in urban areas. Our new sense of the Western Hemisphere permeated everything we did. So I called the book of poems I wrote from that period *Turtle Island* (New York: New Directions, 1974). The introduction says:

> Turtle Island—the old-new name for the continent, based on many creation myths of the people who have been living here for millennia, and reapplied by some of them to "North America" in recent years. Also, an idea found worldwide, of the earth, or cosmos even, sustained by a great turtle or serpent-of-eternity.
>
> A name: that we may see ourselves more accurately on this continent of watersheds and life communities—plant zones, physiographic provinces, culture areas, following natural boundaries. The "U.S.A." and its states and counties are arbitrary and inaccurate impositions on what is really here.
>
> The poems speak of place, and the energy pathways that sustain life. Each living being is a swirl in the flow, a formal turbulence, a "song." The land, the planet itself, is also a living being—at another pace. Anglos, black people, Chicanos, and others beached up on these shores all share such views at the deepest levels of their old cultural traditions— African, Asian, or European. Hark again to those roots, to see our ancient solidarity, and then to the work of being together on Turtle Island.

Following the publication of these poems, I began to hear back from a lot of people—many in Canada—who were remaking a North American life. Many other writers got into this sort of work each on his or her own— a brilliant and cranky bunch that included Jerry Rothenberg and his translation of Native American song and story into powerful little poem events; Peter Blue Cloud with his evocation of Coyote in a contemporary context; Dennis Tedlock, who offered a storyteller's representation of Zuni oral narrative in English; Ed Abbey, calling for a passionate commitment to the wild; Leslie Silko in her shivery novel *Ceremony;* Simon Ortiz in his early poems and stories—and many more.

A lot of this followed on the heels of the back-to-the-land movement and the diaspora of longhairs and dropout graduate students to rural places in the early seventies. There are thousands of people from those days still making a culture: being teachers, plumbers, chair and cabinet makers, contractors and carpenters, poets in the schools, auto mechanics, geographic information computer consultants, registered foresters, professional storytellers, wildlife workers, river guides, mountain guides, architects, or organic gardeners. Many have simultaneously mastered grass-roots politics and the intricacies of public lands policies. Such people can be found tucked away in the cities, too.

The first wave of writers mentioned left some strong legacies: Rothenberg, Tedlock, and Dell Hymes gave us the field of ethnopoetics (the basis for truly appreciating multicultural literature); Leslie Silko and Simon Ortiz opened the way for a distinguished and diverse body of new American Indian writing; Ed Abbey's eco-warrior spirit led toward the emergence of the radical environmental group Earth First!, which (in splitting) later generated the Wild Lands Project. Some of my own writings contributed to the inclusion of Buddhist ethics and lumber industry work life in the mix, and writers as different as Wes Jackson, Wendell Berry, and Gary Paul Nabhan opened the way for a serious discussion of place, nature in place, and community. The Native American movement has become a serious player in the national debate, and the environmental movement has become (in some cases) big and controversial politics. Although the counterculture has faded and blended in, its fundamental concerns remain a serious part of the dialogue.

A key question is that of our ethical obligations to the nonhuman world. The very notion rattles the foundations of occidental thought. Native American religious beliefs, although not identical coast to coast, are overwhelmingly in support of a full and sensitive acknowledgment of the subjecthood—the intrinsic value—of nature. This in no way backs off from an unflinching awareness of the painful side of wild nature, of acknowledging how everything is being eaten alive. The twentieth-century syncretism of the "Turtle Island view" gathers ideas from Buddhism and Taoism and from the lively details of worldwide animism and paganism. There is no imposition of ideas of progress or order on the natural world—Buddhism teaches impermanence, suffering, compassion, and wisdom. Buddhist teachings go on to say that the true source of compassion and ethical behavior is paradoxically none other than one's own realization of the insubstantial and ephemeral nature of everything. Much of animism and paganism celebrates the actual, with its inevitable pain and death, and affirms the beauty of the process. Add contemporary ecosystem theory and environmental history to this, and you get a sense of what's at work.

Conservation biology, deep ecology, and other new disciplines are given a community constituency and real grounding by the bioregional movement. Bioregionalism calls for commitment to this continent *place by place,* in terms of biogeographical regions and watersheds. It calls us to see our country in terms of its landforms, plant life, weather patterns, and seasonal changes—its whole natural history before the net of political jurisdictions was cast over it. People are challenged to become "reinhabitory"— that is, to become people who are learning to live and think "as if" they were totally engaged with their place for the long future. This doesn't mean some return to a primitive lifestyle or utopian provincialism; it simply implies an engagement with community and a search for the sustainable sophisticated mix of economic practices that would enable people to live regionally and yet learn from and contribute to a planetary society. (Some of the best bioregional work is being done in cities, as people try to restore both human and ecological neighborhoods.) Such people are, regardless of national or ethnic backgrounds, in the process of becoming something deeper than "American (or Mexican or Canadian) citizens"— they are becoming natives of Turtle Island.

Now in the nineties the term "Turtle Island" continues, modestly, to extend its sway. There is a Turtle Island Office that moves around the country with its newsletter; it acts as a national information center for the many bioregional groups that every other year hold a "Turtle Island Congress." Participants come from Canada and Mexico as well as the United States. The use of the term is now standard in a number of Native American periodicals and circles. There is even a "Turtle Island String Quartet" based in San Francisco. In the winter of 1992 I practically convinced the director of the Centro de Estudios Norteamericanos at the Universidad de Alcalá in Madrid to change his department's name to "Estudios de la Isla de Tortuga." He much enjoyed the idea of the shift. We agreed: speak of the

United States, and you are talking two centuries of basically English-speaking affairs; speak of "America" and you invoke five centuries of Euro-American schemes in the Western Hemisphere; speak of "Turtle Island" and a vast past, an open future, and all the life communities of plants, humans, and critters come into focus.

3

The Nisenan and Maidu, indigenous people who live on the east side of the Sacramento Valley and into the northern Sierra foothills, tell a creation story that goes something like this:

> Coyote and Earthmaker were blowing around in the swirl of things. Coyote finally had enough of this aimlessness and said, "Earthmaker, find us a world!"
>
> Earthmaker tried to get out of it, tried to excuse himself, because he knew that a world can only mean trouble. But Coyote nagged him into trying. So leaning over the surface of the vast waters, Earthmaker called up Turtle. After a long time Turtle surfaced, and Earthmaker said, "Turtle, can you get me a bit of mud? Coyote wants a world."
>
> "A world," said Turtle. "Why bother? Oh, well." And down she dived. She went down and down and down, to the bottom of the sea. She took a great gob of mud, and started swimming toward the surface. As she spiraled and paddled upward, the streaming water washed the mud from the sides of her mouth, from the back of her mouth—and by the time she reached the surface (the trip took six years), nothing was left but one grain of dirt between the tips of her beak.
>
> "That'll be enough!" said Earthmaker, taking it in his hands and giving it a pat like a tortilla. Suddenly Coyote and Earthmaker were standing on a piece of ground as big as a tarp. Then Earthmaker stamped his feet, and they were standing on a flat wide plain of mud. The ocean was gone. They stood on the land.

And then Coyote began to want trees and plants, and scenery, and the story goes on to tell how Coyote imagined landscapes that then came forth, and how he started naming the animals and plants as they appeared. "I'll call you skunk because you look like skunk." And the landscapes Coyote imagined are there today.

My children grew up with this as their first creation story. When they later heard the Bible story, they said, "That's a lot like Coyote and Earthmaker." But the Nisenan story gave them their own immediate landscape, complete with details, and the characters were animals from their own world.

Mythopoetic play can be part of what jump-starts long-range social change. But what about the short term? There are some immediate outcomes worth mentioning: a new era of community interaction with public lands has begun. In California a new set of ecosystem-based government/community joint-management discussions are beginning to take place. Some of the most vital environmental politics is being done by watershed or ecosystem-based groups. "Ecosystem management" by definition includes private landowners in the mix. In my corner of the northern Sierra, we are practicing being a "human-inhabited wildlife corridor"—an area that functions as a biological connector—and are coming to certain agreed-on practices that will enhance wildlife survival even as dozens of households continue to live here. Such neighborhood agreements would be one key to preserving wildlife diversity in most Third World countries.

Ultimately we can all lay claim to the term *native* and the songs and dances, the beads and feathers, and the profound responsibilities that go with it. We are all indigenous to this planet, this mosaic of wild gardens we are being called by nature and history to reinhabit in good spirit. Part of that responsibility is to choose a place. To restore the land one must live and work in a place. To work in a place is to work with others. People who work together in a place become a community, and a community, in time, grows a culture. To work on behalf of the wild is to restore culture.

Alice Walker

THE UNIVERSE RESPONDS
Or, How I Learned We Can Have Peace on Earth

Alice Walker makes her home in the San Francisco Bay Area. The author of many novels, including *The Color Purple,* she also has published books of poetry and collections of essays. She has been active in the civil rights and women's move-ments. In the following selection, which is the concluding essay of *Living by the Word: Selected Writings 1973–1987,* Walker describes encounters with ani-mals that demonstrate an amity and intimacy that is possible in our relation-ship with other living beings. These interactions suggest a broader truth: the uni-verse is ever giving, responsive to our actions and desires. This fact forms the necessity and foundation for right livelihood. Nature's generosity allows vastly de-structive exploitation to occur but it also enables us to live in place harmoniously if we practice peace.

To some people who read the following there will seem to be something special or perhaps strange about me. I have sometimes felt this way my-self. To others, however, what I am about to write will appear obvious. I think our response to "strangeness" or "specialness" depends on where we are born, where we are raised, how much idle time we have had to watch trees (long enough at least to notice there is not an ugly one among them) swaying in the wind. Or to watch rivers, rainstorms, or the sea.

A few years ago, I wrote an essay called "Everything Is a Human Be-ing," which explores to some extent the Native American view that all of creation is of one substance and therefore deserving of the same respect. I described the death of a snake that I caused and wrote of my remorse. I wrote the piece to celebrate the birth of Martin Luther King, Jr., and I read it first to a large group of college students in California. I also read it other places, so that by summer (I had written it in winter) it had been read three or four times, and because I cannot bear to repeat myself very much, I put it away.

That summer "my" land in the country crawled with snakes. There was always the large resident snake, whom my mother named "Susie," crawling about in the area that marks the entrance to my studio. But there were also lots of others wherever we looked. A black-and-white king snake appeared underneath the shower stall in the garden. A striped red-and-black one, very pretty, appeared near the pond. It now revealed the little hole in the ground in which it lived by lying half in and half out of it as it basked in the sun. Garden snakes crawled up and down the roads and paths. One day, leaving my house with a box of books in his arms, my companion literally tripped over one of these.

We spoke to all these snakes in friendly voices. They went their way. We went ours. After about a two-week bloom of snakes, we seemed to have our usual number: just Susie and a couple of her children.

A few years later, I wrote an essay about a horse called Blue. It was about how humans treat horses and other animals; how hard it is for us to see them as the suffering, fully conscious, enslaved beings they are. It also marked the beginning of my effort to become non-meat-eating (fairly successful). After reading this essay in public only once, this is what happened. A white horse came and settled herself on the land. (Her owner, a neighbor, soon came to move her.) The two horses on the ranch across the road began to run up to their fence whenever I passed, leaning over it and making what sounded to my ears like joyful noises. They had never done this before (I checked with the human beings I lived with to be sure of this), and after a few more times of greeting me as if I'd done something especially nice for them, they stopped. Now when I pass they look at me with the same reserve they did before. But there is still a spark of *recognition*.

What to make of this?

What I have noticed in my small world is that if I praise the wild flowers growing on the hill in front of my house, the following year they double in profusion and brilliance. If I admire the squirrel that swings from branch to branch outside my window, pretty soon I have three or four squirrels to admire. If I look into the eyes of a raccoon that has awakened me by noisily rummaging through the garbage at night, and acknowledge that it looks maddeningly like a mischievous person—paws on hips, masked eyes, a certain impudent stance, as it looks back at me—I soon have a family of raccoons living in a tree a few yards off my deck. (From this tree they easily forage in the orchard at night and eat, or at least take bites out of, all the apples. Which is not fun. But that is another story.)

And then, too, there are the deer, who know they need never, ever fear me.

In white-directed movies about the Indians of the Old West, you sometimes see the "Indians" doing a rain dance, a means of praying for rain. The message delivered by the moviemaker is that such dancing and praying is ridiculous, that either it will rain or it will not. All white men know this. The Indians are backward and stupid and wasting their time. But there is also that last page or so in the story of Black Elk, in which his anthropologist/friend John Neihardt goes with him on a last visit to the Badlands to pray atop Horney Peak, a place sacred to the Sioux. It is a cloudless day, but the ancient Black Elk hopes that the Great Spirit, as in the real "old" days, will acknowledge his prayer for the good of his people by sending at least a few drops of rain. As he prays, in his old, tired voice, mostly of his love of the Universe and his failure to be perfect, a small cloud indeed forms. It rains, just enough to say "Yes." Then the sky clears. Even today there is the belief among many indigenous holy people that when a person of goodness dies, the Universe acknowledges the spirit's departure by sending storms and rain.

The truth is, in the country, where I live much of the time, I am virtually overrun by birds and animals—raccoons, snakes, deer, horses (occasionally). During a recent court trial at which a neighbor and I both happened to find ourselves, her opening words of greeting included the information that two wild pigs she'd somehow captured had broken out and were, she feared, holed up somewhere on my land.

But at least, I thought, my house in the city is safe.

But no.

One night after dinner, as some friends were leaving my house, I opened my front door, only to have a large black dog walk gratefully inside. It had obviously been waiting quietly on the stoop. It came into the hallway, sniffed my hands, and prepared to make itself at home, exactly as if it had lived in my house all its life. There was no nervousness whatsoever about being an intruder. No, no, I said, out you go! It did not want to go, but my friends and I persuaded it. It settled itself at the door and there it stayed, barking reproachfully until I went to bed. Very late that night I heard its owners calling it. George! they called. George! Here, George! They were cursing and laughing. Drunk. George made no response.

I suddenly realized that George was not lost. He had run away. He had run away from these cursing, laughing drunks who were now trying to find him. This realization meant the end of sleep for me that night as I lay awake considering my responsibility to George. (I felt none toward his owners.) For George obviously "knew" which house was at least *supposed* to be a stop on the underground railroad, and had come to it; but I, in my city house, had refused to acknowledge my house as such. If I let it in, where would I put it? Then, too, I'm not particularly fond of the restlessness of dogs. The way they groan and fart in their sleep, chase rabbits in their dreams, and flop themselves over, rattling their chains (i.e., collars and dog tags). George had run away from these drunks who "owned" him, people no doubt unfit to own anything at all that breathed. Did they beat him? Did they tie him to trees and lampposts outside pubs (as I've so often seen done) while they went inside and had drink after drink? Were all the "lost" dogs one heard about really runaways? It hit me with great force that a dog I had once had, Myshkin, had undoubtedly run away from the small enclosed backyard in which he had been kept and in which he was probably going mad, whereas I had for years indulged in the fantasy that he'd been stolen! No dog in his right mind would voluntarily leave a cushy prison run by loving humans, right?

Or suppose George was a woman, beaten or psychologically abused by her spouse. What then? Would I let her in? I would, wouldn't I? But where to put George, anyway? If I put him in the cellar, he might bark. I hate the sound of barking. If I put him in the parlor, he might spread fleas. Who was this dog, anyway?

George stayed at my door the whole night. In the morning I heard him bark, but by the time I was up, he was gone.

I think I am telling you that the animals of the planet are in desperate peril, and that they are fully aware of this. No less than human beings are doing in all parts of the world, they are seeking sanctuary. But I am also telling you that we are connected to them at least as intimately as we are connected to trees. Without plant life human beings could not breathe. Plants produce oxygen. Without free animal life I believe we will lose the spiritual equivalent of oxygen. "Magic," intuition, sheer astonishment at the forms the Universe devises in which to express life—itself—will no longer be able to breathe in us. One day it occurred to me that if all the birds died, as they might well do, eventually, from the poisoning of their air, water, and food, it would be next to impossible to describe to our children the wonder of their flight. To most children, I think, the flight of a bird—if they'd never seen one fly—would be imagined as stiff and unplayful, like the flight of an airplane.

But what I'm also sharing with you is this thought: The Universe responds. What you ask of it, it gives. The military-industrial complex and its leaders and scientists have shown more faith in this reality than have those of us who do not believe in war and who want peace. They have asked the Earth for all its deadlier substances. They have been confident in their faith in hatred and war. The Universe, ever responsive, the Earth, ever giving, has opened itself fully to their desires. Ironically, Black Elk and nuclear scientists can be viewed in much the same way: as men who prayed to the Universe for what they believed they needed and who received from it a sign reflective of their own hearts.

I remember when I used to dismiss the bumper sticker "Pray for Peace." I realize now that I did not understand it, since I also did not understand prayer; which I know now to be the active affirmation in the physical world of our inseparableness from the divine; and everything, *especially* the physical world, is divine. War will stop when we no longer praise it, or give it any attention at all. Peace will come wherever it is sincerely invited. Love will overflow every sanctuary given it. Truth will grow where the fertilizer that nourishes it is also truth. Faith will be its own reward.

Believing this, which I learned from my experience with the animals and the wild flowers, I have found that my fear of nuclear destruction has been to a degree lessened. I know perfectly well that we may all die, and relatively soon, in a global holocaust, which was first imprinted, probably against their wishes, on the hearts of the scientist fathers of the atomic bomb, no doubt deeply wounded and frightened human beings; but I also know we have the power, as all the Earth's people, to conjure up the healing rain imprinted on Black Elk's heart. Our death is in our hands.

Knock and the door shall be opened. Ask and you shall receive.

Whatsoever you do to the least of these, you do also unto me—and to yourself. For we are one.

"God" answers prayers. Which is another way of saying, "the Universe responds."

We are *indeed* the world. Only if we have reason to fear what is in our own hearts need we fear for the planet. Teach yourself peace.

Pass it on.

Linda Hogan

DWELLINGS

Linda Hogan is a Chickasaw poet and novelist. She lives in a small mountain town west of Denver and teaches in the creative writing program at the University of Colorado, Boulder. In the following selection from her book of essays, *Dwellings: A Spiritual History of the Living World,* Hogan examines the nature of— and the naturalness of—dwellings. The creation of dwellings is part of the architecture of memory in bees and mice, and it is one of the ways they interact with their environment. Human buildings too can be seen as a natural function of being at home on the earth. In such a view, the boundaries between nature and culture, human artifacts and natural processes are blurred. Hogan leaves us with a striking image of our interconnection with the earth: a thread of her skirt and a strand of her daughter's hair form part of a bird's nest.

Not far from where I live is a hill that was cut into by the moving water of a creek. Eroded this way, all that's left of it is a broken wall of earth that contains old roots and pebbles woven together and exposed. Seen from a distance, it is only a rise of raw earth. But up close it is something wonderful, a small cliff dwelling that looks almost as intricate and well made as those the Anasazi left behind when they vanished mysteriously centuries ago. This hill is a place that could be the starry skies of night turned inward into the thousand round holes where solitary bees have lived and died. It is a hill of tunneling rooms. At the mouths of some of the excavations, half-circles of clay beetle out like awnings shading a doorway. It is earth that was turned to clay in the mouths of the bees and spit out as they mined deeper into their dwelling places.

This place where the bees reside is at an angle safe from rain. It faces the southern sun. It is a warm and intelligent architecture of memory, learned by whatever memory lives in the blood. Many of the holes still contain the gold husks of dead bees, their faces dry and gone, their flat eyes gazing out from death's land toward the other uninhabited half of the hill that is across the creek from these catacombs.

The first time I found the residence of the bees, it was dusty summer. The sun was hot, and land was the dry color of rust. Now and then a car rumbled along the dirt road and dust rose up behind it before settling back down on older dust. In the silence, the bees made a soft droning hum. They were alive then, and working the hill, going out and returning with pollen, in and out through the holes, back and forth between daylight and the cooler, darker regions of inner earth. They were flying an invisible map through air, a map charted by landmarks, the slant of light, and a circling story they told one another about the direction of food held inside the center of yellow flowers.

Sitting in the hot sun, watching the small bees fly in and out around the hill, hearing the summer birds, the light breeze, I felt right in the world. I belonged there. I thought of my own dwelling places, those real and those imagined. Once I lived in a town called Manitou, which means "Great Spirit," and where hot mineral springwater gurgled beneath the streets and rose up into open wells. I felt safe there. With the underground movement of water and heat a constant reminder of other life, of what lives beneath us, it seemed to be the center of the world.

A few years after that, I wanted silence. My daydreams were full of places I longed to be, shelters and solitudes. I wanted a room apart from others, a hidden cabin to rest in. I wanted to be in a redwood forest with trees so tall the owls called out in the daytime. I daydreamed of living in a vapor cave a few hours away from here. Underground, warm, and moist, I thought it would be the perfect world for staying out of cold winter, for escaping the noise of living.

And how often I've wanted to escape to a wilderness where a human hand has not been in everything. But those were only dreams of peace, of comfort, of a nest inside stone or woods, a sanctuary where a dream or life wouldn't be invaded.

Years ago, in the next canyon west of here, there was a man who followed one of those dreams and moved into a cave that could only be reached by climbing down a rope. For years he lived there in comfort, like a troglodyte.

The inner weather was stable, never too hot, too cold, too wet, or too dry. But then he felt lonely. His utopia needed a woman. He went to town until he found a wife. For a while after the marriage, his wife climbed down the rope along with him, but before long she didn't want the mice scurrying about in the cave, or the untidy bats that wanted to hang from stones of the ceiling. So they built a door. Because of the closed entryway, the temperature changed. They had to put in heat. Then the inner moisture of earth warped the door, so they had to have air-conditioning, and after that the earth wanted to go about life in its own way and it didn't give in to the people.

In other days and places, people paid more attention to the strong-headed will of earth. Once homes were built of wood that had been felled from a single region in a forest. That way, it was thought, the house would hold together more harmoniously, and the family of walls would not fall or lend themselves to the unhappiness or arguments of the inhabitants.

An Italian immigrant to Chicago, Aldo Piacenzi, built birdhouses that were dwellings of harmony and peace. They were the incredible spired shapes of cathedrals in Italy. They housed not only the birds, but also his memories, his own past. He painted them the watery blue of his Mediterranean, the wild rose of flowers in a summer field. Inside them was straw and the droppings of lives that layed eggs, fledglings who grew there. What places to inhabit, the bright and sunny birdhouses in dreary alleyways of the city.

One beautiful afternoon, cool and moist, with the kind of yellow light that falls on earth in these arid regions, I waited for barn swallows to return from their daily work of food gathering. Inside the tunnel where they live, hundreds of swallows had mixed their saliva with mud and clay, much like the solitary bees, and formed nests that were perfect as a potter's bowl. At five in the evening, they returned all at once, a dark, flying shadow. Despite their enormous numbers and the crowding together of nests, they didn't pause for even a moment before entering the nests, nor did they crowd one another. Instantly they vanished into the nests. The tunnel went silent. It held no outward signs of life.

But I knew they were there, filled with the fire of living. And what a marriage of elements was in those nests. Not only mud's earth and water, the fire of sun and dry air, but even the elements contained one another. The bodies of prophets and crazy men were broken down in that soil.

I've noticed often how when a house is abandoned, it begins to sag. Without a tenant, it has no need to go on. If it were a person, we'd say it is depressed or lonely. The roof settles in, the paint cracks, the walls and floorboards warp and slope downward in their own natural ways, telling us that life must stay in everything as the world whirls and tilts and moves through boundless space.

One summer day, cleaning up after long-eared owls where I work at a rehabilitation facility for birds of prey, I was raking the gravel floor of a flight cage. Down on the ground, something looked like it was moving. I bent over to look into the pile of bones and pellets I'd just raked together. There, close to the ground, were two fetal mice. They were new to the planet, pink and hairless. They were so tenderly young. Their faces had swollen blue-veined eyes. They were nestled in a mound of feathers, soft as velvet, each one curled up smaller than an infant's ear, listening to the first sounds of earth. But the ants were biting them. They turned in agony, unable to pull away, not yet having the arms or legs to move, but feeling, twisting away from, the pain of the bites. I was horrified to see them bitten out of life that way. I dipped them in water, as if to take away the sting, and let the ants fall in the bucket. Then I held the tiny mice in the palm of my hand. Some of the ants were drowning in the water. I was trading one life for another, exchanging the lives of ants for those of mice, but I hated their suffering, and hated even more that they had not yet grown to a life, and already they inhabited the miserable world of pain. Death and life feed each other. I know that.

Inside these rooms where birds are healed, there are other lives besides those of mice. There are fine gray globes the wasps have woven together, the white cocoons of spiders in a corner, the downward tunneling anthills. All these dwellings are inside one small walled space, but I think most about the mice. Sometimes the downy nests fall out of the walls where their mothers have placed them out of the way of their enemies. When one of the nests falls, they are so well made and soft, woven mostly from the chest feathers of birds. Sometimes the leg of a small quail holds the nest together like a slender cornerstone with dry, bent claws. The mice have adapted to

life in the presence of their enemies, adapted to living in the thin wall between beak and beak, claw and claw. They move their nests often, as if a
new rafter or wall will protect them from the inevitable fate of all our returns home to the deeper, wider nest of earth that houses us all.

One August at Zia Pueblo during the corn dance I noticed tourists picking up shards of all the old pottery that had been made and broken there.
The residents of Zia know not to take the bowls and pots left behind by
the older ones. They know that the fragments of those earlier lives need
to be smoothed back to earth, but younger nations, travelers from continents across the world who have come to inhabit this land, have little of
their own to grow on. The pieces of earth that were formed into bowls,
even on their way home to dust, provide the new people a lifeline to an
unknown land, help them remember that they live in the old nest of earth.

It was in early February, during the mating season of the great horned owls.
It was dusk, and I hiked up the back of a mountain to where I'd heard the
owls a year before. I wanted to hear them again, the voices so tender, so
deep, like a memory of comfort. I was halfway up the trail when I found
a soft, round nest. It had fallen from one of the bare-branched trees. It
was a delicate nest, woven together of feathers, sage, and strands of wild
grass. Holding it in my hand in the rosy twilight, I noticed that a blue
thread was entwined with the other gatherings there. I pulled at the thread
a little, and then I recognized it. It was a thread from one of my skirts. It
was blue cotton. It was the unmistakable color and shape of a pattern I
knew. I liked it, that a thread of my life was in an abandoned nest, one
that had held eggs and new life. I took the nest home. At home, I held it
to the light and looked more closely. There, to my surprise, nestled into
the gray-green sage, was a gnarl of black hair. It was also unmistakable. It
was my daughter's hair, cleaned from a brush and picked up out in the
sun beneath the maple tree, or the pit cherry where birds eat from the over-
laden, fertile branches until only the seeds remain on the trees.

I didn't know what kind of nest it was, or who had lived there. It didn't
matter. I thought of the remnants of our lives carried up the hill that way
and turned into shelter. That night, resting inside the walls of our home,
the world outside weighed so heavily against the thin wood of the house.
The sloped roof was the only thing between us and the universe. Every-

thing outside of our wooden boundaries seemed so large. Filled with night's citizens, it all came alive. The world opened in the thickets of the dark. The wild grapes would soon ripen on the vines. The burrowing ones were emerging. Horned owls sat in treetops. Mice scurried here and there. Skunks, fox, the slow and holy porcupine, all were passing by this way. The young of the solitary bees were feeding on pollen in the dark. The whole world was a nest on its humble tilt, in the maze of the universe, holding us.

BIBLIOGRAPHY

Books mentioned, with a selection of writings on place

Abbey, Edward. *Desert Solitaire.* New York: McGraw-Hill, 1968.

Barbato, Joseph, and Lisa Weinerman, eds. *Heart of the Land: Essays on Last Great Places.* New York: Pantheon, 1995.

Bass, Rick. *The Book of Yaak.* Boston: Houghton Mifflin, 1996.

———. *Wild to the Heart.* New York: Norton, 1989.

Berg, Peter et al. *A Green City Program for San Francisco Bay Area Cities and Towns.* San Francisco: Planet Drum, 1989.

Berry, Thomas. *Dream of the Earth.* San Francisco: Sierra Club, 1988.

Berry, Wendell. *The Gift of Good Land: Further Essays Cultural and Agricultural.* San Francisco: North Point, 1981.

———. *Recollected Essays, 1965–1980.* San Francisco: North Point, 1981.

———. *Selected Poems of Wendell Berry.* Washington, D.C.: Counterpoint, 1997.

———. *The Unsettling of America: Culture and Agriculture.* New York: Avon, 1977.

Beston, Henry. *The Outermost House: A Year of Life on the Great Beach of Cape Cod.* New York: Doubleday, 1928.

Blew, Mary Clearman. *All but the Waltz: A Memoir of Five Generations in the Life of a Montana Family.* New York: Penguin, 1991.

Brody, Hugh. *Maps and Dreams.* New York: Pantheon, 1982.

Brueggemann, Walter. *The Land: Place as Gift, Promise, and Challenge in Biblical Faith.* Minneapolis: Fortress, 1977.

Buell, Lawrence. "Place." In *The Environmental Imagination: Thoreau, Nature Writing, and the Formation of American Culture,* 252–279. Cambridge: Harvard University Press, 1995.

Butala, Sharon. *Perfection of the Morning: An Apprenticeship in Nature.* Toronto: HarperCollins, 1994.

Cafard, Max. "The Surre(gion)alist Manifesto." *Mesechabe,* Autumn 1989.

Casey, Edward S. *The Fate of Place: A Philosophical History.* Berkeley: University of California Press, 1997.

———. *Getting Back into Place: Toward a Renewed Understanding of the Place-World.* Bloomington: Indiana University Press, 1993.

Chatwin, Bruce. *The Songlines.* New York: Viking, 1987.

———. *What Am I Doing Here?* New York: Viking, 1989.

Daynard, Jodi. *A Place Within: Portraits of the American Landscape by Twenty Contemporary Writers.* New York: Norton, 1997.

Deming, Alison Hawthorne. *Temporary Homelands.* New York: Picador, 1996.

Dillard, Annie. *Pilgrim at Tinker Creek.* New York: Harper & Row, 1974.

Dodge, Jim. "Living by Life." *CoEvolution Quarterly,* Winter 1981.

Doig, Ivan. *This House of Sky: Landscapes of a Western Mind.* New York: Harcourt Brace Jovanovich, 1978.

Dubos, René. *The Wooing of Earth.* New York: Scribner, 1980.

Durning, Alan Thein. *How Much Is Enough?* New York: Norton, 1992.

———. *This Place on Earth: Home and the Practice of Permanence.* Seattle: Sasquatch, 1996.

Ehrlich, Gretel. *Islands, the Universe, Home.* New York: Penguin, 1991.

———. *Questions of Heaven: The Chinese Journeys of an American Buddhist.* New York: Beacon, 1997.

———. *The Solace of Open Spaces.* New York: Viking, 1985.

Finch, Robert. *The Primal Place.* New York: Norton, 1983.

Gallagher, Winifred. *The Power of Place: How Our Surroundings Shape Our Thoughts, Emotions, and Actions.* New York: Poseidon, 1993.

Haines, John. *Fables and Distances: New and Selected Essays.* St. Paul, Minn.: Graywolf, 1995.

———. *Living Off the Country: Essays on Poetry and Place.* Ann Arbor: University of Michigan Press, 1981.

———. *The Owl in the Mask of the Dreamer.* St. Paul, Minn.: Graywolf, 1993.

———. *The Stars, the Snow, the Fire: Twenty-five Years in the Northern Wilderness: A Memoir.* St. Paul, Minn.: Graywolf, 1989.

Hardy, Thomas. *Far from the Madding Crowd.* Greenwich, Conn.: Fawcett, 1960.

Hay, John. *The Run.* Revised Edition. Garden City, N.Y.: Doubleday, 1965.

———. *The Undiscovered Country.* New York: Norton, 1981.

Hiss, Tony. *The Experience of Place.* New York: Knopf, 1990.

Hoagland, Edward. *Red Wolves and Black Bears.* New York: Random House, 1976.

Hoagland, Edward, and Gretel Ehrlich. *City Tales: Wyoming Stories.* Santa Barbara, Calif.: Capra, 1986.

Hogan, Linda. *Dwellings: A Spiritual History of the Living World.* New York: Norton, 1995.

hooks, bell. *Sisters of the Yam: Black Women and Self-Recovery.* Boston: South End, 1993.

Hubbell, Sue. *A Country Year: Living the Questions.* New York: Random House, 1986.

Jackson, John Brinckerhoff. *A Sense of Place, a Sense of Time.* New Haven: Yale University Press, 1994.

Janovy, John, Jr. *Keith County Journal.* New York: St. Martin's, 1978.

Jerome, John. *Stone Work: Reflections on Serious Play and Other Aspects of Country Life.* New York: Penguin, 1989.

Kemmis, Daniel. *Community and the Politics of Place.* Norman: University of Oklahoma Press, 1990.

———. *The Good City and the Good Life: Renewing the Sense of Community.* Boston: Houghton Mifflin, 1995.

Kittredge, William. *Hole in the Sky.* New York: Random House, 1992.

Kroeber, A. L. *Cultural and Natural Areas of Native North America.* Berkeley: University of California Press, 1947.

Leopold, Aldo. *A Sand County Almanac.* New York: Oxford University Press, 1949.

Light, Andrew, and Jonathan M. Smith, eds. *Space, Place, and Environmental Ethics: Philosophy and Geography I.* Lanham, Md.: Rowman & Littlefield, 1996.

Lopez, Barry. *Arctic Dreams: Imagination and Desire in a Northern Landscape.* New York: Scribners, 1986.

Maclean, Norman. *A River Runs Through It and Other Stories.* Chicago: University of Chicago Press, 1976.

McPhee, John. *Coming into the Country.* New York: Farrar, Straus & Giroux, 1977.

Martone, Michael, ed. *A Place of Sense: Essays in Search of the Midwest.* Iowa City: University of Iowa Press, 1988.

Masumoto, David Mas. *Epitaph for a Peach: Four Seasons on My Family Farm.* San Francisco: HarperSanFrancisco, 1995.

Mitchell, John Hanson. *Ceremonial Time: Fifteen Thousand Years on One Square Mile.* New York: Anchor/Doubleday, 1984.

———. *Walking towards Walden: A Pilgrimage in Search of Place.* Reading, Mass.: Addison-Wesley, 1995.

Momaday, N. Scott. "A First American Views His Land." *National Geographic* 150 (July 1976): 13–18.

———. *House Made of Dawn.* New York: Harper & Row, 1968.

———. *The Way to Rainy Mountain.* Albuquerque: University of New Mexico Press, 1969.

Morrison, Toni. *The Bluest Eye.* New York: Holt, Rinehart and Winston, 1970.

Moscow, Ann. *A Sense of Place.* New York: HarperCollins, 1993.

Nabhan, Gary Paul. *Gathering the Desert.* Tucson: University of Arizona Press, 1985.

Nelson, Melissa. "Becoming Métis." *Orion: People and Nature* 16.2 (Spring 1997): 62–64.

Nelson, Richard. *The Island Within.* San Francisco: North Point, 1989.

———. *Make Prayers to the Raven: A Koyukon View of the Northern Forest.* Chicago: University of Chicago Press, 1983.

Nemiroff, Robert. *To Be Young, Gifted, and Black: Lorraine Hansberry in Her Own Words.* Englewood Cliffs, N.J.: Prentice-Hall, 1969.

Nollman, Jim. *Why We Garden: Cultivating a Sense of Place.* New York: Henry Holt, 1994.

Olson, Sigurd F. *Reflections from the North Country.* New York: Knopf, 1976.

Perrin, Noel. *First Person Rural: Essays of a Sometime Farmer.* Boston: Godine, 1978.

Pyle, Robert Michael. *Wintergreen: Listening to the Land's Heart.* Boston: Houghton Mifflin, 1988.

Raise the Stakes. Journal of the Planet Drum Foundation. P.O. Box 31251, San Francisco, Calif., 94131.

Reichard, Gladys. *Navaho Religion: A Study of Symbolism.* New York: Pantheon, 1950.

Rodriguez, Richard. *Days of Obligation: An Argument with My Mexican Father.* New York: Viking, 1992.

Rushdie, Salman. *Imaginary Homelands: Essays and Criticism, 1891–1991.* New York: Viking, 1991.

Sale, Kirkpatrick. *Dwellers in the Land.* San Francisco: Sierra Club, 1985.

Sanders, Scott Russell. *Staying Put: Making a Home in a Restless World.* Boston: Beacon, 1993.

———. *Writing from the Center.* Bloomington: Indiana University Press, 1995.

Sauer, Peter. "Water under American Ground: West 78th Street." *Orion* 15.4 (Autumn 1996): 62–64.

———, ed. *Finding Home: Writings on Nature and Culture from* Orion *Magazine.* Boston: Beacon Press, 1992.

Seamon, David, and Robert Murgerauer, eds. *Dwelling, Place and Environment: Towards a Phenomenology of Person and World.* New York: Columbia University Press, 1985.

Silko, Leslie Marmon. *Ceremony.* New York: Penguin, 1986.

———. "Landscape, History, and the Pueblo Imagination." In *The Nature Reader,* edited by Daniel Halpern and Dan Frank, 72–83. Hopewell, N.J.: Ecco, 1996.

Slovic, Scott H., and Terrell F. Dixon, eds. *Being in the World: An Environmental Reader for Writers.* New York: Macmillan, 1993.

Snyder, Gary. *No Nature: New and Selected Poems.* New York: Pantheon, 1992.

———. *The Old Ways.* San Francisco: City Lights, 1977.

———. *A Place in Space: Ethics, Aesthetics, and Watersheds.* Washington, D.C.: Counterpoint, 1995.

———. *The Practice of the Wild.* San Francisco: North Point, 1990.

———. *Turtle Island.* New York: New Directions, 1974.

Stafford, Kim. *Having Everything Right: Essays of Place.* Seattle: Sasquatch, 1997.

Starhawk. *Truth or Dare: Encounters with Power, Authority, and Mystery.* New York: Harper & Row, 1987.

Stegner, Wallace. *The Sound of Mountain Water.* New York: Doubleday, 1969.

Stine, Annie. *The Earth at Our Doorstep: Contemporary Writers Celebrate the Landscapes of Home.* San Francisco: Sierra Club, 1996.

Tall, Deborah. *From Where We Stand: Recovering a Sense of Place.* New York: Knopf, 1993.

Tuan, Yi-Fu. *Space and Place: The Perspective of Experience.* Minneapolis: University of Minnesota Press, 1977.

———. *Topophilia: A Study of Environmental Perception, Attitudes, and Values.* Englewood Cliffs, N.J.: Prentice-Hall, 1974.

van der Post, Laurens. *The Lost World of the Kalahari.* New York: Morrow, 1958.

Vinz, Mark, and Thom Tammaro, eds. *Imagining Home: Writing from the Midwest.* Minneapolis: University of Minnesota Press, 1995.

Vitek, William, and Wes Jackson, eds. *Rooted in the Land: Essays on Community and Place.* New Haven: Yale University Press, 1996.

Walker, Alice. *The Color Purple.* New York: Washington Square, 1982.

———. *Living by the Word: Selected Writings 1973–1987.* San Diego: Harcourt Brace Jovanovich, 1988.

Wallace, David Rains. *The Klamath Knot.* San Francisco: Sierra Club, 1983.

White, Gilbert. *The Natural History and Antiquities of Selborne.* London: Macmillan, 1970.

Williams, Terry Tempest. *Pieces of White Shell: A Journey to Navajoland.* New York: Scribner, 1984.

———. *Refuge: An Unnatural History of Family and Place.* New York: Pantheon, 1991.

Zwinger, Ann Haymond. *The Mysterious Lands.* New York: Dutton, 1989.

ACKNOWLEDGMENTS

Excerpts from "The Place, the Region, and the Commons" from *The Practice of the Wild* by Gary Snyder. Copyright © 1990 by Gary Snyder. Reprinted by permission of North Point Press, a division of Farrar, Straus & Giroux, Inc.

"The Rediscovery of Turtle Island," from *A Place in Space* by Gary Snyder, published by Counterpoint Press. Copyright © 1995 by Gary Snyder.

"Fantasy of a Living Future," from *Truth or Dare* by Starhawk. Copyright © 1987 by Miriam Simos. Reprinted by permission of HarperCollins Publishers, Inc.

"The Universe Responds: Or, How I Learned We Can Have Peace On Earth," from *Living by the Word: Selected Writings 1973–1987*, copyright © 1988 by Alice Walker, reprinted by permission of Harcourt Brace & Company.

"Prologue: A Sprig of Sage," reprinted with the permission of Scribner, a Division of Simon & Schuster from *Pieces of White Shell: A Journey to Navajoland* by Terry Tempest Williams. Copyright © 1983, 1984 by Terry Tempest Williams. Reprinted by permission of Simon & Schuster.

DESIGNER	Nola Burger
COMPOSITOR	Integrated Composition Systems
TEXT	11/13.75 Adobe Garamond
DISPLAY	Gill Sans
PRINTER AND BINDER	BookCrafters, Inc.